'Wonderfully entertaining … Trust me, it's hilarious …
Every page pulses with humour, ephemeral research and
irresistible nuggets of useless information … His book is
your life, examined by a post-modern academic in fluent
and breezy style, social history at its most accessible'
Val Hennessy, *Daily Mail*

'Here is a book for everyone … It is crammed with
arresting facts and insights. Joe Moran writes more
elegantly than a social historian has any right to … I kept
wanting to read out bits of this book to my children.
Partly because it sets in context the activities that will take
up most of their life – and partly because it might teach
them just how little that is dismissed as "boring" truly
deserves the description' Andrew Martin, *Sunday Times*

'His magnifying-glass focus makes the banal and
everyday surprising and often riveting … Fascinating
stuff, and Moran delivers it in a relaxed and often
hilarious style. It makes you yearn for a revival of
the Mass-Observation projects of the late 1930s'
Kate Colquhoun, *Daily Telegraph*

'An affectionate tribute to British life that's very funny
and bang up to date with chapters on email etiquette and
the seven-minute lunch break. It made me want to take
the author to the pub, where I'd ask him why we drink
beer in pints' Sam West, *Independent*

'A thoroughly novel and refreshing way of looking at
our recent history. This is "mundane" as a good thing. It
is a daybreak to bedtime story told further from "them",
and nearer to "us". Almost every page has its "yes! …
I'd forgotten" moment. I loved his book enormously'
Andrew Marr

Joe Moran is a reader in cultural history at Liverpool John Moores University. His academic research is on everyday life, and he writes regularly for the *New Statesman* and the *Guardian*. He lives in Liverpool.

Queuing for Beginners

The Story of Daily Life from Breakfast to Bedtime

Joe Moran

PROFILE BOOKS

This paperback edition published in 2008

First published in Great Britain in 2007 by
Profile Books Ltd
3A Exmouth House
Pine Street
Exmouth Market
London EC1R 0JH
www.profilebooks.com

3 5 7 9 10 8 6 4

A CIP catalogue record for this book is available
from the British Library.

ISBN 987 1 86197 841 7

Text design by Sue Lamble
Typeset in Palatino by MacGuru Ltd
info@macguru.org.uk

Printed and bound in Great Britain by
CPI Group (UK) Ltd, Croydon, CR0 4YY

MIX
Paper from
responsible sources
FSC® C020471

For Tom and Charlie

Contents

Acknowledgements

Writing about the minutiae of daily life must seem like a very strange habit. So I am grateful to all the friends, family and colleagues who have indulged me in various ways during the writing of this book, either by reading draft chapters or offering various forms of help: Jo Croft, Elspeth Graham, Glenda Norquay, Michael Moran, Winifred Moran, Liam Moran, Catherine Wainhouse and Joanna Price.

I would also like to thank Caroline Pretty, Penny Daniel and Nicola Taplin for their help in preparing the manuscript; and particularly my editor Daniel Crewe, who has supported this project from the very beginning and been a wonderfully rigorous but encouraging reader throughout.

The Mass-Observation material quoted in this book is reproduced with the kind permission of the Trustees of the Mass-Observation Archive, and is copyright © the Trustees of the Mass-Observation Archive. The extract from 'September 1, 1939' is taken from *The English Auden* published by Faber & Faber Ltd.

And the dedication is for my nephew and niece, whose daily habits are always a delight to observe.

them in their 'day surveys', in which they simply described what happened to them on the twelfth day of each month, however mundane. It was part of a project called Mass-Observation, which investigated the hidden significance of people's routine lives. This project began in January 1937, when three young men – Tom Harrisson, Humphrey Jennings and Charles Madge – wrote a joint letter to the *New Statesman*, inviting volunteers to co-operate in a new research project, an 'anthropology at home'.[3] Harrisson had spent a year with a tribal community in Malekula in the western Pacific, where he found that cannibals were at least as civilised as his fellow Old Harrovians, and he vowed to apply the insights he had acquired there to a study of 'the cannibals of Lancashire, the head-hunters of Stepney'.[4]

Mass-Observation wanted to thwart the tendency in modern mass society to live our daily lives deadened by habit, 'with as little consciousness of our surroundings as though we were walking in our sleep'.[5] It soon became notorious for paying minute attention to apparently trifling topics. Its researchers counted the average number of chips in each portion at Bolton fish-and-chip shops, recorded the conversations taking place in Blackpool's public lavatories at 5.30 p.m. each day, and wrote reports on 'The application of face cream' and 'Upper and middle-class soup-eating habits'. And they combined a voracious thirst for arcane knowledge with an ingenious approach to research methodology. A researcher in Bolton, for instance, took the subject of one of his investigations to the pictures, and ended up making love with her in a shop doorway[6] – a form of participant-observation not generally recommended in scholarly anthropology. But while the press dismissed them as 'busy-bodies', 'snoopers' and 'psycho-anthropologic nosey-parkers',[7] Mass-Observation captured the public imagination. Thousands of people signed up as volunteers, and one of its early books, *Britain* (1939), sold 100,000 copies in the ten days after publication.[8]

Why did Mass-Observation have such an intense impact? The main reason, I think, is that it is very rare to explore routine daily life in this detailed, ambitious way – to shine what one atypically appreciative newspaper article called 'a searchlight on living'.[9] For this is a world that we normally regard as too prosaic to be worthy of notice. The French author Georges Perec calls it the 'infra-ordinary': that part of our lives that is so routine as to become almost invisible, like infrared light.[10] Perec spent his whole career trying to make the 'infra-ordinary' more visible by lavishing it with the kind of painstaking attention we normally reserve for earth-shattering events and grand passions. His book *Species of Spaces* (1974) simply lists all the objects he can see in his apartment and neighbourhood. He urges his readers to do the same with the contents of their own lives, looking afresh at how streets are named, houses are numbered and cars are parked – and not worrying about whether these subjects have some pre-agreed significance. This kind of research project is so unusual that when we read the findings – whether on the parked cars in a Parisian street or the size of the portions in a Bolton chippie – we experience both the shock of recognition and the shock of the new.

This book is also about the 'infra-ordinary' – the unremarkable and unremarked upon aspects of our lives. I should begin by warning you that, if you profess an interest in this overlooked research area (which to a certain extent you have already done by picking up this book), you will probably need to develop a thick skin. Some people may accuse you of trying to rediscover what a certain strain of English pragmatism likes to call 'the bleeding obvious'. I am often asked, with benevolent bemusement, why I study such obscure topics as the symbolism of the lunch break, the history of crossing the road or the politics of sitting on sofas. Sometimes, perhaps while investigating a recherché fact about the prawn mayonnaise sandwich,

I have wondered this myself. We expect scholars to have a specialism, a particular expertise that marks them out from non-experts – and when it comes to familiar things like eating prawn sandwiches, crossing the road or sofa-sitting, everyone is a sort of expert.

But while we all experience these activities, we rarely give much thought to them, largely because they are social habits rather than individual idiosyncrasies. Working away at our office desks, sitting in meeting rooms, eating ready meals, flipping through the TV channels with the remote control – these are all part of what the German critic Siegfried Kracauer calls 'a life that belongs to no one and exhausts everyone'.[11] We share these habits with others but have little personal investment in them. Activities like queuing and commuting cannot easily be appropriated as part of a consumer 'lifestyle', one of the ways in which, since at least the 1950s, we have deliberately sought to give meaning to our otherwise unconscious daily lives by making them serve a specific self-image or creative impulse. Instead, they make up the constant, unnoticed background noise of our lives.

The silence of daily life can be deafening – and you can tell a lot about a society from the things it does all the time but rarely examines. Meaning lies buried in the most unlikely places. What Mass-Observation's homegrown anthropology showed was that the divide between the 'meaningful' rituals of so-called primitive societies and the 'meaningless' routines of modern Britain was not as straightforward as people assumed. When we use the word 'ritual' in its anthropological sense we tend to imagine some kind of significant tribal occasion like a marriage, funeral or rite-of-passage ceremony. But rituals can be found in daily activities like holding a fork, tying shoelaces or shaking hands, which people do forgetfully without seeing them as meaningful at all. In fact, the meanings we attach to these activities are all the more powerful because they are ignored. Our daily habits are mechanical actions that we do unthinkingly; but they can also tell us about our collective attitudes, ideas and mythologies – our ways of making sense of the world and our lives.

Habits are traditionally associated with repetition and inertia. But habits also have histories; it's just that we are rarely aware of them. 'The history of the Victorian Age will never be written,' argued an overly pessimistic Lytton Strachey in 1918, because 'we know too much about it'.[12] The same problem of over-familiarity applies to the history of daily life. The very nature of habits and routines, as activities that we do again and again, makes it hard for us to think of them as taking place in historical time. Daily life seems to be endless and without origin: the way things have always been, always will be. Even in the very recent past, however, we come across the most bizarre, mysterious routines that seemed entirely normal and uninteresting to contemporaries. Thanks to Mass-Observation and other sources, we have some idea of what it was like to smoke a cigarette or drink beer in a pub in the 1930s and 1940s. But we don't know much about how those habits changed in the intervening years. So in this book I try to unravel a sort of alternative history of post-war Britain – one that does for habits and routines what other historians have done for more momentous political, social or lifestyle changes. Although the focus is on Britain, part of the story I want to relate is how our national routines became caught up with international trends, particularly from across the Atlantic. The smallest details of mundane life can tell us stories about much larger national and global changes. Unconsidered trifles can be clues to more significant, subterranean shifts in society. There is always a reason why we carry out even the most habitual activities – and those reasons are rooted in history, politics and culture.

This book owes its title not only to the fact that queuing is a seminal daily experience – which I analyse in more detail later on – but also to the sense that investigating the quotidian involves unlearning the obvious, looking again at what we think we have noticed already. And one way of paying this kind of sustained attention to the banal is to focus on the pattern of the day itself – the daily grind, what Parisians poetically call '*métro, boulot, dodo*' (commuting, working, sleeping). Writers have for a long time used the structure of the day to paint a kaleidoscopic picture of society and look again at neglected areas of everyday life. In a 1712 *Spectator* essay, 'The hours of London', an early example of this genre, Richard Steele claims that we can learn much 'from the enumeration of so many insignificant matters and occurrences'.[13] The anonymous bestseller *Low Life* (1752) extended Steele's idea into a book-length tour through twenty-four hours of London life. The young Charles Dickens, an inveterate metropolitan perambulator, wrote chronological accounts of a morning and night of London street life in *Sketches by Boz* (1836).[14] His protégé, George Augustus Sala, went on to publish *Twice Round the Clock* (1858), a kind of tourist's guide to ordinary London life which begins at 4 a.m. in Billingsgate market and ends at 3 a.m. the next morning with the night charges at Bow Street Magistrates' Court. Modernist classics like James Joyce's *Ulysses* (1922) and Virginia Woolf's *Mrs Dalloway* (1925) also use the structure of a single day in a modern city to juxtapose the profound and the banal, the weightiest matters of life and death with the most trivial quotidian detail. All these books use chronology as a great leveller, a way of deferring the question of whether these familiar activities are significant enough to write about. In the structure of a single day, everything receives roughly the same amount of attention – however dull or boring it might at first seem.

This book similarly uses the pattern of a single day in order to explore the hidden meanings and histories of daily life. It has sixteen chapters, each covering a routine activity, roughly one for each hour of the day from getting up to going to bed. Some of these routines would be immediately familiar to anyone alive at the end of the Second World War: having breakfast (although they would be horrified by our propensity to skip it or skimp on it), commuting (although they didn't call it that) and queuing (although it took up much more of their time, and the queuing barriers and recorded voices announcing 'cashier number *one*, please' would have seemed like sci-fi inventions). Other habits – checking emails, watching telly, eating ready meals – would be almost entirely new and strange to them, but they might detect some residue of older social habits even in these activities. All the habits I explore have been included for two reasons: they are near-universal (my apologies if you do not work in some sort of office, but the majority of workers do and the proportion is rising) and are done without much deliberation, and certainly without giving much thought to their histories.

In the following chapters, I investigate a series of uninteresting events that unfolded recently across Britain. Millions of people woke up and had instant coffee and a cereal bar for breakfast. They all rushed for the train and stood pressed up against each other in a crowded carriage. They all arrived at the office, went to their desks and spent the morning there, occasionally getting up to go to the photocopier or the staff kitchen for a gossip. At lunchtime, they all stood in the queue at the bank, then they all bought a sandwich and came back to eat it at their desks. They all checked their emails, and then nipped outside for a smoke. They all had to attend a boring staff meeting. At half past five, they all walked out of the office, weaving in between the rush-hour traffic. They all had a quick, after-work drink with each other, then they all went home and stuck a ready meal in the microwave. They all ate it on the sofa while zapping through the television channels. After they had all watched the late-night weather forecast, they all

1   Bacon and eggs to go

> *'You must set about it more slowly, almost stupidly.*
> *Force yourself to write down what is of no interest, what*
> *is most obvious, most common, most colourless ... Make*
> *an inventory of your pockets, of your bag ... Question*
> *your tea spoons'*
>
> Georges Perec[1]

Traditionally, a 'proper' breakfast is the one meal that the
British are supposed to do well. We are still fond of evoking
some more complete version of it – an inviting mirage of
sizzling bacon, runny egg, succulent sausage and tender
tomato – against the bleaker reality of a half-cup of instant
coffee and the first cigarette of the day. As early as 1952, the
culinary historian Arnold Palmer wrote that 'about eggs and
bacon for breakfast there still lingers, for many honest men,
something of the sanctity of the Union Jack and Stratford-
upon-Avon'.[2] But this timeless symbol of nationhood, 'the
full English breakfast', is actually quite a recent invention.
It was not until the 1840s that breakfast came to be eaten on
rising, and to have a distinctive menu of porridge, bacon,
eggs, toast and marmalade – a product of the more rigid
routines of work and commuting adopted by middle-class
professional men in the early Victorian era.[3]

The mythology of the full English breakfast only really
developed as this tradition was dying out. In 1925, the
comic writer A. P. Herbert wrote a verse entitled 'Bacon
and Eggs':

While paltry pale foreigners, meagre as moles,
Must crawl through the morning on coffee and
    rolls ...
We fight to the finish, we drink to the dregs
And dare to be Daniels on bacon and eggs[4]

But even when Herbert wrote these words, lighter breakfasts were becoming more common. The two modifiers 'full' and 'English' differentiated this breakfast from the Continental and American versions that now existed. In 1961, *The Times* complained about this 'new-fangled expression "a cooked breakfast" – no one, after all, talks about "a cooked luncheon" or "a cooked dinner"'.[5]

The modern, two-course breakfast – cereal followed by toast – fully established itself during the Second World War. With fewer imported cereals available to feed their pigs and poultry, many farmers had to sacrifice these animals and replace them with crops and dairy farming. Bacon and eggs grew scarce and were generally reserved for lunch – now named the 'Wooltonian breakfast' after the minister for food, and reinvented as the most important meal of the day. The enterprising company Weetabix promoted its cereal as 'your every-occasion food in this time of emergency'. As well as being good with milk in a bowl, it could be used to make Weetabix fishcakes or spread with marmalade, grated cheese or sardines. 'Introduce the family to Weetabix sandwiches,' advised another advertisement, 'Weetabix split, buttered and spread with your favourite fillings.'[6]

After the war, the return of a decent supply of bacon and eggs was as much a cause for national celebration as the first shipment of bananas. But the symbolism of the fried breakfast was now outweighing the more prosaic reality. With more women going out to work and more people in sedentary occupations, the lighter breakfast of cereal and toast remained the norm except at weekends.

In 1948, twice as many people had eggs for breakfast on Sunday as in the middle of the week.[7] The British embraced convenience in the morning in a way that they were still reluctant to do with more leisurely meals. Before the war, the middle classes had carefully hidden the origins of shop-bought food at the breakfast table. Servants or house-wives would spoon the marmalade into special pots and then, after breakfast, scrape what was left back into the jar and wash the pots. One academic remembers from his pre-war middle-class childhood 'the frowns which met a glass marmalade pot which appeared on the breakfast table just as it had left it the previous day'.[8]

By the 1950s, the brand name ruled even at the middle-class breakfast table – a quotidian reminder of the rapid triumph of the free market over wartime state controls. A seminal moment was the appearance in July 1949 of Mr Cube the sugar lump, Tate and Lyle's aggressive response to the Labour Party's pledge to nationalise the sugar-refining industry. A cube-shaped man with spindly arms and legs, he appeared on the back of sugar packets, spouting speech-bubble slogans like 'State control will make a hole in your pocket and my packet' and angrily crossing out the S in 'State' to leave 'Tate'. One newspaper cartoonist depicted the 1950 general election as a bicycle race between Clement Attlee and Winston Churchill, with Attlee hampered by Mr Cube clinging to his coat tails.[9] Mr Cube not only made breakfast political, he showed how even the most generic and ubiquitous foods were now synonymous with the leading brands. More items appeared at the breakfast table in their packaging: marmalade in jars, margarine in tubs and finally (horrors!) milk in bottles.[10]

The item that went most commonly undisguised at the breakfast table, however, was the cereal packet. Invented at the end of the nineteenth century, breakfast cereal was a new kind of food which had to be promoted vigorously to convince people to change their habits. The cereal industry, dominated almost from the beginning by a handful of multinationals, was a pioneer in promotional packaging. Breakfast cereals were packaged in sealed bags inside brightly coloured cardboard boxes, which served as a kind of advertising hoarding. After the arrival of supermarkets in the mid-1950s, the cereal aisle became a riot of colour and an incitement to pester power.

There were two main types of cereal packet. First, there were the ones that housed traditional family cereals like Kellogg's Corn Flakes and Weetabix. On the front of the packet there might be an idyllic scene of a prairie field of wheat or corn swaying in the breeze and glistening in the sun; and on the back a pleasing family tableau of bread-winner father, home-making mother and child of each sex, all tucking into their cereal. In a controversial series of BBC Reith Lectures in 1967, the Cambridge anthropologist Edmund Leach attacked what he saw as the 'soppy propaganda about the virtue of a united family life', later defining this as the 'cereal packet image of the family'.[11] People began referring to the 'cornflake family', either to censure or celebrate this cosy image of domestic bliss.

The second, more garish type of packet was used for the sugar-coated cereals aimed at children, like Kellogg's Frosties and Quaker Oats' Sugar Puffs, which were both launched in Britain in 1954. These packets wooed baby-boomer kids with mail-in offers and free gifts, known in the trade as 'insert premiums'. The mail-in offers were items such as combination pen-watches or dog whistles, which you could get in the post in return for a bargain price and a number of packet tops or other proofs of purchase. These offers were called 'self-liquidators' because the 'bargain' price covered the cost of the item, postage, packing and administration. Free gifts began as cheap versions of conventional toys: miniature bandsmen, space rockets or 'atomic' submarines powered by baking powder. Then the cereal companies followed the shrewd American example of linking them with children's TV series, from Lone Ranger Sheriff's Stars to Thunderbirds figurines. The cheap free gift became a symbol of the tacky promises of consumerism, the disappointing content never living up to the delicious expectation of the packaging. Designing tatty gifts for cereal boxes was the seminally unfulfilling job that Tom Good (Richard Briers) gave up in the first episode of the 1970s self-sufficiency sitcom *The Good Life*.

The other element of the two-course breakfast, toast, evoked more ambivalent feelings. Toast had long been a classic element of the full English breakfast, but the electric toaster and its corollary, sliced bread, were inter-war American inventions. After the war, the American toaster conquered Britain while other countries resisted. (It is still uncommon in Italy, for example.) For many years, a toaster was the most popular wedding present in both Britain and America. Toaster adverts showed young women in bridal dresses, with captions like 'Years of blissful break-fasts', 'Love, honour ... and crisper toast!' and 'Toast for the bride! ... may all your breakfasts be happy ones'.[12] But many British people associated the toaster with the brashness and vulgarity of America. 'American toast is horrible,' wrote the New York correspondent of *The Times* in 1961. 'Whisked from the pop-up toaster, it is laid prone on a plate, where it becomes as soggy as a wet blanket. We émigrés have to send home for toast-racks, unknown in this land of super-gadgetry.'[13]

Feelings about the toaster were bundled up with anxieties about the evolution of British bread. During the war, the government banned refined white bread to save grain, and introduced a subsidy and set price for the 'National Loaf'. Widely resented for tasting of sawdust, it was heavily promoted ('smiling through with national bread') and commended for its magical effects on bowel movements and even libidos.[14] Following the recommen-dations of a 'Conference on the Post-War Loaf' in December

1945, the government continued to control the quality of flour and bread, barring white bread from the subsidies still enjoyed by the National Loaf.

In 1956, bread became the last food except milk to stop being subsidised. Sliced white bread could at last compete on a level playing field with its wholewheat rivals. There was a wave of consolidation among the big milling-baking combines, and branded varieties like Mother's Pride and Sunblest filled the shelves. After years of scraping away with a knife at the hard, brown National Loaf, many people loved the sliced white variety. One Manchester woman later recalled, 'The bread came all wrapped in paper, we showed it off in the street. No one could believe how many slices you got with it, people were looking at it like it was something from space.'[15] The Chorleywood Process, a high-speed method of mixing and kneading dough introduced in the early 1960s, made bread even quicker and cheaper to make, but also more spongy and aerated. 'Pre-sliced factory bread,' complained the food writer Derek Cooper in 1968, was 'a sort of chewy wadding much favoured by the British housewife'.[16] This new era of abundance was the point at which middle-class connoisseurs went off the white loaf and began to pine for freshly baked, unsliced bread. 'For centuries the working man envied the white bread of the privileged,' wrote Elizabeth David, doyenne of English cookery writers and champion of good bread, in 1977. 'Now he may very soon grow to envy them their brown wholewheat bread.' No wonder that David judged electric toasters, indelibly associated with the white sliced, to be 'machines with which I cannot be doing'.[17]

As late as 1998, David's successor as the maharishi of the middle-class cook, Delia Smith, was trying to teach television viewers the proper way of making toast, by placing it on a grill which had been pre-heated for ten minutes, and then slotting it into 'this wonderful little gadget', a toast rack.[18] The influence of Delia Smith on British cookery at the end of the last century was unequalled. She simply had to mention mildly exotic ingredients like cranberries or bouillon powder, or recommend a particular type of omelette pan or lemon zester, and the shops ran out almost overnight, a phenomenon known as the 'Delia effect'. But there was no similar run on toast racks after this television performance. Instead, viewers seemed puzzled that she was trying to tell them how to make such a simple item as toast, and giving them such a long drawn-out way of doing it. If even Delia could not challenge it, the toaster's ascendancy was surely complete. It helped that there were now bravely heretical voices like the cookery writer Nigel Slater, who claimed that you needed the extra-hot element of the toaster to make perfect toast, crispy on the outside and soft on the inside.[19]

But the toaster was never merely functional. As the design critic Reyner Banham pointed out in a 1970 *New Society* essay, a modern housewife now had the 'same amount of mechanical assistance (about two horsepower) as was deployed by the average industrial worker around 1914'. But whereas the factory worker's machinery had run for twenty-four hours over three shifts, the housewife's was almost always turned off. 'Mechanically idle for most of their life,' Banham argued, 'domestic appliances must, of necessity, be more symbolic than anything else.'[20] The pop-up toaster, employed for perhaps a few minutes each day, was the most self-consciously designed of all kitchen appliances. Early models mimicked the aerodynamic, curvilinear style of American cars, with rounded Bakelite handles and chrome finishes. Some turned the toasting into a piece of theatre, with holes in the side to watch the bread turn brown, and a melodramatic judder as the toast popped up.

The designer toaster truly arrived in the Thatcher era. The British company Dualit had been making toasters since 1946, durable models aimed at the new wave of post-war Italian cafés. Then, in the 1980s, the Dualit became a modish yuppie gadget. Its retro industrial look was both quirkily English and ideal for the minimalist kitchens of young middle-class professionals. It brought together efficiency and homeliness, the idea of cooking as both science and art. In this sense it was a kind of microcosm of the modern fitted kitchen, which sought to blend the shinily contemporary with the reassuringly retro (cast-iron cookers, fireclay sinks, butcher's blocks) to suggest a room that was both the control centre and emotional heart of the home. The Dualit had nothing so vulgar as a pop-up mechanism; its spring-loaded timer, with its satisfying whirrs and clicks, turned the element off but kept the toast warm inside its slot until someone was ready to press the chunky eject lever to retrieve the toast. Most importantly, the Dualit's generous dimensions could accommodate home-baked or unsliced bread, not just the supermarket varieties of sliced white. Even Elizabeth David might have approved.

Sigmund Freud once wrote that human-made technologies are 'auxiliary organs' that turn humans into 'prosthetic gods', giving us the illusion of power but making us feel unnatural and unhappy in our omnipotence.[21] Today's stylish kitchen appliances, like Alessi whistle kettles, electric coffee grinders, espresso machines and centrifugal juicers, make us feel happier in our godlike mastery. Most of them add to labour rather than save it; they turn a routine activity into a celebration of high style or a comforting ritual of culinary authenticity. Similarly, the designer toaster turns toast-making into a major strategic operation. It can defrost bread, toast the bread on one side only or warm croissants on its special bun rack. It has microchip controls, 'high-lift' facilities that raise the bread right out of the toaster, and removable trays to collect crumbs. It comes in a 'cool-wall' model with a white plastic shell that doesn't get hot on the outside. All these features disguise the reality of the toaster as a very simple piece of technology. Unlike other kitchen appliances, such as microwaves and food processors, we only really need it to do one thing: make toast.

Ironically, the rise of the designer toaster coincided with the decline of the classic cereal-and-toast combo breakfast, to be replaced by one of the two, or neither. Kellogg's Breakfast Bureau, established in September 1975 'to encourage public and professional awareness of the nutritional and social benefits of breakfast' (and, presumably, of Kellogg's breakfasts in particular), conducted a survey of 6,000 homes in 1976 that revealed the changing patterns of breakfast over the previous twenty years. It found that, in 1956, half of all adults and teenagers had a cooked breakfast each morning, even if it was only a boiled egg. From 1957, the Egg Marketing Board's famous advert urged people to 'go to work on an egg', but it was fighting a losing battle. By 1976, only 20 per cent had a cooked breakfast, 40 per cent had cereal, and a further 25 per cent had neither of these but something else to eat, such as toast. The rest managed with tea, coffee, milk or nothing.[22]

In spite of all this, bacon and eggs still symbolised the national morning dish, particularly in politics. During the inflationary years of the 1970s, the rising price of bacon and eggs was evoked in Parliament and the press as shorthand for the effects of inflation on ordinary households. 'This is scandalous,' said one Labour member in the Commons in 1973 in response to an answer from a minister about the current price of bacon and eggs. 'Having got rid of the traditional English dinner, she is now getting rid of our traditional breakfast ... Is it an integral part of the acceptance of the common agricultural policy that we all eat continental breakfasts?' Another Labour MP protested: 'Are the Government determined to price proteins out of my constituents' diet? Do they suggest my constituents eat ice cream, lollies and potato crisps for their main meals?'[23] 'Save your great British brekker!' cried the *Daily Mirror*, above a story that the rising cost of bacon and eggs had led 20 per cent of British hotels to stop serving a full English.[24] Bacon and eggs had stopped being the standard breakfast decades earlier – but humbug was still on the menu.

In 1984, the anthropologist David Pocock noted that breakfast in Britain was still an important meal but was no longer eaten by the family together. Breakfast times were staggered according to individual work or school timetables. On the rare occasions that cooked breakfasts were eaten, they were almost always prepared for men by women, who were more likely to have a light breakfast or skip it altogether.[25] Even children could prepare their own cereal, which made the idea of a synchronised family breakfast anachronistic. As Christina Hardyment writes, 'it is ironic, considering that classic image of the "cornflake packet family", that few products have accelerated the decline of eating breakfast together more than packaged cereals.'[26]

By the end of the century, the market for breakfast cereals, which had risen steadily since the late 1930s, had begun a slow decline. 'Have you forgotten how good they taste?' was the slightly needy advertising slogan used by Kellogg's Corn Flakes in the early 1990s. The baby-boomers had all grown up and the children's market for cereals was now saturated. Consumers were also more sophisticated: in 1987, the market researcher Mintel found that nearly two out of three women were no longer persuaded by their children to buy cereals because of the free gift inside.[27] One cereal that bucked the downward trend was muesli, which finally shook off its cranky image of the 1970s, when gentrified urban areas had been known as muesli belts, and middle-class left-liberals as sandals, beards and muesli-eating types. As breakfast lost its familial associations and developed more individualistic associations with health and fitness, the kinds of products that thrived were one-portion porridge sachets, bran cereals and 'luxury muesli' – surely an oxymoron.

For younger people, breakfast has become the 'deskfast', the portable snack taken into the office and eaten there. The default deskfast, the cereal bar, arrived in Britain from America in the late 1990s and within five years accounted for about a fifth of the total breakfast cereal market.[28] Cereal bars have been promoted as a convenient, portable snack for the harassed and hurried, 'the best solution to a missed breakfast'.[29] A 1998 London Underground poster for Kellogg's Nutri-Grain bars went: 'Circle line … 4 mins. Breakfast … 1 min.' A 2002 advert for Alpen bars showed commuters trying to eat a bowl of cereal on their way to work, with the slogan: 'Now available in rush hour.'

In the morning we are juggling different tasks (washing, dressing, shaving, eating) in the face of immovable deadlines (transport timetables and the start of work), so we are particularly receptive to the promise of convenience. Marketing people try to persuade us that we have no time to pour milk into a cereal bowl, or butter our toast, or boil a kettle. At the end of the millennium, an American marketing firm said of the modern breakfast: 'Going from hand to bowl to mouth is out. Going from hand to mouth is much more in sync with lifestyles built on mobility.'[30] Many of the newer 'breakfast solutions' are American in origin: frozen fry-ups in microwaveable trays, bacon-and-egg toasties and 'Drink'n'Crunch' portable cereals with an inner cup containing cereal and an outer cup filled with milk. But even the humblest and handiest deskfast respects the integrity of breakfast, by compressing the different elements of a traditional breakfast into one package. In spite of our restless quest for convenience, we seem to be reluctant to dispense with the sense that breakfast is a little meal rather than just a snack. The cereal bar is a dry, rectangular-shaped bowl of muesli, with yoghurt substituting

19

for milk; the smoothie is a 'meal in a glass' for those who wish to avoid the tiresome chore of peeling fruit, chewing it and dispensing with the remains; the all-day-breakfast sandwich is the traditional fry-up in cold, portable form.

In his novel *Flaubert's Parrot* (1984), Julian Barnes calls Britain 'the land of embarrassment and breakfast'[31] – an interesting juxtaposition, since breakfast has traditionally been the least sociable meal of the day, meant to be eaten in near silence. The mutating British breakfast reflects the perennial pull between inertia and change in daily life, our desire to cling to the comfort of old habits while embracing speed and expediency. The full English breakfast is no longer a private, family ritual but a kind of public indulgence. It survives in hotels, for foreign tourists or the English on vacation, or as the weekend treat of brunch. In greasy spoon cafés it is the 'all-day breakfast', the universal cure for student hangovers. Thanks to low-carb diets like the Atkins, it is not even derided as a heart attack on a plate any more. But if bacon and eggs is still held up as a national archetype, it stopped being part of our daily routine long ago. From the National Loaf to the Egg Marketing Board, post-war governments have done their bit for the traditional breakfast, but we were never quite hungry enough for it when it mattered. Nothing is keeping us from a full English breakfast except our grudging acceptance of Americanisation and social change.

The chain-owned gourmet coffee and sandwich bars that have sprung up in city centres since the mid-1990s have cannily brought together all these different ideas about breakfast: as a movable feast, a hurried afterthought, a lifestyle statement and a comforting ritual. Give us your tired, your time-poor, breakfastless masses, their welcoming fascias seem to say. On your way to the railway station, you just have time to nip into Starbucks or Pret a Manger to buy a 'Rise and Shine' muffin, an egg and tomato breakfast baguette or a 'Very Berry Breakfast Bowl' (spoon supplied); a cappuccino in a polystyrene cup with a corrugated cardboard sleeve to protect your hand from the heat; and a dinky little smoothie bottle from the neatly stacked shelf in the chiller cabinet. All this will cost you a good chunk of your daily salary, but it has given you an extra five minutes in bed and sold you a sense of yourself as a thoroughly modern, busy professional. Then you run for the train with both hands full, praying you can get a seat.

2 Standing room only

> 'It's not catastrophes, murders, deaths, diseases, that age
> and kill us; it's the way people look and laugh, and run
> up the steps of omnibuses'
>
> Virginia Woolf[1]

If you think things were bad on your journey to work
today, then try transporting yourself through time on to
a busy commuter train in the autumn of 1945. After six
years of war, the railways are in a terrible state, wholly
unprepared for the mass return to work. Your dirty, ageing
train is hopelessly overcrowded. The queue for the tea at
the station café was too long to join, and there is no buffet
car or trolley. The only form of ventilation is opening a
window, at a time when people only tend to take a bath
once a week, men rely on a change of collar each day rather
than a change of shirt, and deodorant is an exotic rarity.
One Mass-Observation diarist wrote of a train journey in
September of that year when she had to sink to the floor
twice, her legs under the luggage space, to inhale some
breathable air amidst the fug of body odour and tobacco
smoke.[2]

The train carriage has always brought people together
in an awkward mix of tolerance and irritation, proximity
and distance, kinship and anonymity. Its predecessor, the
stagecoach, was a garrulous mini-community by compar-
ison. In his 1818 essay 'On the Ignorance of the Learned',
William Hazlitt remarked that 'you will hear more good

things on the outside of a stage-coach from London to Oxford, than if you were to pass a twelvemonth with the Under-graduates or Heads of Colleges of that famous university.'[3] When the train arrived in the 1830s, it soon became a more anonymous form of travel. The greater comfort of a railway carriage encouraged musing and window gazing, and made solitary activities like reading, writing, sewing and sleeping easier. By 1862, the *Railway Traveller's Handy Book* was complaining:

Generally speaking, the occupants of a railway carriage perform the whole of the journey in silence ... This is most unnatural and unreasonable. Why should half a dozen persons, each with minds to think, and tongues to express their thoughts, sit looking at each other mumchance, as though they were afraid of employing the faculty of speech? Why should an Englishman ever be like a ghost, in not speaking until he is spoken to?[4]

This anonymous author then rather undermines his own argument by pointing out that reading on the train 'forms an excellent weapon of defence against bores, that impertinent, intrusive, and inquisitive race, who can only be silenced by levelling a volume or a journal at their heads'.[5]

When people began to stand on commuter trains towards the end of the nineteenth century, there was some debate about whether they should even be allowed to do so. In 1906, in one of the first references to the term, a reporter complained that '"straphanging" on the railway has become a recognised institution, and the law provides no penalty'.[6] In the inter-war era, London Underground accepted straphanging as a reality and tried to make it more comfortable for passengers. They replaced the leather loops, which chafed the hands and shook the passenger about, with aluminium handles or brass rails attached to seat backs.[7] On overground commuter trains, however, it was generally felt that a middle-class passenger who had paid for his season ticket should at least be entitled to a seat, preferably some distance away from the hoi polloi.

It is a myth, however, that the class division of carriages on British railways was an especially pernicious reflection of the class system. Most European countries, even the Soviet Union, kept three or four classes of carriage long after the British had learned to get by with two. The class divisions on British railways had less to do with social snobbery than with the logistical relationship between physical space and profit. It took nearly seventy years, after all, for railways to accept that passengers might like to have toilets, buffet cars and heating, all of which inconveniently took up space and added to the weight of the train.[8] On the one hand, the private companies who ran the railway system up until the Second World War wanted to make money by cramming in as many people as possible, thus keeping shareholders happy; on the other hand, they did not want to risk alienating passengers too much, particularly those in first class who had paid more for their tickets and for whom the emptiness of the carriage was presumably part of its attraction.

During the Second World War, all classes of passengers simply had to put up with late, crowded trains because, as the poster said, 'food, shells and fuel *must* come first'. But the shabbiness and unreliability of trains after 1945 was a constant reminder of the unevenness of post-war renewal. British Railways, nationalised in 1948, soon became a collective running joke, from its overcrowded carriages to its lame excuses for lateness. The railways became tied up with a pervasive sense of national decline, particularly during the awkward decade after 1955, when electric and diesel trains replaced the old steam engines. Others saw the semi-hostile atmosphere of a train carriage as a symbol of the return of English reserve after a brief flowering of wartime communality. In a 'Demob diary' for the *New Statesman* in 1946, Tom Harrisson complained that daily life was retreating again into 'the restricted circle of private western experience'. After returning from war service in Borneo, he was horrified at having to 'face your fellows in the train speechless, almost ashamed. One longs to reach out and talk a little to the elderly gentleman with the checked waistcoat reading Kafka, to strike up an unambitious, inter-station intimacy with the nice, dumb-looking blonde.'[9]

When did the bored commuter become a symbol of the drudgery and alienation of daily life in this way? The word 'commuter' had been in use in the United States since the late nineteenth century, a 'commutation ticket' being the American name for a season ticket. The transatlantic poet W. H. Auden, who never had to do much commuting, was one of the first to introduce the word to a British readership, along with its connotations of dull conformity. 'From the conservative dark / Into the ethical life / The dense commuters come,' he writes in the poem 'September 1, 1939'.[10] But the word 'commuter' did not replace the older 'season-ticket holder' in Britain until the 1950s. By 1960, it was so familiar that it was being used confusingly to cover anyone travelling to and from work, including motorists.[11]

The shift in terminology was significant. The season-ticket holder had a certain cachet, sharing friendly greetings each day with the stationmaster and a sense of camaraderie with his fellow travellers. Given that daily train travellers were mostly middle-class and male, the railway carriage had elements of the gentleman's club, as passengers read the newspaper headlines to each other or did the crossword together. The season-ticket holder was, *The Times* remembered nostalgically in 1963, 'an ample, solid citizen going about his business with a complacent knowledge of his status'. The commuter, on the other hand, was 'a sharp-faced, bustling, impatient fellow with little time for the traditional courtesies of life'.[12] After the war, there were simply too many commuters for the role to retain any sense of social distinction. The commuter might cling to 'certain snobbish consolations – flatter himself that he is not as the bus riders are, or those inferior beings who take a "daily return"'. But, deep down, he knew that he was a drudge like everyone else, as even the sound of the wheels moving on the rails seemed to tell him: 'You'll-go-on-doing-this-for-the-rest-of-your-days.'[13]

Some male commuters still wore a distinctive uniform: a pin-striped suit, briefcase, furled umbrella and bowler hat under which, at least according to the cartoonists, they kept their packed lunches. The bowler hat was fairly common in the earlier part of the century, but by the post-war period it was worn almost exclusively by gentlemen in the City, or by men who wished to associate themselves with this world. The Irish writer Sean O'Faolain remarked that 'between England and Revolution there will always stand an army of bowler hats'.[14] From Monty Python to Reggie Perrin, British TV comedy of the 1960s and 1970s was fascinated with this slightly anachronistic figure of the faceless, stockbroker-belt commuter, sometimes giving him a dark or anarchic side. Perrin is the tortured office drone whose wife hands him his umbrella and briefcase and pecks him on the cheek each morning, before he travels to work on the same crowded commuter train, which is always exactly eleven minutes late for some obscure reason ('Badger ate a junction box at Effingham').

As it struggled with a reputation for running unreliable, congested trains, British Railways tried to improve its rolling-stock, streamline its operations and market itself more effectively. In the 1960s, the older, pre-war carriages, with long corridors leading into a series of smaller compartments, began to be replaced by open saloon coaches with wide vestibule entrances. These new carriages created more standing space, but fewer doors meant that it also took longer for passengers to board and alight. They also made it even less likely that passengers would talk to each other, as they were no longer placed in a small compartment with a few other commuters. Meanwhile, the 1963 Beeching report ordered the closure of many branch lines and the prioritising of the more profitable main lines. In 1965, British Railways rebranded itself 'British Rail', adopting a new double-arrow logo and dressing its staff in dark-blue suits and dinky caps like Continental policemen. TV adverts extolled the virtues of InterCity services, including a famous campaign beginning in the mid-1970s with the DJ Jimmy Savile proclaiming in stentorian tones that this was 'the age of the train'.

But the Thatcherite view of recent British history refused to accept that the train's time had come. Margaret Thatcher, first elected as prime minister in 1979, believed that the country had suffered since the war from the British disease of mediocre management and unmotivated employees, and that national decline could only be averted if the public sphere was transformed by the incentives of the market. British Rail seemed to slot into this narrative perfectly – that is, if you conveniently forgot that it had been trying to commercialise itself since the mid-1960s. For good measure, Mrs Thatcher also disliked trains, travelling on them just once in her eleven years in power, and championing instead what she called 'the great car economy'.[15] During the 1980s and early 1990s, British Rail was subjected to every form of market discipline short of privatisation: reduced budgets, performance targets, consumer charters, and more emphasis on PR and advertising.

In 1984, BR dispensed with Jimmy Savile's services and came up with the alternative advertising slogan 'We're getting there', a clever play on words which conceded that they hadn't actually got there yet. One TV commercial by Saatchi and Saatchi had a sweaty, cramped plane turn magically into an expansive train, with business people stretching their legs out and tucking into full English breakfasts. Another award-winning commercial from the late 1980s, made by future Hollywood director Tony Kaye, used Leon Redbone's somnolent song 'Relax' and showed people on a train becoming so relaxed that their shoes morphed into slippers, the Penguin logos on their paper-backs rolled over and fell asleep, and their chess pieces snored contentedly.

When compared with a distinctly unrelaxing daily commute, these adverts were hostages to fortune. We're getting there? We're going nowhere in the middle of a tunnel, actually. Relax? That's a bit tricky when your face is buried in someone else's armpit. The point was that these adverts weren't addressed at commuters at all, who were largely captive customers. They were aimed at business people on long-distance trains who had to be wooed away from the aeroplane and the motorway. InterCity trains had much nicer carriages than those on suburban lines, even in standard class: more spacious, reclining seats with folding tables, air-conditioned interiors and sound insulation.

Thatcherite policy encouraged the different areas of BR to function as separate businesses. By the late 1980s, InterCity services were in profit, but the provincial and commuter services still relied on massive subsidy (as they do even after privatisation).[16] Thatcherite economics came up against the intractable nature of the railway as a subsi-dised, fixed capital industry. When the government made huge cost-cutting demands in the 1980s, the cuts could not simply be compensated for by greater efficiency and better marketing. To make matters more difficult, there was a huge increase in commuters in the South-East in the 1980s and 1990s, as London became more important as a financial and business centre. These prosperous, southern season-ticket holders, struggling into work on old, crowded trains, were unlikely losers from Thatcherism. Their misfortune was to be caught in the middle of the unresolved conflict between an enterprise economy demanding ever-greater mobility, and a deteriorating infrastructure struggling to provide it.

At the same time, the new language of PR tried to massage and appease these disgruntled commuters. You were now no longer in 'second' but in 'standard' class (the airline adjectives of 'economy', 'tourist' and 'coach' having been considered but wisely rejected), and no longer a 'passenger' but a 'customer'. Whatever you were called, the train was just as likely to be overcrowded and late. According to most industry experts, by the late 1980s British Rail was more efficient and better organised than it had ever been.[17] On the railways, however, there is a more obvious disparity between bold PR claim and depressing reality (late trains, cancellations) than in any other business. Among other things, this disparity helped to soften up the public for the privatisation of British Rail in 1994.

Commuter carriages became still more crowded after privatisation, a period of economic growth and high employment. The rush hour expanded, as the new rail companies offered 'early bird' discounts for travelling on quieter trains. On suburban lines, the differentiation of first from standard class had long been a symbolic one, perhaps marked by a few more inches of seat, a slightly thicker cushion or a bigger headrest. The distinction now eroded further, as companies crunched their passenger numbers in different ways. 'We don't do sociology,' said one train company director, when asked about the meaning of these developments, echoing the pragmatic line in the Victorian era when the railway companies would refer to 'charging what the traffic would bear'.[18] Of course, financial decisions still have sociological consequences. Some companies on prosperous commuter lines in Surrey and Hampshire retained first class and made it swankier, with roomy seats, sockets for laptops and internet connections. On others, first and standard class remained, but the distinction was simply marked by headrests bearing a 'first-class' doily. The grottiest lines dispensed with first class altogether because they reasoned that it would be empty much of the time. Seats, aisles and legroom all became smaller as they squeezed in more passengers.

But the various passengers' charters of the privatised rail companies have displayed more concern about punctuality than the less quantifiable experience of being on the train. Although people might quibble over degrees of lateness, a train is generally either late or on time. But when exactly does a train become overcrowded? A 2003 Commons Transport Committee report complained that train travellers faced the 'daily trauma' of 'intolerable' and 'positively frightening' conditions that left them arriving at work feeling 'tired, stressed and uncomfortable'. There are no national measures of train overcrowding, and some companies prefer the euphemism 'crowding'. Modes of transport that rely on advance bookings, like planes and long-distance trains, are full when all the seats are sold. But commuter trains are designed to be filled to capacity, what some experts call 'crush loading'. Most train companies work with a rough allowance, dating from the days of British Rail, of 0.55 square metres of space for each standing passenger, but this is difficult to measure because a crowded railway carriage is a fluid, ever-changing entity.[19]

What can be done to alleviate 'crowding'? You can make the trains longer, but this might mean extending station platforms. You can introduce double-decker trains, which run on the Continent and were used on certain British lines as early as 1949, but this might entail the expensive business of raising bridges. There is a simpler solution, favoured by the Transport Committee report: rip the seats out. In 2002, Connex South Eastern, which ran commuter services in south London and Kent, became the first train company to announce that it was creating space for 'humane standing room' on its busiest trains. It would introduce London Underground-style carriages with longitudinal rather than transverse seating, with a large gangway in the middle, and straps and rails on to which passengers could cling. Connex handed out leaflets on station platforms, asking for passenger feedback: 'The painful reality is that peak-time passengers on south London journeys usually have to stand, and may well feel like cattle. We can't find a way to make that not true. We can, with your help, find a way to make it more bearable.'[20] But when people have to get to work, it is amazing what they will find bearable. Certainly, they would rather hang from a strap, pressed up against several complete strangers – however sweaty and unpleasant the experience is – than wait around on a platform for the next train. Soon, other rail franchises began to 'reconfigure' their trains, installing more handholds and replacing seats with 'perches'.[21]

The social etiquette of congested commuter trains has always been knotty. In the 1960s, the Canadian sociologist Erving Goffman came up with the term 'civil inattention' to describe the polite ways in which we ignore other people's presence in these temporarily shared environments, from thousand-yard stares to burying ourselves in newspapers.[22] Goffman went on to pose the following dilemma. As the bus or train carriage fills up, you only sit next to someone else when there are no other seats available. But if the numbers thin out again, do you give up the double seat you are sharing with a stranger for a double seat of your own, at the risk of seeming hostile?[23]

A similar and particularly British predicament concerns the circumstances under which you give up your seat to the elderly, the infirm or (if you are a man) a woman. Whatever era they were written in, newspaper articles on the relinquishing of seats always seem to suggest that it was more common a generation ago, to the extent that one wonders whether it was ever common at all. 'May I suggest that the time has come for gentlemen travelling in the tubes and elsewhere to give up their seats to the ladies as they did in the pre-war days?' wrote a vicar to *The Times* in 1937. 'If I remain seated my conscience upbraids me; if I rise and go through the polite forms I feel a prig and a traitor to my glumly sitting sex.'[24] Two years earlier, there had been a fistfight involving several dozen people at West Kensington Underground station, which ended up in the police courts: a retired army captain had remarked that youngsters ought to give up their seats to an elderly woman, to which several young men had taken exception.[25] Perhaps the problem was not the decline of courtesy but that this particular courtesy presented a whole series of Goffmanesque dilemmas. Should an elderly man give up his seat to a fit young woman? How near to the sitting man did the standing woman have to be? What happened if the woman, infected by new-fangled ideas about sexual equality, refused the seat? 'To have one's offer of a seat declined, however graciously,' wrote one *Times* correspondent in 1961, is 'most unlady-like and always embarrassing to the donor.'[26]

In the chronically crowded commuter train, these quandaries can seem rather quaint. Here there are more acute problems of personal space. What happens when your neighbour takes up all of the plastic armrest between the seats, falls asleep on your shoulder or tries to use a laptop in a confined area? The question of how best to ignore our fellow passengers has also been displaced by another dilemma: how to talk to those who are not there. When the earliest, brick-like mobile phones appeared in the late 1980s, they were seen as flash yuppie props, attached to self-confident, braying voices making offers on Docklands apartments or closing deals with Tokyo. By the early

1990s, as mobile phones became more common, it was the banality rather than the theatricality of the conversations that began to grate – the classic example being the people who simply announced that they were 'on the train' to absent friends or family. What might have been seen only two decades ago as un-English self-display is now grudgingly accepted, although those brave souls who wear hands-free headsets still receive the occasional double-take, and listening to one side of a telephone conversation will always be either boring or maddening (because we cannot hear half the conversation whether we want to or not). Not only do strangers on trains disagree about the nature and value of silence, but mobile phones also occupy the user and repulse strangers more comprehensively than books or newspapers. In doing so they have subtly altered the already fragile social dynamic of the train carriage, making us seem even more absent to each other. When the train is delayed, we are now much more likely to phone friends than moan collectively with our fellow passengers.

Using our state-of-the-art mobile phones to explain to a friend or colleague that our dilapidated train is running late is a perfect illustration of the unevenness of progress in daily life, the way changes to our mundane lives often lag behind more spectacular transformations – something that is rarely captured in fictional attempts to imagine the future. In the early 1960s, Hanna-Barbera made a cartoon called *The Jetsons*, a sort of space-age version of *The Flintstones*. Its paterfamilias, George Jetson, commuted from the family home in the Skypad Apartments to his job at Spacely Space Sprockets in a nuclear-powered space car, which looked like a flying saucer with a see-through lid. His son, Elroy, had to make do with a low-tech method of travelling to school: sliding down a pneumatic tube. The series was set at some unspecified point in the twenty-first century, and, when I watched the series as a child, I fondly imagined that this was how we would all move

3   A lifetime behind a desk

> *'This boundless region, the region of le boulot, the job,*
> *il rusco – of daily work, in other words – is less known*
> *than the Antarctic'*
>
> Primo Levi[1]

After the cattle-truck incarceration of the commuting train, you arrive with some relief at your own mini-fiefdom which, according to UK law, must occupy at least eleven cubic metres: the office desk and its environs. With the possible exception of our beds, many of us spend more of our lives here than anywhere else. But if work is a territory that is too familiar to be colonised by knowledge, as Primo Levi suggests, then the office desk is a true *terra incognita*. No unintrepid explorer has yet planted his flag on its laminated top. Like much to do with modern office life, it is an American invention – and its design, contents and location are a little primer in office politics.

Billy Wilder's classic film *The Apartment* (1960) is, among other things, a narrative about the role of the desk in post-war office life. As the film begins, the camera pans across a huge office made up of serried rows of identical desks, all facing the same way and receding into apparent infinity. In America, this layout was known unflatteringly as the 'bullpen', to suggest either the stockyard or the sweaty, crowded area where baseball pitchers warm up. Somewhere in this endless sea of desks, the camera finds our hero, C. C. 'Bud' Baxter (Jack Lemmon), a lowly insurance clerk in a large corporation called Consolidated Life, working at desk number 861 on the nineteenth floor. Desk number 861 is, like all the others, a descendant of the Modern Efficiency Desk, first made in 1915 by Steelcase Inc. for the New York offices of Equitable Assurance. This desk, which was a simple, rectangular table with small drawers, replaced the cabinet-like desks, with their high backs made up of little drawers and cubby holes, which dominated office life before the First World War. At their new efficiency desks, office workers could be watched, monitored and subjected to time-and-motion studies. They had to keep files and letters moving quickly from their in-trays to their out-trays, rather like a factory assembly line.

By lending his apartment to his seniors for their extra-marital affairs, Baxter begins to move up the corporate ladder. Promoted to 'second administrative assistant', he puts his few belongings – Rolodex, diary, pen, papers – in a cardboard box, and the camera follows him as he walks through the ocean of desks into his own office, one of the small rooms around the side of the floor, with large windows for easy surveillance of the bullpen. Eventually, he is promoted to the twenty-seventh floor, where female secretaries serve as gatekeepers to the male executive's hallowed private space. Baxter's final reward at the end of the film is a panelled corner office, with an artfully angular desk and a leather swivel chair. Naturally, he gives all this up at the end of the film for the charms of a lift attendant played by Shirley MacLaine.

That is what work desks used to be like. The American *Business Etiquette Handbook* for 1965 advises employees:

> Avoid over-decorating your desk or area. When your desk shelves and wall space are covered with mementos, photographs, trophies, humorous mottoes and other decorative effects, you are probably not

beautifying the office; rather you may be giving it a jumbled, untidy look. You may also be violating regulations against using nails in the walls … [2]

Before the Second World War, executive desks were dark-wood, Georgian, pedestal types. When high-status office furniture began to be made for the mass market in the US in the 1950s, it deliberately eschewed this antique style in favour of light-coloured desks with rounded or angled corners, not unlike dining tables.[3] The executive's office became like a domestic interior, no longer burdened with the fuss and mess of bureaucracy: 'Anyone who entered would immediately perceive that this was a man, freed from mundane traffic with papers and pretensions, who had attained a state of pure function.'[4] Unlike the office drone's desk, executive desks were heavily accessorised with things like cigar lighters, electric pencil sharpeners and Newton's Cradles (those clacking steel balls that demonstrate the law of conservation of momentum). America pioneered this market in prestige, but the same basic rules applied elsewhere: you won status with a larger desk, more space around it, and best of all your own office. The British civil service, for example, measured the subtlest distinctions in service grades through precise allocations of desk type, carpet and square feet of floor space.

Around the time that *The Apartment* was made, however, the nature of the office began to change. The salaries of office workers had fallen behind those of many manual workers and, rather than trying to compete on pay, firms tried to brighten up their offices to attract staff. Adverts for clerical jobs in London in the 1950s began to use phrases like 'modern' and 'friendly' to describe offices, particularly to attract women.[5] Much of the new office technology was marketed at women, from lipstick-coloured telephones to Marcello Nizzoli's much-imitated, curvaceous designs for Olivetti typewriters. One 1960 typewriter advert showed a female secretary dressed in black tie and tails at a type-writer blown up to the size of a grand piano: 'You are the artiste ... Your touch on the keys, your virtuosity produce the accomplished results which ensure your Chief's "applause" and a universal ovation!'[6]

At around the same time, in the late 1950s, the German consultancy Quickborner was developing the concept of *Bürolandschaft* (office landscaping), which reinvented the office as a free-flowing, open-plan space, with desks arranged not in regimented rows but in 'islands'. All workers, including executives, were given roughly the same amount of space, and could personalise it with pot plants, photos and keepsakes. In America, the designer Robert Propst had a similar idea while employed as director of the research division of the furniture company Herman Miller. 'Today's office is a wasteland,' he wrote in 1960. 'It saps vitality, blocks talent, frustrates accomplishment. It is the daily scene of unfulfilled intentions and failed effort.'[7] Propst developed 'Action Office 2', a modular office system marketed by Herman Miller in 1968. Its chief innovation was the partition panel, a screen between four and six feet high, covered in padded fabric, which became an omnipresent means of dividing space and providing some privacy in open-plan offices. For Propst, it was a way of giving workers control over 'exposure overload' and the 'continuous idiot salutations' necessary in bullpen offices where workers had to 'invest in a recognition act every time someone goes by'. The panel was also a blank canvas on which people could stick pictures and notices, to 'explain our work, define our individuality and relieve our memory'.[8]

Of course, the new open-plan office had another advantage: it saved money. In traditional offices, there is a lot of redundant square footage taken up by linking corridors and the areas behind doors. An employee sitting in an enclosed, one-person office is literally a waste of space. Conveniently, partitioned spaces also have higher tax write-offs than offices with fixed walls.[9] The open-plan office is supposed to sweep away outdated hierarchies and inefficient bureaucracy, fostering teamwork and creative interaction. The unsurprising reality is that, however our desks are arranged, our colleagues can be irritating as well as helpful, and the competition for status and hierarchy is as resilient as ever. At Hewlett-Packard, a pioneer of open-plan office spaces, one of the most common items supplied by the corporate nurse was earplugs.[10] The partition panel became the raw material not for Action Offices but for cubicles, those universal signifiers of American white-collar alienation, immortalised in Scott Adams' Dilbert books. Propst realised to his horror that 'not all organiza-tions are intelligent and progressive. Lots are run by crass people who can take the same kind of equipment and create hellholes. They make little bitty cubicles and stuff people in them.'[11]

In Britain, there were other, unforeseen problems with communal offices. In 1968, the *Observer* magazine ran a feature titled: 'Would you let your daughter work in an open-plan office?' One male employee, it discovered, 'suffers from visual distraction. He has to turn his desk sideways to avoid seeing the miniskirts.'[12] In an age when good secretarial skills were at a premium, women could demand a 'modesty board' – a piece of plywood stretching across the desk front – as a perk and status symbol. Two out of three secretaries, the *Daily Mirror* reported, wanted modesty boards 'to stop the boss peering at their legs'.[13] A simpler solution – allowing women to wear trousers to work – did not arrive in most British firms until the mid-1970s.

The dilemma of the open-plan was how to gesture towards egalitarianism while satisfying the human need for status-markers. In the late 1960s, for example, the British civil service tried to economise on desk size. A range designed for the Ministry of Public Buildings and Works broke the desk up into separate units for different tasks, such as a space for writing work, a telephone table, a storage unit, and so on. [14] A worker who needed more space could put in an application for more units, which could be added to the original in a honeycomb pattern. Rather than fretting about different types and sizes of rectangular desk, civil servants gained kudos by adding units. Hierarchies remained, but they had been rationalised. A similar compromise occurred in some open-plan Japanese offices. The desks of the higher-ups were at one end of the room, with their subordinates arranged in hierarchical order all the way down to the 'bottom' of the room, near the entrance. If you wanted to talk to people at the 'top', you had to make your way through the human shield of their underlings, which protected executives from routine inquiries.[15]

IBM's launch of the personal desktop computer in 1981 created a new type of desk: the workstation. And an unintended consequence of the arrival of the workstation was that it made office chairs more important. Before the 1970s, it was generally believed that there was a textbook way to sit in a chair, with both feet flat on the floor, knees together, legs bent at right angles and the back straight. Since it was up to the worker to sit up straight, chair designers focused on creating designs that symbolised status rather than on improving posture. The contrast between high-backed, throne-like executive chairs and small-backed, armless secretarial chairs for dainty ladies survived well into the 1960s. Height had such status value that few chair seats would screw down below eighteen inches, even though the average woman's leg was more like sixteen inches from the underside of the thigh to the floor.[16] This status-consciousness was complicated by the new science of ergonomics (from the Greek *ergon* 'work' and *-omics* 'to manage'), first used in cockpit design during the Second World War and then applied to offices, which sought a more efficient relationship between people and their working environments. By the 1970s, this science was suggesting that chairs should not support one 'correct' posture but encourage motion, allowing workers to spread the strain of sitting across their various body parts. All this emerged at the same time as the computer was encouraging workers to hunch forward and move about less. Mindful of ever-more stringent health and safety regulations, companies took note.

The father of the modern, ergonomic office chair was Bill Stumpf, who as an academic and designer at the University of Wisconsin in 1966 began studying orthopaedic data and examining the movements of office workers at desks with the aid of time-lapse photography. After joining Herman Miller, Stumpf wrote a paper called 'A chair is a chair is a problem' which argued that 'many of us spend eight hours a day in a chair that is uncomfortable, that restricts our movement and inhibits our performance'.[17] Stumpf's solution came in 1976 with the Ergon chair. It had all the essentials of today's swivel chair: moulded, foam-filled back and seat, armrests up at desktop height, gas-lift levers to adjust the height and tilt, and five-star legs on easy-glide castors. One sceptical customer said it looked 'like two hemorrhoid pillows put together to make a chair'.[18]

The ethos of ergonomics is egalitarian: a comfy chair is seen as an inalienable human right. But the distinction between basic operator chairs and smarter managerial chairs survives. The latter tend to be higher-backed with wider seats, leather covers and more generous padding, including 'memory foam', which responds to the sitter's body shape. Sophisticated specifications also denote status gradations. Don Chadwick and Bill Stumpf's bestselling Aeron Chair, first produced in 1994, is the ultimate, de luxe place to park your behind. It is 'biomorphic' to adapt to the curves of the human body, and minutely adjustable with levers and pulleys. It comes in three sizes to accommodate (the promotional material says tactfully) 'those in a broader range of the anthropometric scale'. Its back and seat are made up of a flexible mesh, which prevents heat build-up and adapts to the sitter's shape. Trendy companies like the Aeron chair not only because it shows how much they care about their workers' delicate bottoms, but also because the mesh seat lets more light into the office.[19]

Even an entry-level Aeron, without all the fancy extras like tilt limiters and extra back-support options, will cost several hundred pounds. So it has tended to inhabit the loft-office spaces of dotcom entrepreneurs rather than, say, the offices of impoverished academics. (Like most people, I have to make do with a bog-standard descendant of the Ergon.) In 2004, the *Sun* expressed outrage that the Ministry of Defence had bought an Aeron chair for each of the 3,150 civil servants in its main building in Whitehall, at the same time as 'squaddies in Iraq have to buy their own boots and sleeping bags'.[20] Infinite adjustability is all very well, it seems, but not for public servants at the taxpayer's expense. Give them an Ergon, and they can swivel on that.

The arrival of the PC also meant that the main purpose of the desk was now to provide a home for the computer. The computer is usually bulkier than the typewriter, it comes with all sorts of paraphernalia like mouse mats and wrist rests, and its cables need to be neatly hidden round the back of the desk, routed down its hollow table legs or tucked inside nearby partition panels. With the rainbow-coloured, translucent iMac an honourable exception, the desktop computer is generally a grey, standard-issue box. The Olivetti approach to office appliance design, which valued originality in each item, has been roundly trounced by the IBM approach, which promoted the virtues of predictability and standardisation. Office design is now all about how objects fit together as part of a system. Beauty has been sacrificed for order.

This suits most office designers and companies, who have long been suspicious of desk clutter. Some firms do not even allow employees to have personal items on their desks, in case their idiosyncratic mess scrambles the signals of the company's corporate branding. And these advocates of clean designer workplaces have found an unlikely ally in the fashionable mind-body-spirit movement. Guides to office Feng Shui advise workers that 'keeping your personal space in order opens the flow of chi and stimulates your creativity'.[21] Firms of 'deskologists' offer to cure you of 'irritable desk syndrome', de-cluttering your workspace if you are too lazy or inept to do it yourself.[22]

Look around any office today, however, and you will see that this war against clutter has been lost. An academic survey of office workers in Orange County, California, found that they displayed an average number of 9.6 personal items on their desks and that the more they were allowed to personalise them, the happier they were with their workspaces.[23] One of the main effects of these desk accessories is to subvert the functionalism of the office. There is a whole office supplies industry that answers to this need for uselessness in the form of banana-shaped pens and nose-shaped pencil sharpeners. Workers display deliberately bizarre items like nodding dogs, ugly trolls or grow-a-heads (heads with grass growing out of the top instead of hair) which they would regard as far too kitsch to have in their homes. The infamous sign 'You don't have to be mad to work here … but it helps' is now extinct, but its successors are everywhere: 'So far today I only made one mistake … I got out of bed.' 'I'm busy now, can I ignore you some other time?' 'I can only please one person per day: today isn't your day and tomorrow doesn't look good either.' Like much generic office humour, these signs are both subversive and fatalistic: they gesture towards the messy politics of work and then universalise them, making them seem like a feature of offices everywhere. Some jokey

office worker, interviewed for a study by the Work Foundation on office space, argued that there was method in his mayhem: 'My in-trays are always full and I have since abandoned them to simply hold desktop detritus. I have different degrees of "in", depending on how many things I need to get through … I try to operate a hierarchy of surface areas …'[26] In this more fluid, unstructured environment, the sticky note reminds us of some job we need to do when we get round to it.

But our nesting instincts, which can turn the desk into such a chaotic personal space, conflict with one of modern office life's harsher realities: our desk is no longer our own. In 1985, Philip Stone and Robert Luchetti wrote a seminal essay, 'Your office is where you are', in the *Harvard Business Review*. Stone and Luchetti came to bury what they called 'Cubicleland'. Offices should be redesigned as 'activity settings', they argued, with a private 'home base' for each worker supplemented by access to shared facilities and communal areas. They even suggested giving employees an expense budget with which they could purchase access to these spaces as and when they needed them.[27] This article spawned a movement known as 'alternative officing'. It gained momentum during the economic boom of the late 1990s, when trendy ad agencies and PR companies in London and New York redesigned their offices, dividing them up into quiet 'chill-out' or 'Zen' zones with beanbags and sofas, 'chaos' spaces with meeting tables for exchanging ideas, and 'touchdown areas' with breakfast-style bars and laptop connections.

The sworn enemies of the alternative office are territoriality and permanence. Office space needs to be adaptable to 'churn', the term used for moving workers or equipment around, the rate of which grew by 14 per cent during the 1990s.[28] In the words of one New York consultant, new office furniture tries to be 'less Dilberty'.[29] Office furniture companies offer a basic 'vocabulary' which allows desks and workstations to be 'highly configurable ... with flowing, fluid shapes, that grow, flex and adapt to change over time'.[30] Screens and canopies are not boringly right-angled, but at 120-degree angles to produce pleasing honeycomb shapes. Desks are rounded to form a kidney-bean shape, with employees seated in the centre of the curve so that they are surrounded by work surface. Overhead poles, tiles and panels offer various 'wire management solutions', but the ultimate dream is the cableless office, which will detach computers from desks and unchain workers from workstations. There is an architectural evangelism about alternative officing which assumes that people's ways of working will be transformed by a curvy desk or a translucent work surface. For all the revolutionary rhetoric, the British economy is dominated by small companies with limited budgets, which manage to get by with desks that are tediously rectangular.

The alternative office has suffered the same fate as the 1960s open-plan office: its loftier ideals have lost out to the more prosaic aims of saving space and money. In the 1990s, under pressure from shareholders and rising rents, many firms tried to cut 'occupancy costs' – that is, the costs of renting, servicing, lighting and heating their buildings. They looked for measurable notions of a building's 'performance', such as comparing the money earned by employees for the firm with the expense of housing them at their desks.[31] On these purely utilitarian grounds, the desk is an under-used resource, occupied for an average of 45 per cent of office hours. The rest of the time its occupant will be in meetings, seeing clients, training or off work.[32]

One solution is for workers to share their desks. In the system known as 'hotelling', they book in each day with a 'concierge'. The concierge takes their possessions out of a locker, wheels them in a portable filing cabinet to their designated desk, uses a smart card to reroute telephone calls, and sets up personal items such as stationery and even family photographs.[33] Once the desk is vacated, the concierge clears and cleans it for the next occupant, just like a hotel room. In 'hot-desking' – a term possibly derived from 'hot-bunking', where sailors on watch share bunks, sleeping in the warm pit left by the last man rather than bothering to change the sheets – workers simply have to grab the first desk that is available. The sexy names given to these cost-effective forms of musical chairs suggest the libertarian, nomadic ethos of the alternative office. Certainly, 'hot desk' sounds more exciting than 'shared desk' or 'no desk'.

For all their passionate advocates, however, hotelling and hot-desking have not yet made any great inroads into the resilient territorialism of the office. Shared workspaces have given rise to the predictable phenomenon of 'warm-desking', where workers deprived of a permanent desk lay claim to a temporary one, spreading their coats, mobile phones and general mess around according to the law of first possession.[34] Surveys of workers invariably suggest that, although they do not necessarily want the seclusion of their own private offices, they do want control of their personal space, which means their own desk.[35] When firms try to wrestle their employees from their desks in the name of creativity and innovation, the employee is entitled to respond: work is work. It is fine to make it more pleasant and agreeable, but dishonest to pretend that it is something else entirely. If you want me to work, I need somewhere to do it. So please, if it's not too much to ask, can I have my desk back?

4 The word from the water cooler

> 'The Office in the twentieth century was becoming ...
> as important as The Land in the Middle Ages or The
> Factory in the nineteenth century. Yet there had been no
> Office Dickens or Office Langland'
>
> Jonathan Gathorne-Hardy[1]

If workers are no longer to be chained to their desks, then
they can hardly be criticised for getting up occasionally to
have a natter with their colleagues. In the late 1990s, the
British media identified a new phenomenon inspired by
this habit: the 'water-cooler moment'. The phrase seems
to have originated among American television executives,
who wanted their programmes to generate conversation
the next day as workmates filled their little plastic cups at
the office watering hole. The water cooler soon came to be
seen as the office equivalent of the old parish pump or the
tribal campfire: the place where vernacular knowledge,
folklore and gossip were exchanged.

Water coolers have been around in American offices
since the beginning of the twentieth century, early models
using a big block of ice to cool the water. Firms have long
been suspicious of the time that workers waste filling up
from them. In Sinclair Lewis's office-life novel, *The Job*
(1917), an efficiency expert arranges to have office boys
deliver glasses of water to work desks four times a day:

Thitherto, the stenographers had wasted a great deal

of time in trotting to the battery of water-coolers, in actually being human and relaxed and gossipy for ten minutes a day. After the visitation of the expert the girls were so efficient that they never for a second stopped their work – except when one of them would explode in hysteria and be hurried off to the rest-room.[2]

The idea of water-cooler gossip has a long history: 'scuttlebutt' is an old nautical term for a cask of fresh water on deck from which crew members could drink, and it became a synonym for idle gossip in the US navy.[3] As a metaphor for workplace tittle-tattle, however, 'water-cooler moment' is misleading. A water cooler is not a good place to gossip, because it tends to be placed in prominent areas like receptions or common rooms, and there is no excuse to stop and chat because you can fill up your cup quickly. The office gossip needs somewhere to pause, out of general earshot, in front of a noisy photocopier or over a boiling kettle in the staff kitchen. So how and why has this phrase become such a powerful cultural metaphor? In part, it is because of a shift in how workers have thought and felt about what their firms suspiciously call 'non-productive working time'.

Traditional factory discipline in Britain clamped down on idle talk, limiting conversation among workers to fixed breaks. Up until the 1960s, the British equivalent of the water-cooler moment was the tea break, as dearly loved a national institution as the drink itself, immortalised in songs like 'Everything stops for tea' (1935) and 'I like a nice cup of tea' (1937). During the Second World War, the mass-observer Celia Fremlin provided a vivid account of the British attitude to tea breaks in her book *War Factory* (1943). Fremlin spent several months with women conscripted to do factory work in Wiltshire, where she discovered that her fellow workers were demoralised by long hours and tedious routines. Between three and five o'clock in the afternoon was the worst time for what managers called 'lavatory-mongering', when workers drifted off to the cloakroom, spending half an hour or more there, talking or just doing nothing. But after five o'clock, there was a marked improvement in morale, with the feeling that a tea break was imminent. Fremlin heard one worker console a newcomer during her first tea break: 'You'll be all right now, the time goes ever so quick after tea.' 'That's right,' her friend agreed. 'It goes lovely after tea. Funny, isn't it? It never drags, not after teatime.'[4]

In factories, the klaxon or foreman's whistle gave the signal for workers to down tools for the tea break. Trade union tea-tasters would test the quality of the members' tea before it could be distributed. If tea was served in the canteen, workers would be given a five or ten-minute allowance for 'walking time'. There were frequent tea strikes in the 1950s and 1960s, Byzantine disputes about the timing of the break or the quality of the brew. For proto-Thatcherites, they symbolised how much British industry was enslaved to idle workers and bolshy unions. The genteel office version of the fixed break was the shout of 'Trolley!' which announced the arrival of the tea lady with elevenses or afternoon tea. In his touching memoir of 1950s office life, *Exciting Times in the Accounts Department*, Paul Vaughan remembers finding comfort in the clockwork regularity of these visits: at 10.30 a.m., a woman would wheel in a large trolley with tea and sandwiches, returning again at precisely 3.30 p.m. with tea and cakes.[5] Higher-ups in offices would follow the same routine, but would receive their tea in china cups on a tray rather than a trolley. Whether you gave a chit to the trolley lady or had your secretary brew up for you, the tea break was a little encapsulation of office hierarchies.

In the 1960s, the fixed tea break began to be abolished and 'free' or flexible breaks introduced instead. The key catalyst for this change was the hot drinks vending machine, which arrived from America in the 1950s. After a tea strike at Ford's Dagenham plant in 1962, Primapax's general manager wrote to Ford, pointing out that his vending machines could help avoid future industrial strife.[6] Vending machines could be placed throughout workplaces, dispensing with the mass trek to the canteen or the long wait for the tea trolley, and workers could refill according to their own unique 'fatigue curve'. In 1960, fewer than 500 British factories had vending machines; by the end of 1966, 6,000 had them.[7] Break times now had to be staggered because vending machines could not cope with a rush on their services in fixed breaks. The machines also helped to develop the public's taste for instant coffee: stewed vending-machine tea was virtually undrinkable. There were some demonstrations against the substandard 'robot cuppa', though, and, as late as 1978, one firm's employees queued up in protest every morning and afternoon to wait for their (non-existent) tea trolley after it was axed.[8] Most workers were won over eventually, as trade unions negotiated days off work in lieu of the time saved from abolishing fixed breaks.

When offices began to go open-plan in the 1960s, space formerly given to cellular rooms and corridors made way for communal areas with comfy seating, vending machines and mini-kitchens. Robert Propst, the inventor of the Action Office, claimed that one of his aims was to make workers get up from their desks and interact: 'It's truly amazing the number of decisive events and critical dialogues that occur when people are out of their seated, stuffy contexts, and moving around chatting with each other.'[9] The first automated photocopiers arrived in American and British offices in the 1960s, and they soon became havens for gossips – particularly since people had to wait for longer at the machines then, when copy speeds were slower and jams more frequent. Photocopiers also inspired a new sort of written gossip. Workers used them to reproduce cartoons, jokes and fake memos, giving rise to a genre of urban myth, 'photocopylore', first identified by an academic folklorist, Michael J. Preston, in 1974. As bits of paper got repeatedly copied and amended with crossings out, doodles and speech balloons, the myths changed subtly just as they did in oral retellings.[10] Unlike official memos, which were attached to prestigious individuals within a company, photocopylore spread the common knowledge of office life. Two things made it possible: the anonymity of new technology, and the waning of the most obvious office hierarchies. By the 1970s, bosses and secretaries routinely addressed each other by their first names. There were fewer signs saying 'Less talk, more work', because work itself involved more talking. As the role of the typist-secretary declined, office workers had to leave their desks to photocopy, file papers or put letters in the post, making casual encounters with colleagues more likely. Breaks became briefer and less formal but more frequent.

By the early 1990s, most British offices had installed American-style water coolers, partly because of a small number of enterprising firms like Watersplash, which saw how popular they were in the US and spotted a marketing opportunity in the UK. These new-look water coolers were the product of a series of laws about accessibility and hygiene passed in America in the 1980s. Water coolers now had to be barrier-free, disabled-access units, with no traces of lead, which meant using plastic rather than metal. A whole industry sprang up to supply these designer water coolers, with one-touch plastic taps and upendable, blue-tinted refill bottles. Firms realised they were a cheap and cheerful way to smarten up the workplace and give waiting clients a general impression of a caring employer. 'Water-cooler moment' became a popular phrase not because people actually talk at water coolers, but because it captured the snatched, accidental nature of interaction in modern offices.

The changing nature of the work break also transformed the way that advertisers marketed drinks and snacks. Take 'Hunk', a celebrated TV commercial of the mid-1990s for Diet Coke. Over a steamy Etta James soundtrack, a group of women gather by the floor-to-ceiling window of an open-plan office for their '11.30 appointment'. They gaze longingly at the glistening bare torso of a hunky window cleaner as he drinks from an ice-cold Diet Coke. At the end of their break, the women all chorus, 'Same time tomorrow, girls.' The Diet Coke commercial inspired many imitators, all suggesting that work breaks were now fleeting but precious pauses to be exploited to the full. Numerous adverts used images of office workers, usually women, enjoying surreptitious pleasures like celebrity gossip magazines, luxury yoghurts or chocolate treats at their desks. In 2004, Nestlé briefly replaced its long-running slogan 'Have a break, have a KitKat' with the blander 'Make the most of your break', in response to market research about office breaks. Nestlé explained that 'the workplace break is now less structured and formal' but 'even if it is for five minutes, you can maximise your enjoyment with a KitKat'.[11]

This shift in the pattern of work breaks also altered the nature of workplace gossip – although such changes are difficult to analyse because gossip is simultaneously the most common and elusive of social habits. By its very nature, it leaves behind little in the way of evidence. Most surveys about gossip simply ask people when and where they gossip. According to one rather speculative study, based on a 47-week working year, the average office employee spends 24 days complaining about the boss, 21 days gossiping about colleagues and flirting with them, 19 days making personal phone calls, 14 days daydreaming and 8.8 days hiding in the toilets.[12] But gossip, which is conducted out of someone else's earshot and tends to merge with other forms of conversation, is almost impossible to measure and define. People may not be fully conscious, or may be keen to deny, that they have been gossiping.

If it is hard to study gossip in the present, then it is harder still to uncover its history. Most academic studies of gossip have seen it as hardwired in our evolutionary psychology, and the eternal necessity for hunter-gatherers to be social animals. But clearly the subject matter of gossip changes over time – outside of its immediate time and place, it is likely to seem petty and insignificant. We don't know whether workers talked about different things in their tea breaks in the 1940s, but a reasonable surmise (confirmed partly by Fremlin's account of the ritual whingeing about supervisors in the Wiltshire factory) is that they gossiped more about their bosses and less about each other. Open-plan office space, first-name etiquette and relaxed dress codes may create a friendlier working environment, but they also mean that workers are less sure about their status and roles. In the modern office, hierarchies and rewards are fluid and uneven. The classic topics of modern office gossip emerge out of these anxieties: restructuring, redundancies, takeovers, favouritism, other people's salaries and perks.

The word on gossip is that it is a disagreeable habit which does no one any good. In recent years, however, sociolinguists and social anthropologists have talked up its virtues. They argue that gossip is a vital means of sharing information, forming social alliances and oiling the wheels of office relationships so that we can deal with more serious issues when they arise. Most gossip, far from being idle tittle-tattle, is both true and useful. In the mid-1990s, the anthropologist Robin Dunbar developed a much-discussed theory of gossip. Beginning with the observation that monkeys groom each other to consolidate alliances and hierarchies, Dunbar argued that gossip evolved as a sort of 'vocal grooming', suitable for the larger groups in which humans live. Around two-thirds of conversation is taken up not with intellectual or practical matters but with gossip about personal relationships, likes and dislikes and the behaviour of others.[13] People who do not gossip, instead of being admired for their fine, upstanding characters, are seen as either aloof or insignificant by their peers.

According to the business ethnographer John Weeks, there is even a purpose to that unloved subset of office gossip, whingeing. In 1994, Weeks spent several months working in a leading British bank. He gave it a pseudonym (the British Armstrong Bank, or BritArm) for obvious reasons: this was a company about which nobody who worked for it had a good word to say. But Weeks argued that this culture of complaint was a form of 'lay ethnography', a way for people to make sense of their own lives.[14] Moaning was a kind of melancholy amusement which allowed fellow moaners to join in a common vision and purpose without rocking the boat too much. Weeks distinguished between two types of complaint: deprecations and derogations. Deprecations genuinely solicited redress or change, but workers rarely voiced them because they raised difficult issues about power and resources. Derogations were simply insults or put-downs which signalled a fatalistic acceptance of the firm's failings, a way of establishing empathy between the moaners rather than achieving a solution to the complaint.[15]

Surprisingly, Weeks found that the moaniest workers were also the most vociferous in defending their company against external criticism. Complaining about the bank's culture was a way 'to display affinity with it, not alienation from it. You must know the culture well and be a part of it to be able to complain about it and get away with it.'[16] Weeks's ethnography of whingeing cocks a snook at contemporary management theory, which makes such capital out of training and motivating workers to have a positive, can-do attitude. At BritArm, these happy-clappy training sessions just became another thing to moan about. Workplaces now have so many emptily ritualistic official communications that it is hardly surprising when workers come to prefer authorless, unofficial gossip.

Some apologists for office gossip suggest that it is becoming harder to talk casually in modern workplaces. Dunbar argues that much modern work involves tenuous connections with people on the other end of a telephone line or email server, and that the desire to cut occupancy costs encourages firms to get rid of communal spaces. This devalues the 'chance encounters over the coffee machine, idle chatter around the photocopier', where casual contacts can function 'like a parallel-processing supercomputer', generating ideas that individuals could never have on their own.[17] Sociologists like Richard Sennett and Ray Pahl claim that flexible, insecure patterns of employment have created low-trust, rivalrous workplaces where friendships with colleagues are more difficult.[18]

But this pessimistic analysis is only part of the story. One of the aims of new office designers has been to distinguish between different types of office, which they call 'cells', 'dens' and 'hives' according to the different types of work that go on there. Cells are individual offices for people such as barristers or academics who need to work quietly on their own or have one-to-one meetings. Dens are bustling places where people need to exchange ideas, like newspaper offices or advertising agencies. Hives are places like call centres or data-entry offices, where employees are supposed to get on with their jobs like 'busy worker bees'.[19] In these low-status offices, employers control their workers closely, by monitoring toilet and smoking breaks, watching over them with video cameras, tracking the rate of their computer key strokes and arranging their desks in serried rows like the old-style bullpens. Unsurprisingly, the opportunities for idle chatter are rather limited.

In den-like offices, however, gossip is seen as a social

good. The rationale goes like this: as companies use technology to automate their routine tasks, or farm them out to low-status workers in hive-like back offices, higher-status workers are left with more complex tasks that can only be conducted in teams.[20] A study by the London School of Economics found that, across a wide range of white-collar jobs, the time spent talking with colleagues and generally dealing with other people increased by about a third in the five years up to 1997.[21] Many open-plan den offices now have 'break-out areas' with café-style tables, chairs and sofas, a decor and ambience clearly influenced by the cappuccino culture of the high street.

Not all workers are seen as worthy of access to this cappuccino culture, however. In December 1996, the London Underground almost shut down when maintenance workers demanded the right to a cappuccino break. Three years earlier, they had relinquished their twice-a-day, twenty-minute tea break in return for a free drinks vending machine. Keen to save money, LU management then withdrew the most popular but costly options, cappuccino and hot chocolate, before climbing down when threatened with a strike. The rail union's general secretary, Jimmy Knapp, said, 'Cappuccino might not be everyone's cup of tea, but a deal is a deal.'[22] In 2001, there was a fully-fledged strike on the Underground as train drivers' unions demanded that water-boilers be supplied in their mess rooms, so they would not have to spend their breaks waiting for kettles to boil.[23] For much of the media, these strikes were simply a throwback to the bad old days of petty industrial disputes. But is any more time 'wasted' during tea breaks in messes than during coffee breaks in modern offices? White-collar professionals are supposed to be sufficiently self-motivated, and reliant on the creative exchange of ideas, to make time spent talking inherently useful. Semiotically, the tea break denotes relaxation, idling and switching off, while the coffee break denotes stimulation, sociability and conversation. Coffee has retained some of its traditional associations with metropolitan, middle-class sophistication, and its even older reputation as 'the thinker's drink'.[24]

The downside of gossiping in coffee breaks in den-like offices is that work and leisure time blend into each other. It might be fun to spend the day exchanging information and bouncing ideas around with one's colleagues. But workplace chatter is still work, albeit of a kind that is difficult to quantify. Much office conversation in open-plan spaces is spontaneous and unstructured. Research by the design consultancy Space Syntax suggests that around 80 per cent of work conversations happen when one person simply passes another's desk.[25] An earlier MIT study conducted in the 1970s found that office workers are four times more likely to talk if they are sat six rather than sixty feet apart, and that people seated more than seventy-five feet apart hardly speak at all.[26] The informal nature of office encounters may be a source of uncertainty, since workers have to invent the rules as they go along. How much time should busy workers actually spend gossiping, and at what point should they extricate themselves from a corridor chat without seeming unfriendly? They may feel justified in cutting off a conversation because they have work to do, but gossiping has social and career benefits that are less tangible than making a deadline.

The way we gossip at work is an effect of the way we work. From tea breaks to water-cooler moments, gossip can only happen when office space is arranged in particular ways. The communal areas where workers congregate to talk – office designers call them 'magnet facilities' – have their own special rites and customs, not unlike those of shared student houses. Informal protocols and open-plan offices have only made these rites and customs more complicated. I once saw a handwritten sign in an office kitchen, stuck on the wall above the kettle: 'Please do not fill this kettle with more water than you need. The planet is already weeping, people!' Few workers would ever express an opinion about even the messiest desk of a colleague, let alone order them to tidy it. But in this no-man's-land of the office, the staff kitchen, workers feel connected and implicated in each other's lives. Not only do they gossip here, they also feel the need to communicate with their colleagues when they are not there. Even boiling a kettle is a political act. Office gossip is the daily habit most commonly derided for its triviality and gratuitousness. On the contrary, it seems to be both compulsive and compulsory.

5 Cashier number *one*, please

> 'We must rid ourselves of the delusion that it is major
> events which most determine a person. He is more
> deeply and lastingly influenced by the tiny catastrophes
> of which everyday existence is made up'
>
> Siegfried Kracauer[1]

Some firms might worry about the working time wasted
through office gossip. But few workers spare a thought to
how much of their day is taken up by unpaid labour, from
the hard graft of commuting to the routine tasks that fill
up our lunch breaks. Of these, perhaps the most tedious is
queuing. Waiting in line is a universal routine of daily life,
and the peak hour for doing it is lunchtime. It is then that
many of us queue at cafés, snack bars, post offices, banks
and holes in the wall. There is an obvious reason for long
lunchtime queues, a classic problem of synchronisation in
a consumer economy: workers are only able to queue up
in their lunch hour, which is precisely when there are less
likely to be servers or cashiers, who have inconsiderately
decided to take their lunch break at lunchtime as well.

Queuing is never just experienced and endured, it is
loaded with meaning – especially for Britons, who are
supposed to be so wonderful at doing it. Where does this
myth of the British (or, more particularly, the English) as
virtuoso queuers come from? The orderly queue seems to
have become an established social form in the early nineteenth century, a product of more urbanised, industrial-

ised societies which brought masses of people together in one place. But in 1837, when the historian Thomas Carlyle referred to the new habit of waiting in line for service, he was praising not his own countrymen but the French for their 'talent ... of spontaneously standing in queue'.[2] It was not until the end of the Second World War that a number of writers on the English character turned their attention to queuing. In his essay 'The English people' (1944), George Orwell envisaged an imaginary foreign observer who would be struck 'by the orderly behaviour of English crowds, the lack of pushing and quarrelling, the willingness to form queues'.[3] The Hungarian émigré George Mikes claimed in his bestselling book *How to be an Alien* (1946) that 'an Englishman, even if he is alone, forms an orderly queue of one'. Queuing, he claimed, was 'the national passion of an otherwise dispassionate race', the daily embodiment of our eternal sense of fairness and civility.[4] Writing a year later, the historian Ernest Barker commended the English urban crowd for its 'good sense, a species of self-discipline and a tactic of "fitting in" neatly on a little space ... there will be some bad manners and a little thrusting; but the institution (for the queue is of that order) will be made to work.' [5]

For all these writers, queuing is essentially apolitical: it may rely on the threat of legal enforcement but, as Barker puts it, any policeman who is on hand to preserve order 'melts easily into the general system of voluntary tactics'.[6] The queue is seen as an organic formation, a series of semi-improvised, tacit understandings between ordinary people. Its self-regulating aspect allows it to be allied with a certain kind of English liberalism which values the compromises of everyday life as a guarantor of social solidarity. Waiting in line is not a technique to be learned; there are no guides to 'queuing for beginners'. The queuer is simply supposed to draw intuitively on British traditions of decency, fair play and democracy.

It is no coincidence that the myth of the British as patient queuers developed during the Second World War. In this time of rationing and shortages, there was nothing trivial or decorous about queuing etiquette. Waiting in line was a fraught, politically charged activity rather than the minor irritation in daily life that it is today. Housewives would join a queue without knowing what was at the end of it, in the expectation (not always fulfilled) that it must be for sought-after goods. Queues, far from being celebrated as egalitarian, were widely seen as inequitable. People queued for unrationed but scarce foods like fruit, vegetables and fish, or rationed food like meat when they wanted better cuts. Working women, the elderly and mothers with babies thought this unfair because they were less able to queue for long periods. The government was sufficiently worried about the health consequences of women standing in line for long periods that it introduced a scheme to give priority to expectant mothers, by affixing a label to their ration books saying, 'Queue priority, please.' In one Second World War joke, a shopkeeper says to a young woman, 'Excuse me, miss, are you pregnant?' She replies, 'Well, I wasn't when I joined the queue.' A Mass-Observation survey reported in September 1948 that there was 'no other current topic that arouses such immediate and fierce reaction ... as the subject of queues ... which clearly to many is the symbol of all the frustrations of this post war era.'[7]

The Conservative leader Winston Churchill exploited these popular frustrations, symbolically identifying queues with the Labour government. During a 1949 by-election in South Hammersmith, he insisted that 'the queues of housewives outside the shops are the essence of Socialism and the restrictive system by which it and its parasites hope to live'. In an election radio broadcast of January 1950, Churchill invented the term 'Queuetopia' (a word which is still in the *Oxford English Dictionary*, although now rarely used) to describe a Britain under Socialist rule. The Labour Party Women's Organisation clearly blamed disgruntled housewives for the party's defeat in 1951, complaining that 'the last election was lost mainly in the queue at the butcher's or the grocer's'.[8]

The abolition of rationing in 1954, and the introduction of self-service supermarkets like Sainsbury's around the same time, finally put paid to endless shop queues. Government advisers, seeing the importation of this American retail method as a way of coping with labour shortages, cutting costs and increasing sales, energetically promoted 'the gospel of self-service'.[9] But many housewives were sceptical about this new form of shopping, worried about the loss of personal service, the temptation to overspend and even being accused of stealing goods bought in other shops. Drawing on memories of rationing, self-service advocates reassured them with the promise of queueless shopping: they would only have to queue to pay, with no time-consuming weighing and wrapping of food, and 'those requiring few items could obtain them speedily, while others could shop at their leisure'.[10] One upbeat newspaper article of 1959 claimed that self-service 'saves thousands of hours of queuing time every day', and that even a queue was now only 'a queue in one store as opposed to queues in four or five shops'.[11] This optimism proved to be premature. By 1964, the Consumer Council was reporting that the most common complaint of supermarket shoppers was the length of queues at the checkouts.[12]

If queuing slipped off the political agenda in these years, it still remained a significant annoyance in everyday life. For a long period from the late 1950s to the late 1970s, for example, readers of *The Times* complained endlessly in its Letters page about the queues in branches of high street banks and post offices. The main complaint was their restricted opening hours, which meant that customers had to form long queues at peak periods such as lunchtime. Many were also frustrated at the series of multiple queues for different cashiers, so that unlucky people might be stuck for ages behind a child paying in all the small change from a piggy bank. Since a queue forms when there is a failure to match supply with demand, its stubborn visibility in daily life could be seen as another symptom of the 'British disease' of badly trained, poorly motivated employees and mediocre management. The queue had become a symbol of national decline, a recurring issue for political and cultural commentators at the time.

It did not help that, in the 1960s, more information began to filter out about the daily lives of people behind the Iron Curtain, so that long queues became metaphorically linked to the inefficiencies of command economies. In Eastern bloc countries, people still had to queue up for scarce items that westerners now regarded as essential. Russian shops had an infamous three-queue system which required customers to line up firstly to view goods, secondly to pay for them and finally to obtain them. In East Germany, this experience of waiting was justified by the principle of deferred gratification: if ordinary citizens made sacrifices now and lived up to revolutionary ideals, it was argued, they would be rewarded later with a more equal society. During the last years of the GDR, though, the attempts by the regime to suggest that waiting was a practical lesson in collectivity – describing a queue, for example, as a *Wartekollektiv* (waiting collective) or a *sozialistische Wartegemeinschaft* (socialist waiting-association) – came to seem like the laughable death-knell of an increasingly ineffective thought police.

In Britain, it became a journalistic cliché to say that the queues in banks and post offices were longer than anywhere 'this side of the Iron Curtain'. Correlli Barnett, chronicler of national decline and a favourite historian of Thatcherites, was still making this analogy in the mid-1990s as part of his argument that Britain's post-war problems stemmed from the 'New Jerusalemism' of the liberal idealists of the 1940s who committed the country to a welfare state. 'In the emptiness of its shops and the length of its queues,' he wrote, 'Britain in the late 1940s much resembled Russia in the 1990s.'[13] The Churchillian idea of the queue as the quotidian manifestation of meddling socialism had proved remarkably persistent.

In the 1970s and 1980s, one particularly compelling symbol of national decline was the dole queue. This image was immortalised in Saatchi and Saatchi's famous Conservative Party poster of 1978–9, which was widely credited with helping Margaret Thatcher win her first general election victory. It was a photograph of a long, snaking queue leading to an unemployment office, accompanied by the slogan: 'Labour isn't working'. This long line was actually made up not of jobless people, but of various members of Hendon Young Conservatives and their parents.[14] They were asked to assemble at a north London park for the photo shoot, but only twenty loyalists turned up. So the photographer used a rope to mark out a meandering line and the volunteers gradually moved along it. These images were then brought together in a composite photograph, with the faces out of focus to conceal the duplication.[15] The poster's memorable image and its caption's clever double meaning – referring to both unemployment and a more general national malaise – once again equated queues with government incompetence and socialism.

But these images of long dole queues were based more on folk memory than contemporary reality. The term 'dole queue' was coined in the 1930s, and references to it in the Thatcher era recalled earlier images of men in northern towns queuing up outside 'the labour' in cloth caps and overcoats – images which had become part of the collective national psyche. In his 1941 essay 'The lion and the unicorn', Orwell included 'the queues outside the Labour Exchanges' in his list of characteristic 'fragments of the English scene'.[16] (This was the same passage about 'old maids biking to Holy Communion' famously quoted in a 1993 speech by John Major, who strangely neglected to include the line about dole queues.) By the 1980s, though, unemployed people received 'giro' cheques in the post rather than cash handouts, and they sat down and waited to be called in 'job centres' rather than queuing up outside dole offices.

As the dole 'queues' lengthened in the Thatcher era, queuing in many other public spaces was transformed by queue management systems, which drew heavily on a new branch of statistics known as 'queuing theory'. Queuing theory deals with situations in which customers arrive in 'poisson distribution': in unpredictable numbers, at variable intervals, and requiring different periods of service. This academic sub-discipline took off with the advent of computers in the 1950s and had been used since then to deal with large-scale waiting systems such as the rotation of hospital beds, airport runway control or urban traffic jams. In the 1980s, it was increasingly applied to the management of actual queues of people. This was all part of a much wider Thatcherite revolution which meant that both public and private sector companies had to respond more to the needs of the consumer. Managers set themselves the dual, sometimes conflicting, aims of serving the customer and cutting costs. Reducing queues was a painless way for firms to square this circle. Unlike some other aspects of customer service, queuing times were measurable, and the queue management boffins promised to design systems that both served people more quickly and minimised costs by cutting down on employee 'idle time'.

The 'thinking ticket machine', for example, aimed to do away with lines of people altogether. It was developed in Sweden in the 1960s, and the British firm Lonsto sold its first model to Tesco and Green Shield in the 1970s.[17] In the 1980s, it began to be used widely in places where people might have a long wait, like train booking centres or passport offices. Queuers took a numbered ticket from a dispenser and waited for their number to appear on an electronic display, thus saving them from having to stand in line for long periods. By the early 1990s, banks and post offices had introduced the 'electronic call forward' system for those who did still have to wait in line. Cashiers pressed a button when they were free, which activated dot-matrix displays and a recorded voice ('cashier number *one*, please') informing the person at the head of the queue where to go.

This cutting-edge technology was accompanied by a more mundane piece of queuing furniture: a metal pole with a rounded base and a strip of retractable webbed tape at the top, which was drawn out and attached to other poles to form queuing channels. In some hotels and cinemas, though, they had posher poles with a chrome finish and twisted, coloured rope – an altogether classier waiting experience. These queue barriers – what the sociologist Barry Schwartz calls the 'ecological supports' of queuing[18] – transformed the activity of waiting in line into a marketing opportunity. Trapped behind these barriers, we could not escape invitations to impulse-buy from shopping baskets strategically placed in the channels, or those irritating videos informing us of new services from the Post Office that we didn't want. Even the retractable tape on the queuing poles could be printed with promotional messages and logos. At around the same time, supermarkets began using assistants to pack bags for customers, and made pledges to open more checkouts by calling on 'queue busters', staff on the shop floor who would stop what they were doing and operate checkouts at busy times. Less publicly, they invested money in training checkout operators to work more quickly.[19]

But the Thatcherite queuing revolution was a very uneven phenomenon. At bus stops, where consumer satisfaction was not so easily measurable or highly valued, people still had to fend for themselves and work out their own shambolic queuing etiquette. The absence of a proper queue at bus stops could lead to near-anarchy, as hordes of passengers clambered on to already packed buses in no particular order, and drivers with half-full buses sped past stops teeming with angry commuters, because they knew they would have to let everyone board or no one at all. It was not that people who queued up for buses were ruder or angrier than those who queued up in shops or banks (they were, after all, often the same people) but that bus users had been left to improvise their own queuing discipline.

Perhaps because of its continued associations with unglamorous activities like waiting for a bus, the queue remained a symbol of national decline. In a speech in April 1994, the Conservative minister Michael Portillo invoked 'the still small voice of Britain's quiet majority' which is 'dismayed by much that goes on around it', offering the example of hard-working citizens 'standing in the post office queue watching handouts going to people who seem capable of work ... In a world turned upside down, they ask where is the encouragement for self-reliance, where is the punishment for wrong-doing, where is the incentive to achieve?'[20] The typical post-office queue was grist to Portillo's mill because it brought together such an eclectic mix, of poor people cashing benefits and the more prosperous buying stamps, posting parcels, or depositing takings from small businesses. Portillo's snap judgements about other people in the queue exploited the nature of the post office as a point of middle-class contact with the 'giro economy'.

But all this was changing: from the late 1990s onwards, most state benefits were paid directly into bank accounts.

Telephone and internet banking also removed the need for high street banks to deal with their customers in person. Since these services were mainly used by the well-off, banks began launching online accounts that cream-skimmed their wealthiest clients and offered them preferential rates. Indeed, for those with access to money and technology, queuing is increasingly a personal choice. People still have to wait in line for service, of course, or this chore is displaced into other forms of waiting like queuing at ATMs and traffic jams. But there are more opportunities to opt out of the experience of queuing by buying online or shopping outside peak hours. Queuing is a way of rationing goods or services – and in post-Thatcherite Britain, the rationing is not necessarily done with the same egalitarianism as the wartime fish queue. In the future, for instance, those who want to queue up to be served by a cashier in a bank may have to pay a surcharge, because the favoured customers will all be logging on to their e-accounts. Only the poor will be queuing up for their money, and they will have to pay for the privilege.

But the mythology of the British as enthusiastic queuers, forged in wartime, has survived. In the millennial anthology *British Greats*, the writer Shyama Perera argues that the queue captures 'the timeless essence of the British spirit'. The actual organisation of the queue might have changed, she writes, but the basic notion of egalitarian turn-taking has not. In London's 'multicultural hotch-potch', we sometimes see 'members of more assertive or less organised races trying either to test or to buck the system'. But they soon acknowledge that the queue is 'a totem of patience, practicality and a sense of fair play'.[21] For Perera, our national tradition of queuing exists outside of politics and history: the technology, method and personnel may vary, but the etiquette is never-ending.

At the same time, we often hear the claim that British queuers have become increasingly impatient in recent years, and that this is a more general sign of the decline of civility in public life. These accounts typically explain the phenomenon of 'queue rage' – the willingness to queue jump or to shout abuse at other people waiting in line – as an effect of an accelerated, time-poor society. As one management psychologist puts it, 'The culture of queuing is changing in Britain. You're becoming more like the Americans – more intolerant, more impatient. We lead increasingly frenetic lives and that freneticism makes us more driven, more time-conscious.'[22] In the absence of any longitudinal studies of queuing behaviour, this claim is largely unverifiable. Unfortunately, we have no hard evidence of how well-mannered people were in bus queues in 1950. Politeness and stoicism are subjective qualities, improvised in the routine acts of daily life, and leave behind few historical traces. We do know, however, that people have been complaining about the disintegration of queue discipline for almost as long as they have been lauding the queue as the essence of British decency – perhaps because this myth carries such symbolic weight that it cannot be sustained by the necessarily messier reality.

How can all these different ideas about the queue co-exist? Because not all queues are the same. Those who like to see the queue as an essentially British civic ritual can see their theories confirmed in those interminable lines of good-natured people waiting to buy tickets for Centre Court at Wimbledon, sign books of condolence or get pole position in the January sales. Some of these dedicated queuers even turn their little patch of pavement into a home from home, complete with tent, sleeping bag, flask and reading matter. These semi-domestic settings are a favoured subject of television vox pops, as reporters interview people in line, preferably in the rain which invariably fails to make them 'downhearted'. The queue becomes an end in itself and queuers are rewarded with the amused attention of others and a sense of camaraderie. But the queues we experience in everyday life – like waiting for the bus or at the bank or post office – rarely have this recreational aspect and certainly do not give us the same warm glow of togetherness.

Britons who travel abroad may discover something rather surprising: other nationalities seem to have grasped the complex activity of queuing. These foreigners do not generally riot, push, jostle, harass or abuse those in front of them when forced to wait in line. Perhaps, on reflection, the ability to stand patiently in a queue is not so uniquely wonderful after all. And however much we elevate the queue as the embodiment of quintessential Britishness, it will remain tiresome and boring to stand in it – which is why the more privileged among us will go to such lengths to avoid joining it. So let's hear two cheers for the carefully managed queue. There may be an infantilising quality to queue barriers and automated voices, like the condescending sign at the head of the queue in my local bank which says, 'Nearly there: thanks for waiting.' But when faced with the tedium of queuing, anything that makes waiting in line quicker and visibly fairer for everyone is surely a good thing. Long may we hear that singsong chant, 'Cashier number *one*, please.'

6 Dining al desko

> 'Objects and words also have hollow places in which a
> past sleeps, as in the everyday acts of walking, eating,
> going to bed, in which ancient revolutions slumber'
>
> Michel de Certeau[1]

If much of our lunch hour is eaten up by routine tasks like queuing, how much time do we actually have to eat? Each year, surveys of British workers map an apparently inexorable trend: the incredible shrinking lunch break. The average lunch 'hour' fell from 36 minutes in 2000 to 19 minutes and 42 seconds in 2006. Seven out of ten workers practise 'desk-dining', the average time taken to eat their lunch in front of the computer being 3.5 minutes. One in four claims never to take a lunch break at all.[2] With a bathetic nod to Continental pavement cafés, lunching in the office has been given a name, 'dining al desko', which captures both our puritanical attitude to work and a vague sense that we are missing out on a better life elsewhere. Desk-dining is the ultimate symbol of our workaholism and indispensability to the firm. But feeling too busy and harassed to have a proper lunch is a state of mind. No one is telling us we can't have a lunch break; most employers are rather more generous than the 1998 EU Working Time Regulations, which entitle workers to a twenty-minute meal break if they work for more than six hours. The reasons for the decline of lunch are not so much economic and rational as psychological and historical.

Britons have been worrying about the paucity of their midday meal for decades, particularly for those lower-middle-class office workers who could not rely on expense accounts or the subsidised staff canteens found in factories. Complaints about unappetising white-collar lunches date from just after the Second World War, when food was on everyone's mind in an era of rationing and scarcity, and a hot lunch was seen as vital preparation for the rest of the day. During the war many people went out for lunch, so they could be guaranteed at least one substantial meal, particularly in the winter when air raids interrupted the dark evenings. The growth of industrial canteens in wartime led people to expect a hot lunch. But canteens and restaurants were also rationed, and their customers soon learned to arrive before the food ran out. This helped to push back the traditional time of lunch from a 1 p.m. start to 12 noon, or even 11.45 a.m. by the end of the Second World War. As rationing continued after the war, the hegemony of lunch, and its earlier starting time, continued.[3] People tried to eat as big a meal as possible at midday, making do with a lighter evening meal in their homes.

Getting hold of a big meal was not always easy, however. In 1947, a querulous leader appeared in the *Daily Mail* headed 'Four jam sandwiches'. It told the heart-rending tale of the respectable-looking, middle-aged man who travelled each morning on the commuter train to London. He had such an air of quiet distinction that his fellow passengers began wondering about the contents of his rather smart briefcase. Then, one morning, the train suddenly jolted and the briefcase fell open, spilling on to the floor of the carriage, wrapped up in brown paper, four jam sandwiches – the gentleman's sorry excuse for a lunch. The tale of this unfortunate fellow was meant to illustrate the descent of the middle classes into genteel poverty, a fate that particularly agitated newspapers like the *Daily Mail* in the late 1940s (not to mention today).[4]

Even after rationing ended, there was still the question of how to feed the growing number of white-collar workers in city centres, particularly London. In the 1950s and 1960s, many new office blocks were built on former bombsites as the economy boomed and the capital emerged as the centre of the world's financial markets. The clerks and secretaries who serviced this new economy could not always afford the prices for a sit-down meal at traditional eating places like the Lyons Corner Houses, and such formality was becoming outmoded anyway. To fill the gap in the market, hundreds of cheap and cheerful sandwich bars sprang up all over London, many run by Italians who had emigrated there after the Second World War.

The luncheon voucher, introduced just after rationing came to an end in 1954, was a godsend for this emergent sandwich business. Luncheon vouchers, which firms liked because they were tax-deductible, were supposed to guarantee a hot meal for young office workers on modest salaries. Ubiquitous press adverts promoted their virtues: '"Good afternoon" she said – and it was! Thanks to Luncheon Vouchers, she'd eaten well that lunch-time. So she was attentive, looked alive, felt active. A good hot lunch had made all the difference between afternoon apathy and afternoon efficiency.'[5] But in some parts of the country, particularly pricey London, the luncheon voucher could only buy a couple of rolls and a drink at a sandwich bar.[6] A letter to *The Times* in 1960 blamed the luncheon voucher's meagre ration for 'the listlessness and, indeed, exhausted look of the average office junior'.[7]

Why was the sandwich so frowned upon? It is the perfect lunch on the hoof, and can be as nourishing as a hot meal. It is a proudly British invention (if such a simple, imitable thing can be said to be 'invented' at all), attributed to John Montagu (1718–92), the fourth Earl of Sandwich. According to the *Oxford English Dictionary*, he 'once spent twenty-four hours at the gaming-table without other refreshment than

some slices of cold beef placed between slices of toast'
– thus acquiring an unjustified reputation as an idler and
libertine (and a pedant might insist that he invented the
toastie rather than the sandwich). The sandwich initially
had an upmarket reputation – its purist incarnation being
the cucumber sandwich, the thin, crustless, unappetising
morsel which, in the novelist Compton Mackenzie's words,
felt and tasted 'like a damp handkerchief'.[8] The cucumber
sandwich was a genteel anti-food eaten at cricket matches
and tea parties, its nearest modern-day equivalent being
the breadless sandwich.

With the arrival of mass-produced bread in the inter-
war period, the sandwich went rapidly downmarket. In
1944, H. D. Renner argued in *The Origin of Food Habits* that
'the sandwich is a poor substitute for a single slice of bread,
spread with something one can both see and anticipate in
advance', without 'the coffin-lid which spells death to the
flavour'.[9] In the post-war era, the shop-bought sandwich
came to stand for all that was wrong with our national
cuisine and lifestyles. It was often a wretched affair of
spongy, pre-sliced bread stuffed with preservatives, coated
with margarine and filled with processed cheese, fish paste
or luncheon meat. For something so simple to make, a lot
could go wrong with a sandwich, mainly in the interval
between manufacture and consumption. Even a well-made
sandwich could be ruined if it was left out for too long in
those glass bell covers found in cafés and railway buffets,
the last resting place for sandwiches with leathery ham,
rubbery egg, limp lettuce and curled corners.

While the luncheon voucher threatened to kill off the
hot midday meal for lowly office workers, the lunching
tradition survived for those higher up the food chain. In
London, the 'city lunch' had been an institution since the
early years of the twentieth century. Businessmen would
entertain their associates at their club on the Mall or in
long-established restaurants like Simpson's Tavern and

Sweetings. These restaurants, open only for weekday lunchtimes, served a posh version of school dinners or nursery food – steak and kidney pudding or fish and chips, followed by plum duff or treacle tart and custard. The city gents would linger over cigars and brandy, finally stumbling out, a little unsteady on their feet, around three o'clock in the afternoon. In the 1965 Finance Act, the new Labour government abolished the expense allowance tax relief on most of these business lunches. Such was the chorus of outrage against this flagrant act of class war – Egon Ronay's *Good Food Guide* lamented the ensuing 'acres of white untenanted tables'[10] – anyone would have thought the government had made lunch illegal, rather than simply abolishing a tax break. Of course, the business lunch survived. The writer and journalist Godfrey Smith wrote in 1982:

> If the left is serious in its aim to make us one nation, it could do worse than start by abolishing lunch. For lunch is a social divider of infinite power. It distances husbands from their wives and bosses from their workers. It is a gauge of the gap between the haves and the have-nots, the inner temple of the expense-account cult and the last bastion of the male chauvinist. It is a perk of privilege and a symptom of decadence. Down with lunch! Death to all noonday noshers![11]

If the left did not kill off the leisurely city lunch, then Thatcherism and the less clubbable American business culture it embraced dealt it a significant (but not fatal) blow. The executive dining room, which had been endangered since the 1970s, finally bit the dust in the 1980s in favour of single-status dining at staff canteens. Doing away with such executive perks was a way for firms both to cut costs and to present themselves as informal and non-hierarchical. 'Big Bang' of October 1986, a classic Thatcherite reform that ended restrictive practices in the City's dealing rooms and computerised the Stock Exchange, was also an important event in the history of lunch. Rather than meeting on trading floors, brokers now moved bonds and shares around using computers and telephones. The new-era traders were too busy making deals with Hong Kong to break off for a leisurely three-course meal. They needed something that was portable, filling and amenable to multitasking. Fortunately, something like this had already been invented.

In order to rid itself of its painful associations with British naffness, though, the sandwich needed to posh up drastically. In 1980, in the words of the deskbound narrator of Michael Bracewell's office-life novel, *Perfect Tense*, 'the world of takeaway sandwiches was still a cold and benighted place, enduring its darkest hour before the dawn of new fillings. And how those fillings would stand for an epoch!' Then, in the early 1980s, 'a long low band of light began to shine across the far horizon of this dark world'.[12] The first rumblings of this bourgeoisification occurred within London's Square Mile, where Robin Birley opened a sandwich bar in Fenchurch Street in September 1979. Birley was a well-connected old Etonian with suffi-cient social cachet to begin the high-class rehabilitation of the sandwich. His chain of shops soon spread all over the City, and spawned many imitators. By 1985 there were at least a hundred other sandwich bars in the Square Mile.[13]

These upmarket establishments were different from their more plebeian antecedents. They used natural ingre-dients: real mayonnaise instead of salad cream, unproc-essed cheese, and freshly baked bread from baguettes to bagels. The striking combos offered as fillings – mashed avocado and bacon, pastrami and aged parmesan – over-compensated for the formerly humble status of the sandwich. The posh sandwich bars took orders over the phone and delivered all over London. One of the familiar mid-morning sights in the capital in these years was the burly young men, many of them Antipodean, carrying baskets of sandwiches on foot or bike to beat the traffic, or stalking office corridors like old-fashioned hawkers, yelling, 'Sandwiches!' As the city dealers munched on their lunches at their VDUs, the power sandwich came to stand for a new work ethic. In the famous opinion of Gordon Gekko in Oliver Stone's 1987 film *Wall Street*, lunch was for wimps.

The new-style sandwich bar was partly modelled on the New York deli, where the customer was king and the motto was 'have it your way'. New York delis sold pile-it-high, doorstop sandwiches with layers of cold cuts, cheese and salad, nicknamed 'Dagwoods' after an American comic-strip character who often made this kind of oversized snack. In a cartoon, a foot-high sandwich can fit inside a human jaw; in real life, the deli sandwich often had to be artificially supported by giant cocktail sticks (which, some might say, rather defeats the point of a sandwich). Queues at delis were long, as customers ordered complicated, tailor-made sandwiches like 'a triple-decker pastrami on rye, with mustard on one side, and hold the mayo'. London's posh sandwich bars began exporting this philos-ophy of consumer choice to Britain, but it would take a much bigger operation to change the British sandwich for ever – and it needed to break into the ready-made rather than the smaller made-to-order market.

At around the time that Birley opened his first sandwich bar, the ready-made sandwich also underwent a trans-formation. Before about 1980, the template for the pre-packed butty was the British Rail sandwich, a metaphor for national decline since it became a running joke on *The Goon Show*. Until pub food started to improve in the 1970s, many leftover BR sandwiches were also sold in public houses.[14] But when, in May 1997, the *Wall Street Journal* launched an unprovoked broadside on our nation's sandwiches, invoking the spectre of the 'infamous British Rail sandwich' and claiming that 'barely edible sandwiches dominate the dietary landscape of Britain like nowhere else',[15] this newspaper was surely behind the times. The British Rail sandwich had died with the privatisation of the railways, and in fact it had been surprisingly edible (if ruinously expensive) in its twilight years. In any case, the *Journal* was evoking an era BMS – before Marks & Spencer.

The Marks & Spencer sandwich was born in the late 1970s, when one of the firm's managers, Henry Lewis, was involved in an abortive scheme to run cafés in stores. The first café was earmarked for the Croydon branch, but the shop refit was behind schedule, so Lewis had staff trained to prepare sandwiches but no café to sell them in. Instead of wasting their expertise, he put them to work making sandwiches for the food hall.[16] They sold like hot cakes – or rather, like cold sandwiches. So M&S began to sell sandwiches properly in 1980, using its stores in Croydon, Kilburn and Oxford Circus to test the market.

The M&S sandwich benefited from a kudos that the store had accumulated over many years. After the Second World War, in the words of one historian, M&S had 'burst from its somewhat dull chrysalis to emerge as the classless, efficient, decently functional, distributive model of the new age', a place where 'doctor's wife and docker's wife' could 'avail themselves of the growing range and quality of mass-produced goods the new market made available'.[17] M&S stood for reliability, reasonable prices and unshowy middle-classness. Its sandwiches, produced by small catering firms under constant M&S supervision, set new standards of meticulousness and cleanliness. When the workers who made the sandwiches returned from foreign holidays, they even had to provide stool samples to show they had not acquired any dangerous bugs while abroad.[18]

M&S cut its sandwiches diagonally into triangular

wedges and then placed them in rigid plastic containers, an improvement on the sweaty cellophane and greaseproof paper that had previously held the pre-packed sandwich together. The triangular containers could be easily stacked (two triangles made a rectangle) so the sandwiches weren't squashed and had space to breathe. Initially, there were only four varieties of M&S sandwich, all reminiscent of tea at the vicarage: salmon and cucumber, prawn and cream cheese, egg and tomato, and ham salad.[19] M&S soon carved out a niche by pioneering fillings that were slightly quirky without being too outlandish, such as prawn mayonnaise or BLT, the American favourite that crossed the Atlantic in the 1980s. Neither conservative nor revolutionary, they epitomised M&S's knack of innovating unthreateningly. By 1990, its sandwich shop at Oxford Circus was selling two million sandwiches a year.[20] Soon Boots the Chemist, supermarkets and petrol stations realised they could make big profits from cold, takeaway food and began selling the triangular sandwich wedge as well.

This new type of 'sand-wedge' did not entirely kill off the long business lunch. Stockbrokers might now be chained to their computer screens and too busy to go out for lunch; but the newer professions that did well out of the 1980s, like PR, marketing and advertising, entertained clients to drum up business. If Thatcherism made a fetish of longer hours, it also valued entrepreneurial networking and deal-making. Diners might opt for the 'menu rapide' and forgo the three brandies after pudding, but a 1980s lunch could still go on late into the afternoon. What changed in these cases was the purpose of lunch – a shift encapsulated by the term 'power lunch', which originated in New York's eateries in the late 1970s. Books appeared about how to schmooze successfully in restaurants, with titles like *Power Lunch: How You Can Profit from a More Effective Business Lunch Strategy* and *Do Lunch or Be Lunch*. Lunch had to have an ulterior motive, like fishing for a contract or closing a deal. In his 1986 book *The Theory and Practice of Lunch*, Keith Waterhouse deplored this soulless, utilitarian attitude. Lunch, he argued, should be purely pleasurable and leisurely ('three hours is about right'), and should certainly not be confused with business, particularly if this involved 'overseas persons you have never clapped eyes on before' and 'briefcases stuffed with printouts or samples'.[21] Waterhouse's book was a kind of valediction for a dying tradition – specifically, for the journalist's boozy lunch. It was published in the year that Rupert Murdoch's newspapers moved from Fleet Street to Wapping and undermined this tradition for ever.

The final death of the long business lunch came not in the wheeler-dealing 1980s but in its aftermath, the recession of the early 1990s. Even in a recession, of course, people still have to eat. (Historically, sandwich consumption has risen in times of economic difficulty, such as the depression of the 1930s, because the sandwich is a cheap meal.) Firms began to cut back on their staff restaurants and expense accounts, and sandwich bars took more boardroom deliveries for 'business platters', those little plastic trays of tiny triangular sandwiches, with a few chocolate marshmallows thrown in if you were lucky. In a sense, the business platter was a classic form of outsourcing, a popular strategy of the post-Thatcher era which allowed firms to farm out their routine operations (in this case, providing lunch) and concentrate on their core business. When the recession lifted in the mid-1990s, the long business lunch never really returned. The new trend was for what Americans called 'fast-casual' dining, which offered fresher, nicer food than a fast-food joint but was quicker and cheaper than a restaurant. When Pret a Manger opened in London in 1986, it provided a model for the gourmet sandwich chains which spread across the capital and then the country in the 1990s. These chains sold a hybrid of the posh, made-to-order sandwich and the mass-produced wedge. Their sandwiches were ready-made and wrapped, but prepared in store each day, with only a few hours' shelf life.

Thanks to Pret a Manger and its imitators, the sandwich shop is now a cornucopia of exotic fillings and bread types, with lots of organic, free-range, low-carb options for middle-class metropolitans, and even the most ordinary ingredients rendered interesting with the aid of redundant adjectives: 'peppery watercress', 'crunchy iceberg lettuce', 'ripe tomato', 'shredded cucumber', 'dolphin-friendly tuna'. The way of attracting custom in an increasingly crowded market is to emphasise both quality and diversity. Assailing the customer with choice undermines the last selling point of the independent sandwich shops: that they can make any sandwich to order, just like the New York delis. M&S now offers over eighty varieties of sandwich, surely enough to satiate even the most cosmopolitan consumer. Some chains, like Subway, will make up any sandwich filling for a customer in a few minutes. This diversifying strategy seems to work: the market for sandwiches has levelled out in recent years, but the number of chain-owned sandwich shops continues to grow at the expense of the independents.[22]

Despite the increase in choice, however, the top five sandwich fillings chosen by British consumers actually seem quite mundane. These five fillings – BLT (with a 14 per cent market share), prawn mayo (11 per cent), egg mayo (10 per cent), tuna mayo (10 per cent) and ham and cheese (7 per cent) – make up over half the market. The choices are fairly consistent across class, region and gender; only with the more unusual options do real variations emerge. Conservative supporters, for example, are nearly twice as likely as the average consumer to buy a smoked salmon sandwich, while Labour supporters generally opt for more prosaic fillings. Londoners, who buy the most sandwiches, are also the most exploratory in their tastes.[23]

The prawn mayonnaise sandwich, the second most purchased variety and the most popular among women, has become a sort of cultural metaphor for the lunchtime revolution. In 1991, the jeweller Gerald Ratner made a famously ill-advised joke that his firm's 99p earrings cost the same as a prawn sandwich but 'maybe the prawn sandwich would last longer'.[24] Nine years later, the Manchester United footballer Roy Keane, furious with the poor atmosphere at a midweek game at Old Trafford, complained about supporters who 'have had a few drinks and their prawn sandwiches and do not realise what is going on out on the pitch'.[25] Ratner saw the prawn sandwich as cheap and disposable; Keane saw it as food for snobs on executive freebies, not 'real' football fans. The prawn sandwich is successful because it is neither: it is a bit nicer than something we would make ourselves, but not too intimidatingly different. It is food for what Barry Schwartz calls 'satisficers', people who simply look for a product that is 'good enough' and do not worry about all the alternatives.[26] The 'paradox of choice', as identified by Schwartz, is that endless variety is not necessarily a liberation for the consumer – there comes a point at which too much choice causes self-doubt, confusion and even misery. When it comes to buying sandwiches, though, we seem to be creatures of habit: life is too short to waste any existential despair on a cheap lunch. In any case, the exoticising of fillings is offset by the now universal practice of refrigerating sandwiches, which gives them all a slightly wet, insipid taste. Unlike revenge, the sandwich is not a dish best served cold.

The gourmet sandwich, pioneered in London by M&S and Pret a Manger, has now conquered the whole of Britain. It has done so partly at the expense of northern-style rolls and baps, which now seem rather staid and stodgy compared with the trendier varieties of bread pioneered in the capital, such as paninis, ciabattas, pittas and wraps.

7   The dread of the inbox

'The everyday receives our daily inattention'

Georges Bataille[1]

There is one habit that we all seem to like doing while desk-dining. Surveys of internet traffic have suggested that the peak time in the working day for checking and answering emails is lunchtime.[2] This is not very surprising: the nature of email means that it can be left until there is a lull in the activity of the office, and it is also an amorphous, many-headed beast that merges work time and free time. Email allows you to sort out your office diary, your personal life and your daily chores all at once. Since having an email address has only been de rigueur in Britain since the mid-1990s, any office worker over thirty-five should remember a time before the inbox ruled their lives in this way. However did we do without this instantaneous messaging system, which brilliantly obliterates time zones, eliminates 'phone tag', and allows us to send everything from one-line hellos to book-length documents with a single mouse click? Hardly anyone can remember. The rapid success of email has not made us more aware of its history – if anything, it has produced a kind of collective amnesia about the work revolution it produced. Email has vastly expanded the number of people who write to each other, but these people have learned how to use it through trial and error. It has created new ways of thinking, feeling and relating to others – but not ones of which we are usually aware. To begin to understand the nature of the problem, it is worth thinking first about the daily habit it usurped: letter-writing.

Letter-writing manuals, which emerged in the medieval era and boomed in Britain from the eighteenth century onwards, served as guides to writing for the barely literate, and introductions to the rules of polite society for the aspirational. There were Byzantine, constantly shifting rules about how to open and sign off a letter, depending on one's social status and familiarity with the recipient. The most cumbersome sign-offs ('I have the honour, Sir, to remain your obedient servant') originated in the sixteenth century. Two centuries later, however, people began using '&c' at the end of their letters as a substitute for this stock phraseology. The number of sign-offs, each with its own specific meaning, proliferated. 'Yours', for example, evolved as a halfway house for people who were unsure whether to write the formal 'Yours sincerely' or the effusive 'Yours ever'. The tweaking of rules and the improvisations of individual letter-writers anticipated some of the strategies of emailers. Until the penny post arrived in 1840, the letter's recipient had to pay for the postage. So it could be bad manners to send either a very short or a very long letter (since extra sheets of paper cost more). You could save space by using abbreviations – not unlike the shorthand used in contemporary email and text messaging.[3] In the mid-nineteenth century, when the post began to be delivered by train several times a day, letters were often as brief and trivial as emails. A city gent might send a note to his suburban home at lunchtime, announcing to his wife that he would be late home that evening[4] – the equivalent of people today declaiming that they are 'on the train'. The postcard, which arrived in the late nineteenth century, also anticipated the informality of email and was similarly laid-back about spelling, syntax and conjunctions ('Hving wndrfl time').

As the rules loosened up further in the first half of the twentieth century, there was a long debate about whether to retain the wordier conventions. A common topic to write to the editor of *The Times* about, for example, was how to write to the editor of *The Times*. One correspondent, signing himself simply 'Victorian', complained about the growing habit of writing 'Yours, &c.' in such letters, 'a deplorable concession to the slovenly made by those who are not slovenly'.[5] 'Another Victorian' protested that '"Yours sincerely" from some individual of whom one has never heard is highly irritating.'[6] Other people would conduct surveys of hundreds of letters published in the newspaper, and write to the editor about the percentage of correspondents who had signed off 'Yours faithfully' or 'Yours truly', and had preceded this with 'I am' or 'I remain'.[7]

One form of address now common in emails between strangers, and which excited more ire than any other, was 'Dear [first and second name]'. In the early 1950s, the linguist Alan Ross identified this 'non-U' (non-upperclass) convention as an invention of intellectuals in the 1930s.[8] Nancy Mitford complained that 'this unspeakable usage sometimes occurs in letters – Dear XX – which, in silence, are quickly torn up, by me.'[9] In 1962, an MP wrote to *The Times* to protest at being addressed in such a way: 'You, Sir, once in the thirties, used your great power to stop laundries from putting pins into the shirts they had cleaned. Will you now thunder again to choke this form of address which I find odious?'[10] Just as the right people are supposed simply to 'know' the correct form, it was rarely explained why this salutation was so offensive, on a par with the despicable practice of putting pins in shirts, but presumably it was to do with the assumption of first-name familiarity by one's social inferiors.

It is easy to laugh at these snobberies. With its reputation for informality and spontaneity, however, email threatened to throw out centuries of letter-writing etiquette and put nothing in its place. The problem was that no one was quite sure what sort of message an email was: it was somewhere between a letter, a telex, a fax and a phone call. For a long time it was the very junior partner of these other forms of communication. A Cold War baby, email began as part of efforts by the United States Defense Department to create a dispersed electronic network that could survive a nuclear bomb dropping on a mainframe computer. But for several decades after the computer engineer Ray Tomlinson sent the first email from one machine to another in 1971 (by using the @ sign as a way of differentiating between their locations) its wider commercial success hung in the balance. 'Electronic mail has been on the way for ten years now and is expected soon, a delivery record of which Queen Victoria's postal service would be thoroughly ashamed,' complained one British journalist in 1991.[11]

Even after its commercial introduction in the UK in the mid-1980s, email struggled to compete with the telex and the fax. Telex, which had been running commercially since 1932, was antiquated and expensive: a typed message at one end turned into a pattern of holes punched on to reams of ticker tape at the other end, and even a simple message could take up metres of tape. But telex usage was still expanding well into the 1980s, and early email services allowed you to send an email that came out as a telex at the other end (and vice versa).[12] At this time the fax machine, not email, looked like the future. In 1986 there were only 86,000 fax machines in the UK; two years later there were a quarter of a million.[13] At the same time, the largest email system, British Telecom's Telecom Gold, had only 80,000 users.[14] There were other, much smaller email systems, run by firms like Mercury set up in the wake of the Thatcher government's ending of BT's monopoly. Until a wave of industry takeovers and agreed protocols in the early 1990s, though, all the software systems were incompatible with one another. If you picked the wrong system, you could soon end up friendless, with no one left to write to.

Computer systems in the 1980s were primitive and too much email traffic slowed up the system, so companies would discourage excessive use among their employees. This was always likely to be a difficult area because the ease and confidentiality of email made it an instant ally of the frivolous, illicit message. Computer programmers in California in the 1970s were rumoured to use email to set up their dope deals, and one of the first transatlantic emails, sent by Len Kleinrock in 1973, asked the recipient, Larry Roberts, to retrieve an electric razor that he had left behind at a computer conference.[15] In the 1980s, though, this kind of trivia was frowned upon: in 1986, Hewlett-Packard urged users of its in-house system not to email each other Christmas greetings.[16] But the biggest disadvantage of email in this period was that, unlike a fax or telex, it gave no indication that it had arrived – a problem if you only received one or two messages a week. Some email systems would offer a radio paging service to warn you of a message arriving, but that could double the cost.[17]

Because email co-existed, and still co-exists, with these other forms of communication – letter, telex, fax – users were unsure whether to make up new rules of etiquette or adapt old ones. Email clearly borrowed its header format (To, From, Subject, etc.) from the internal memo, which first emerged in the business world in the 1870s.[18] But it had a more informal character attuned to the less overtly hierarchical organisations of the 1980s and 1990s – a sort of electronic equivalent of the open-plan office. Executives no longer asked their secretaries to take down a letter, type it up and sign it '*per procurationem*' (by proxy); they emailed their underlings, who replied in kind. Email had a New World confidence that invidious distinctions of class and status could simply be swept away by straightforwardness. A 1992 American guide to email urged users to ignore the social niceties of conventional mail: 'E-mail is supposed to be fast, tit-for-tat communication. You ask. I answer. You ask. I answer. You're not supposed to watch the sun set, listen to the surf pound the sun-bleached sand, and sip San Miguel beer as Paco dives for abalone while you craft your e-mail.'[19]

But the absence of an obvious email protocol was not necessarily liberating. It could make those lower down the office hierarchy more uneasy, worried about being either too formal or too casual. In the early days of email, most British office workers simply mimicked the etiquette of the formal business letter, beginning with 'Dear Mr ...' and closing with 'Yours sincerely'. Such sticklers were likely to baulk at including the original message in the reply, on the grounds that you would never reply to a letter by writing at the bottom of it. But more confident souls soon dispensed with such hangovers from snail mail, and even circumvented salutations and sign-offs altogether, batting emails back and forth as though they were having a telephone conversation.

Another uncertainty was how well-written an email needed to be. Until the arrival of Microsoft Outlook in the late 1990s, it was hard to word-process and spell-check emails. In the earliest email systems it was even difficult to move the cursor, so you had to leave the typos or start all over again. Some business cultures not only tolerated spelling mistakes in emails, but even admired them as a sign that the sender was too busy to worry about such fripperies. Typing in e e cummings style, unpunctuated and in lower case, had a slightly macho, no-time-to-press-the-shift-key quality. In the 1990s, an American academic, David Owens, spent a year at a California research and development firm which was a model of team-led egalitarianism. When he looked at a sample of 30,000 email messages sent within the company over a four-year period, however, he found that senior figures tended to send much shorter, abrupt messages with the poorest grammar and spelling.[20] Email might be quick, easy and open to all – but it still conveyed silent status signals.

Email occupied a confusing middle ground between the premeditation of a letter and the expressiveness of a phone call. To compensate for the absence of verbal intonation in email, early users of message boards used 'emoticons' and 'smileys' to denote things like 'only joking' and 'happy', and acronyms such as LOL ('laugh out loud', sometimes embarrassingly mistaken for 'lots of love'). But according to a survey by the linguist David Crystal, this kind of cool, Californian-style shorthand never caught on among the majority of British email users, particularly in the world of work.[21] Over time, as people got used to the technology, a sort of tacit protocol did develop. The email message began with 'Dear' or 'Hi' followed by the name (usually the first name, although when addressing a stranger the rather prim 'if I may' sometimes followed in brackets). The sign-off was something like 'Best' or 'Cheers'. Rules of grammar and punctuation were relaxed, and non-geeky abbreviations like BTW (by the way) permitted. But certain things remained infra dig, like typing in capital letters – the norm on telex, but regarded as a form of virtual shouting on email.

The growth of email did not dispense with the fondness that many felt for the material form of the letter, particularly if it bore the idiosyncratic imprint of the person who had written it. The English upper classes, who invented most of the rules of letter-writing, were particularly reluctant to let go of the handwritten letter. Ever since Nancy Mitford ruled that sending letters by airmail suggested an 'undue haste' which was definitely 'non-U',[22] the guardians of etiquette had been fighting a rearguard action against soulless business correspondence. In their 1982 *Sloane Ranger Handbook*, Ann Barr and Peter York noted the upper-class love of personal 'thank you' letters and other notes sent to friends as a way of defying the impersonality of business letters. Sloanes liked the smell and texture of watermarked paper and Mont Blanc fountain pens, and the eccentricities of handwriting, liberally sprinkled with underlinings and exclamation marks for emphasis and flourish. The ultimate expression of this sensualism was the 'stiffie', the card with engraved lettering ('Sloane Braille') announcing a wedding or an 'at home', displayed like a trophy on the mantelpiece.[23]

But this system of etiquette was thrown into crisis by email. Email's software programs gave little opportunity for personal expression and they jumbled up the most private messages with workaday memos. Eventually even the guardians of good form at Debrett's had to accept the inevitable lure of the inbox.[24] But the nostalgia for the personal letter remained – and not merely in the best circles. There is a natural inclination to assign different levels of importance to correspondence which the more old-fashioned technologies exploit. With the arrival of fax, for example, the telex industry claimed that fax was fine for everyday usage but really important messages had to be signalled by their noisy arrival at a telex terminal.[25] Later on, as email traffic expanded, it was the fax, or better still a letter by first-class post, which assumed this kind of rarity value.

From the beginning, email software programs drew on this nostalgia for the post, mimicking the look and vocabulary of snail mail. America Online, which launched in the US in 1993, was successful because it offered novice users a series of familiar features, including a friendly voice when you logged on saying, 'You've got mail'. When AOL launched in Britain in 1996, subscribers instead heard Joanna Lumley's breathy English voice saying, 'You've got post', later updated to 'You've got email'. In almost all email programs, new messages are denoted by an unopened envelope symbol, read messages by an opened one, and messages sit in your 'inbox' or 'mailbox'. Email has retained an atavistic attraction to the iconography of the letter. (The current *Times* Letters page, still the bush telegraph of the Establishment, advises that 'we take letters by e-mail', which suggests a similar residual attachment.)

However apologetically email usurped the letter, by the end of the century it was the dominant form of mail in the UK. 'If you have no e-mail address you're a walking piece of history, as out of date as papyrus,' decreed one journalist in 1999.[26] Perhaps the most significant effect of the triumph of email has been the sort of personal–professional spillage that upper-class etiquette most feared, in which non-work intrudes into working time and vice versa. Email is provided free by employers to their staff and so can lead to unauthorised spreading of gossip and jokes, the sort of surreptitious fun on the company's time that the French call *la perruque* (which literally means a 'wig'). But the opposite has happened as well: work has invaded other areas of our lives. Unlike the morning post, email arrives at any time of the day or night. In this sense, it is like many of the newer communications technologies, such as answering machines and mobile phones, which promise to help us organise our time but also make us permanently available to others. Just like working through your lunch break, though, the tyranny of email has been socio-psychological rather than directly coercive. No one forces you to log on. If you have a thick skin, you can ignore email more or less indefinitely. Given that universities pioneered the use of email, it is ironic that they seem to have such a disproportionate number of these people (usually male) who never check their emails or do so only on random occasions.

To be fair to these e-fuseniks, you never know what an email contains until you open it, so there is no foolproof way of sorting out relevant emails from the ever-expanding morass of spam – both commercial and occupational. The 'reply all' and 'cc' functions allow work emails to be disseminated willy-nilly. Higher-ups can use them to proselytise, motivate and keep underlings 'in the loop'; subordinates can copy in their superiors to show they are keeping busy. The increase in back-covering, cheerleading or simply redundant emails has inspired what I call 'look-at-me mails', which have exclamation marks or red flags next to them denoting 'high importance'. Look-at-me mails have a slightly admonitory tone, as if implying that we are in the habit of ignoring all our other messages. But the growing use of flags for messages which are neither urgent nor important surely suffers from the law of diminishing returns, particularly since no one sends emails marked 'low priority'. I wonder what attention-grabbing devices emails will need in future (flashing lights? drum rolls?) just to inform us that someone's wallet has been found in the toilets.

Since around the turn of the millennium, there have been countless press articles in Britain about the time workers spend dealing with emails. These articles take a fairly standard form: they use surveys by internet measurement companies to estimate how many minutes or hours a day the average worker spends dealing with emails, how many messages they receive each day or year, or how many billions of emails are sent around the world each day or year. Of course, this last statistic is always going to seem like a big number – but in retrospect some of the numbers in these surveys do not seem so large. As recently as 2001, a MORI survey found that Britain's company directors were 'struggling to stay on top of their inboxes', with a quarter of them receiving 'more than 30 e-mails a day' – a not especially mind-boggling number in hindsight.[27] These surveys often come up with widely differing results. Email traffic is hard to quantify not only because it is virtual but also because so many messages are sent within intranets (private networks within organisations) rather than across the internet. In any case, the statistics are of dubious value because they do not measure how useful all this email activity is, or to what extent it has displaced other time-consuming activities, such as fielding phone calls or answering letters.

Email surveys are a classic example of how, according to the sociologist Joel Best, the media use statistics – by making a fetish of rising numbers and then turning them into 'numeric statements about social life',[28] the statement in this case being that email is spiralling out of control. Workers are suffering from 'mail rage ... crack[ing] under the strain of handling their ever-expanding in-box'.[29] Others are experiencing 'inbox dread', the sick feeling you get before you log on to deal with an insurmountable mountain of emails. Since around half of all office workers are said regularly to email colleagues less than ten feet away, the campaign against email infoglut has even become part of the wider war against obesity.[30] In October 2005, Sport England encouraged employers to ban internal emails and get staff walking round the office in an 'E-mail free Friday' scheme, part of the 'Everyday Sport Office Games'.[31] A less-noticed effect of the proliferation of emails has been a return to the proxy forms of office correspondence briefly banished by email at the end of the last century. Many bosses are now unreachable via their inboxes, using 'e-secretaries' to filter out unwanted contact.[32]

The electronic message has not killed off more traditional ways of working. New technologies never arrive in a vacuum; they mould themselves around the habits we already have. Email was supposed finally to usher in that perennial chimera, 'the paperless office'. One journalist predicted in 1986 that 'the partnership of word processor and e-mail almost eliminates the need for paper'.[33] In fact, a recent study suggests that email has increased paper consumption by about 40 per cent. Rather than photocopy documents to distribute to colleagues, we distribute through email and then expect them all to print it – which is why the increase in printer sales has outweighed the increase in photocopier sales about thirty-fold since the late 1980s.[34] Copying is giving way to what is known in the trade as 'MOPying', producing 'multiple original prints'. It seems that, whatever the advantages of virtuality, you can't beat the portability and navigability of paper.

Email may speed up certain tasks, but it also provides ample evidence of C. Northcote Parkinson's time-honoured law that 'work expands so as to fill the time available for its completion'.[35] Email makes both meaningful and meaningless communication easier, and allows us to conduct electronic conversations that could be more quickly and efficiently conducted by the old-fashioned technology of talking. When I am asked for the nth time at work, 'Did you get my email?', I politely refrain from pointing out that this question defeats one of the main purposes of email, which is to bypass conversation. Emails have not dispensed with the need for human interaction, or the bottomless capacity of work to generate time-wasting and redundancy.

The editors of the *Oxford Book of Letters* point out that 'it is hard to imagine an anthology of faxes, and harder still to foresee an Oxford Book of E-mail'.[36] But if future historians of daily life did manage to retrieve information from obsolescent email servers, they might find that today's trite memo is tomorrow's historical curio. In 2000, the artist Tom Phillips produced an engrossing history of the last century simply by reprinting thousands of postcards and their messages.[37] Like the lines scribbled on the backs of postcards, email messages are batted off without a thought, written in a nondescript, functional style, full of truisms and clichés ('wish you were here… / thanks for yours …'), and preserve in writing something that might normally only be spoken, and thus lost to posterity. Assuming they can hack into my account, those future historians may come to thank virtual hoarders like me, who pointlessly retain old emails. Every so often I receive curt messages from computer services informing me that my inbox is full and that my account will be suspended until I empty it. Half-heartedly, I undertake a mailbox detox. But I can't quite bring myself to delete all those little pieces of trivia about routine lives: lost student essays, missed meetings, out-of-order photocopiers, broken vending machines. In time, like Phillips's postcard messages, they will make for a riveting historical record. All human life is in our inboxes.

8 Puffing al fresco

*'I'm glad I don't have to explain to a man from Mars
why each day I set fire to dozens of little pieces of paper
and put them in my mouth'*

Mignon McLaughlin[1]

It's anti-social, very bad for you and you really should
cut down. But enough about your sixty-a-day email habit
– there is an everyday addiction with a much more undis-
tinguished history. Imagine for a moment that Britain is
a remote island, inhabited by an eccentric tribe of people
yet to encounter any other civilisation. An anthropologist,
arriving on this island for the first time in order to study
our way of life, would be puzzled and intrigued by a ritual
that occurs in workplaces several times a day. Every so
often, a few workers break off from whatever they are
doing in order to huddle outside the office buildings,
perhaps looking slightly sheepish and put-upon as they do
so. This seems to happen regardless of the weather: in the
battle between the unkind elements of this island and the
ferocity of the habit, the latter always wins. The sharp-eyed
anthropologist would soon note that there is one unifying
characteristic of these semi-detached workers. They are all
carrying small, thin, white cylinders, which are burning at
one end, and every so often they put them to their mouths
and inhale.

What the anthropologist would not know, of course, is
that these puffing pariahs have only been a common sight

outside offices over the last decade or so. As scientific evidence and public opinion have ganged up on smokers over the last two decades, the lit cigarette has been gradually expelled from indoor public spaces. In 2006, after much debate about respective rights and liberties, Parliament voted to ban smoking from all indoor public places, including workplaces, pubs and restaurants, with a few exceptions such as private clubs. The smoking room and the communal ashtray were to become instant historical relics, with all smokers exiled to private houses or the open air.

While some smokers consider themselves to be the recently persecuted minority of a politically correct 'nanny state', there is nothing new about their banishment outdoors. Smokers began to be segregated from non-smokers in Britain as early as the 1830s. Smoking was seen as a masculine, private pleasure, and doing it in public places was associated with a boorish disregard for ladies' delicate throats. William Thackeray chivalrously advised his nephew that 'a cigar should be considered, not as preferable to [women's] company, but as consolation for their absence'.[2] At the dinner table, gentlemen had to wait until the ladies had withdrawn before settling down with their cigars and rough talk. Even smoking in the street in the presence of women could have one classed as a cad, and notices in public parks asked cigar smokers to extinguish them when requested by a lady.[3] Smoking was routinely banned on railway stations and trains from the beginning, although this rule was often ignored. Finally, an 1868 Act of Parliament decreed that trains must have special smoking carriages – a clause sponsored by the great libertarian philosopher and MP John Stuart Mill. Smoking carriages were specially marked with a large 'S' painted on the door.[4]

It was the mass-produced cigarette, arriving in Britain in the late nineteenth century, which turned smoking into a more public activity. Male connoisseurs of the pipe and cigar were united in their loathing of the cheap, tasteless 'Virginia cigarette' (named after the state from which the tobacco originated), which they dismissed as 'the finicking toy of the foreigner' and 'a miserable apology for a manly pleasure', suited only for the 'effeminate races of the Continent and the East'.[5] Cigarettes were not only unisex, they were also classless – indeed, their ready-rolled, quick-fix pleasure was suited to the more communal smoking of the working classes in the pub or factory. Smoking was now part of the mundane routine of daily life rather than the after-dinner pleasures of the drawing room. The First World War also saw a huge acceleration in demand for cigarettes because, unlike other smokes, they took no time to prepare and could be enjoyed quickly – the same qualities that still make them ideal for work breaks.

In the inter-war years, the nicotine habit was so rife that hardly anyone campaigned against smoking in public places. With little firm evidence that it was a serious health hazard, opponents of smoking stressed that it was a public nuisance, which linked them in the public mind with the puritanism of the temperance movement.[6] The National Society of Non-Smokers, founded in 1926 to campaign for more non-smoking places, was commonly seen as the last refuge of milksops, killjoys and life-deniers. One *Times* leader even objected to the expression 'non-smoker', which, it argued, suggested something quite different from 'a person who does not smoke': 'It is an aggressive, inter-fering phrase. A non-smoker not merely does not smoke; he will try to see that no one else shall smoke.'[7]

Mass-Observation was particularly interested in smoking at this time because it seemed to divide society into two groups, smokers and non-smokers (or people who did not smoke), which cut across all other divisions of age, class, sex, occupation and belief. Charles Madge and Tom

Harrisson argued that 'if we find sectarian feeling between smokers and non-smokers, it will be significant of man's tendency to distinguish socially between those who share his habits and those who do not'. Sure enough, Mass-Observation found that smokers believed that there was something 'queer' about men who did not smoke. They had 'a milky babies' breath smell' and were 'not quite a man' or 'not one of us'. Refusing the offer of a cigarette created a minor social embarrassment and set up 'a barrier of intimacy', even though, to cover up the awkwardness, the smoker often went on to compliment the smoker on being free of the habit.[8]

By 1949, 81 per cent of men and 39 per cent of women smoked.[9] Even during these years of post-war austerity and shortages, cigarettes were seen as a special, unrationable commodity. After a punitive American loan agreement of Christmas 1945 ended the so-called 'cigarette famine' by allowing the importation of cheap tobacco, the Tory MP Bob Boothby lamented that 'we have sold the Empire for a packet of cigarettes'.[10] By then, many of Britain's smokers were so desperate for a fag that they probably thought this a fair bargain.

The popularity of smoking meant that, even as clear evidence about the link between smoking and lung cancer emerged from the early 1950s onwards, governments focused on measures like increased tobacco taxes and stronger health warnings on cigarette packets rather than the policing of public space. Exhortations not to smoke in public were flexible and permissive. On double-decker buses, smoking was banned on the lower deck and the front seats of the upper deck – but where exactly did the front seats end? The question 'Do you mind if I smoke?' was heard even in non-smoking sections of buses and trains, and since the requester had usually taken the cigarette out of the packet already, it was a brave soul who answered, 'Yes'. (It was a braver soul still who gave the answer suggested by a letter-writer to *The Times* in 1941: 'Not at all, Sir, if you don't mind my being sick.'[11])

There were many ways of asking or ordering people not to smoke through signs. 'No smoking please' started to replace 'Smoking' signs on trains in the 1920s,[12] although these could always be hilariously defaced to say 'smoking please' instead. Hospitals employed the educative 'No smoking, lungs at work'. 'Thank you for not smoking' was seen in taxis and restaurants from the 1970s, an excessive politeness which ended up irritating militant smokers by assuming they had already refrained when they had every intention of partaking. Such niceties were superfluous by the 1990s, when the simple image of a red bar running through a cigarette was universally understood. For a brief period, even this minimalist sign was an endangered species. There was no need to order people not to smoke when it was hardly allowed anywhere, just as there was no need to tell people not to set fire to the building. Under the 2006 Health Act, however, 'no smoking' signs have to be displayed in all smoke-free premises, even if no one has been allowed to smoke in them for years.

If smoking was increasingly frowned upon in public places, smoking in offices was common until the late 1980s. In a survey conducted in 1969, only 3 per cent of young male office workers said they would be prepared to give up smoking at work if threatened with the sack.[13] Smoking was presumably tolerated at work on the same principle that bays are smaller in office car parks than in municipal ones: colleagues are supposed to be able to negotiate more easily than strangers over the etiquette of shared space, an optimistic view of office politics. This all changed with the new anxiety over passive smoking and the arguments about whether and to what extent it causes lung cancer. The campaign against workplace smoking began in Britain in 1988, when the government published *Passive Smoking at Work*, a booklet which urged employers to introduce no-smoking policies in consultation with employees. One of the first companies to do so was the UK division of the Ford Motor Company, which in January 1990 banned its office staff from smoking except in designated areas and only then provided it did not 'adversely affect those in the non-smoking areas'.[14] Employers' fears of being sued by non-smokers were a powerful catalyst for change. In 1990, an asthma-suffering social security worker from Luton won a landmark ruling that she had been made ill by her colleagues smoking at work, and that this could be classed as an industrial accident.[15]

By the early 1990s, the government was publishing stricter guidelines and targets for reducing smoking at work. The phrase 'second-hand smoke' became the preferred way of describing what passive smokers inhaled, a term somewhat loaded with the charity-shop connotations of 'second-hand', which implied that this kind of smoke was inferior to the spanking new kind that smokers themselves enjoyed. Passive smoking moved up the political agenda not simply because of firmer medical evidence about its dangers, but also because the most influential classes in society had been most successful at kicking the habit. In June 2004, the health secretary John Reid said that smoking had become 'a middle-class obsession' and was one of the few pleasures available to some working-class people.[16] He was at least accurate demographically. Since the 1970s, smoking among higher social classes has fallen much more sharply than among lower ones, and today unemployed people smoke most of all.

There was no defining moment in the regulation of smoking, just a slow, incremental extension of indoor bans. As the American precedent shows, regulations beget more regulations because of the logical inconsistencies of partial rules. When New York City began to crack down on smoking in the late 1980s, the authorities initially planned to impose smoke-free zones in common areas and allow smoking in enclosed offices. But this would have meant depriving secretaries of a perk granted to executives, so smoking had to be restricted throughout the workplace.[17] British employers began to introduce smoking rooms (nicknamed 'sin-bins') in the early 1990s. But these rooms, which required separate ventilation shafts, were often prohibitively expensive. Banning all smoking indoors was the simpler solution.

The ethical and legal ambiguities do not end with a blanket indoors ban. An American Benson & Hedges advert from the mid-1990s showed smokers sat at work desks resting precariously on window ledges, with the caption: 'Have you noticed finding a place to smoke is the hardest part of your job? For a great smoke, put in for an office window.' This neatly illustrated a problem raised by the ban on indoor smoking in public places: what constituted a public place, and where did the 'indoors' end? When the small Californian town of San Luis Obispo initiated the modern trend for banning smoking in public places on 2 August 1990, it simply covered all bars, restaurants and workplaces. In the most car-polluted state in America, the legislator joked that 'in San Luis Obispo you have to go inside to get some fresh air'.[18] But other Californian local councils went further, banning smoking from sidewalks and public parks. The statewide law prohibiting smoking inside any public building in California, introduced in 1994, extended to within five feet of the doors and windows of buildings, and ten years later this was extended to twenty feet.[19]

In any case, some employers do not like the entrances to their buildings being cluttered up with smokers, particularly when important clients might be using them, so they order workers to stand well back from the doorways. In one British firm, smokers were banished to a red square painted on the ground at the far end of the backyard.[20] For other employees, the office was everywhere: sales reps were banned from smoking in their cars (a surely unpoliceable rule, unless they tested for nicotine on the uphol-stery), and hospital workers from smoking in uniform, even when they were off-duty.[21] The 2006 Health Act also inspired a series of discussions about what constituted an 'enclosed public place'. The government made it clear that it could include vehicles used as a workplace by more than one person, bus shelters, covered train platforms and even entrances to office buildings.[22]

Workplace smoking bans did benefit some, however. Firms like the No Butts Bin Company emerged to sell the paraphernalia of outdoor smoking that has been such a ubiquitous feature of office courtyards and doorways since the mid-1990s: wall-mounted external ashtrays with narrow openings at the top for fag-ends and an internal 'baffle' system to prevent smoke emissions; and, to protect al fresco smokers, smoking canopies or even glass-panelled 'smoking shelters' that look exactly like bus shelters. The promotional literature for the No Butts smoking shelter claims that forcing workers to stand out in the wind and rain 'can have a bad effect on morale, damaging productivity and threatening your profits. Put a roof over smokers' heads and you will be surprised at how grateful they will be.' [23] Whether or not they are grateful, smokers in these shelters cut rather forlorn figures, as if they are being imprisoned in pens rather than offered protection from the elements. But they seem prepared to put up with these minor indignities for the sake of a smoke.

Smoking has become so entrenched in daily life because it is both a habit and a ritual – something that is done routinely and unthinkingly but that also has elements of self-display and social bonding. As Mass-Observation noted in 1938, there are different stages of developing the habit. People start to smoke to join in and be sociable, but then 'the social cause is forgotten in the nervous need'. Even the smoker could not tell you how much 'the pleasure of the senses' is mingled with 'the pleasure of social conformity'.[24] It was the non-verbal rituals of smoking that made it such a good subject for the kind of visual observation in which Mass-Observation specialised. Tom Harrisson began his career as an ornithologist, and he carried this observational technique over into the study of people, always believing you could learn more by carefully watching than asking endless survey questions. Like drinking (another favourite M-O topic), smoking was actually difficult to do while talking at the same time.[25] Mass-Observation noted in the late 1940s that many smokers found the look and feel of the cigarette, and its accoutrements such as matches and lighters, intensely pleasurable, and did not enjoy smoking in the dark when they could not be seen.[26] Harrisson was fascinated by the largely middle-class ritual of tapping the cigarette before lighting it, a redundant gesture because factory-made cigarettes did not need their tobacco packed any more tightly.[27] Some smokers put the end they had tapped in their mouths; others lit the tapped end in the belief that it would light more evenly. Tapping was rendered still more superfluous by the post-war spread of filter tips. It is uncommon now, but I remember seeing friends doing it as late as the early 1990s, perhaps in unconscious mimicry of their parents.

Non-smoking policies now have to contend with these long-standing rituals. Few companies, however, have developed firm policies on smoking breaks. If smokers have six cigarette breaks a day at five minutes each, for example, they will be spending half an hour more away from their desks than their non-smoking colleagues. Should they be forced to clock off when taking a smoking break, and will non-smokers feel resentful if smokers are not made to do so? Since smoking is addictive, employers have generally decided to tolerate smoking breaks to maintain morale. Just as cigarette consumption has always been encouraged in wartime as the nervous soldier's friend, there is now an implicit acceptance that some people need to smoke to cope with the boredom and stress of work. Workplace smoking is also an ideal way of creating camaraderie because it brings together people of different hierarchies and ranks to gossip and network. But the workplace fag break undermines one of smoking's chief pleasures. A cigarette has traditionally been a fermata, a pause in the treadmill of daily life, the inhalation and exhalation of smoke being repetitive but not quite rhythmic, always within the smoker's control. Now people will say, 'I'm just popping outside for a ciggie' or 'Have I got time for a fag?' during a break in a meeting, and rush out to get their nicotine hit. A smoke is a snatched moment rather than a leisurely interruption.

Also new are the impoverished rituals inspired by open-air smoking. What has traditionally made smoking such an attractive sight for lifetime non-smokers like myself is its absent-minded, peripheral quality. Smoking can be effort-lessly combined with other activities, like holding a drink, typing with one hand or talking on the telephone. In his breathless ode to smoking, *Cigarettes are Sublime*, Richard Klein argues that cigarettes are 'never what they appear to be, may always have their identity and their function elsewhere than they appear'.[28] The cigarette carries such a freight of meaning because it is an apparently meaning-less thing, identical to the thousands of others that the smoker has smoked and will smoke: people rarely claim ownership by referring to 'my cigarette'.[29] But outside, the cigarette and the smoker are suddenly all too visible, not that perfect alignment of unselfconsciousness and conspic-uousness that makes multitasking smokers so charismatic. The outdoor smoker becomes somehow self-conscious and furtive rather than nonchalant and self-possessed.

Klein argues that cigarette smoking is a way of extending the limits of the body so that it is 'no longer fixed by the margin of your skin'. You feel the smoke penetrate deep into your lungs, then you exhale it into a kind of halo which surrounds the body and can be wafted away with graceful hand gestures.[30] Such languorous motions

– posing as a Rive Gauche intellectual in cafés, blowing smoke rings, double-tapping delicately on the ashtray and waving the cigarette around like a burning wand – are now less common as indoor smoking declines. Mass-Observation claimed that middle-class smokers tended to hold their cigarette between the first and second finger, so that it could be wafted about imperiously, whereas working-class smokers, who were more likely to smoke outside, tended to hold the cigarette between thumb and finger with the lit end facing the palm.[31] This latter now seems to be the default option, not because smokers are disproportionately working-class (although they are) but because outdoor smokers often have to protect their cigarette from the elements. Until quite recently, smoking also inspired an elaborate apparatus – ashtrays, spittoons, tobacco pouches, cigarette cases – which extended the smoker's personal space. Smoking outdoors, by contrast, needs to be quick and unfussy. Even loose tobacco and cigarette papers take too long to prepare, are difficult to light and likely to go out. Smoking's accessories are now communally provided, nailed to the wall and designed to dispose of the smoke and ash cleanly. Smokers are left almost empty-handed, with only their cigarette packet and lighter for company.

You might wonder why people still bother to smoke at all, if the poetry of lighting up has been so compromised. But legal restrictions and ethical imperatives are always coming up against the persistence of social habits. In certain parts of America, the smoker is a virtual moral outcast; in France, *le pause café-clope*, the coffee and cigarette break, is such a national ritual that legislation to ban indoor smoking has only dented it slightly. Britain falls somewhere between these two extremes: smoking might be an increasingly endangered practice but it still penetrates everyone's daily life – both smokers and non-smokers – in subtle, pervasive ways.

My office at work is directly above a terrace where

students, and some members of staff, congregate to light up between classes. Smoking has been banned from inside all the university buildings for several years. Actually, it is banned from the terrace as well, which is technically part of the building, but a tacit acceptance that this constitutes 'outside' means that smoking is tolerated there. Looking out of my window, I can see people gossiping, laughing, exchanging cigarettes and lighters, and blowing their smoke into the air. Instead of cigarettes being offered, people now 'cadge' fags off each other because they have given up and have just momentarily lapsed (again). But the *esprit de corps* is the same. The smokers' club may be more exclusive these days, but perhaps that adds to its allure. The rituals and sociability of smoking cannot simply be rationalised or legalised out of existence. Smoking is an international, wordless language that breaks down – if only for a few brief moments – the inevitable awkwardness between people who are not quite strangers and not quite friends. For now, you will have to stub that fag out. It is time to go inside for the one immovable event of the modern working day: the staff meeting.

9 Any other business?

'The regularity of a habit is usually in direct proportion to its absurdity'

Marcel Proust [1]

Everyone agrees: meetings are rubbish. In an age of video conferencing, electronic discussion groups and virtual meeting rooms on the web, they are such an old-fashioned, sedentary waste of people's time. To fans of business-speak, even the word has become embarrassing. They prefer to catch up, huddle, 'share and air' or 'F2F' (face-to-face) with their colleagues – anything other than a boring 'meeting'. Cutting-edge companies invent tactics to keep meetings moving along, like making everyone stand up at breakfast bars, or providing one less chair than required, to encourage punctuality. Intimidating meeting rooms are ditched in favour of 'conversation areas', painted in bright primary colours to encourage lateral thought or serenity. But whatever we call them and however we dress them up as something else, meetings are a hard habit to break. Why?

The problem dates from the end of the nineteenth and the beginning of the twentieth centuries, when new forms of white-collar bureaucracy emerged on both sides of the Atlantic, and the rules of meetings began to be codified and formalised. Two books in particular became classics: *Robert's Rules of Order*, published in America in 1876, and Frank Shackleton's *The Law and Practice of Meetings*, published in Britain in 1934. These books, which have since gone through hundreds of reprintings, set out the familiar conventions which have developed from parliamentary procedures, voluntary organisations and the AGMs of public companies: placing items on agendas, offering apologies for absence, proposing motions, asking for a quorum count, raising any other business, and so on.

The modern idea of the meeting emerged in America in the late 1940s as a way of challenging these rigid procedures. The psychologist Kurt Lewin, a refugee from Nazi Germany who arrived at Iowa State University in the 1930s, has some claim to being the originator of the modern meeting. The war effort had placed a high value on teamwork and collective organisation. It encouraged psychologists like Lewin to move into applied areas, and to study group dynamics rather than individuals. Lewin was inspired by the 'Human Relations' school of management, which argued that workers are more productive when they feel involved in decision-making. He and his colleagues got funding from the Office of Naval Research to found the National Training Laboratories for Group Development (although Lewin died of a heart attack before it was set up). In 1947, NTL held its first summer session in Bethel, Maine – a small, mountain village chosen as a 'cultural island' where delegates could be receptive to new ideas. NTL inspired a new ideal, the 'member-centred' meeting, which was such a radical departure that people had to be taught how to behave in it by teams of 'professional group expediters'.[2] Within fifteen years the summer school had grown into a massive operation, with thousands of delegates and over a hundred trainers.[3]

The 'member-centred' meeting transformed the chairman into a more egalitarian-sounding 'facilitator' or 'moderator', and valued the contributions of all members equally – but it also scrutinised their behaviour more, with the aid of the new science of occupational psychology.

In one training manual of the period, the authors listed numerous 'nuisance types' to be found in 'sick' groups, such as hair-splitters, eager beavers, fence-sitters and doubting Thomases. Unfortunately, you could not escape censure simply by sitting there in silence. Even non-speakers were classified as either 'constructive' or 'destructive'.[4] Since members were supposed to talk, they could now be evaluated for their leadership qualities or lack of them. As another meetings manual put it: 'Each supervisor and each manager above him is on the alert for men who stand out as "comers".'[5] The member-centred meeting did not simply encourage people to participate; it questioned their motives and characters if they did not.

The member-centred meeting was the natural habitat for William H. Whyte's 'organization man', the office worker employed in the large, faceless corporations of post-war America. This man was a master of the 'committee arts'.[6] He was suspicious of authoritarian leadership and viewed the group as the appropriate space for negotiating and resolving problems. But as Whyte noted perceptively, 'if every member simply wants to do what the group wants to do, then the group is not going to do anything'.[7] Whyte invented a term, 'groupthink', to describe the forms of collective psychology that developed in meetings in which the overriding aim was consensus.[8] Groupthink allowed people to make wholly irrational decisions, reassured by the fact that everyone else felt the same way. Groups were most likely to suffer from groupthink if they eschewed formal protocol – a more probable eventuality in a member-centred meeting.

Throughout the 1950s, the proselytisers for the member-centred meeting developed new techniques for encouraging member participation – many of them taken from research in adult education, which found that groups learned more by doing than passively listening. One technique – labelled 'Phillips 66' after its inventor,

J. Donald Phillips, an adult education tutor at Michigan State College – involved dividing large groups into teams of six and giving each team six minutes to discuss a problem. These were soon renamed 'buzz groups' because of the subdued buzzing noise the discussions generated.[9] Another technique was the role-play, used by the US army in the war to see if applicants for dangerous work would crack under interrogation, and adapted for business as a way of demonstrating a concept quickly and simply.[10] But the most popular new technique was creative thinking or 'brainstorming', a method developed by the advertising executive Alex Osborn, in which participants generated ideas without others being allowed to censor or comment on them.[11]

Many of these American techniques had crossed the Atlantic by the mid-1950s, although at first some British observers viewed them rather archly. One 1959 newspaper article, about experiments in brainstorming at John Lewis, quoted the head of its vocational training department: 'In brainstorming you speak first and think afterwards.' The article concludes, 'The assumption is that out of this intellectual orgy something of value will emerge … So far, Mr Pennell conceded, no "startlingly new" ideas of great value appear to have come to light, but he emphasizes that some results are still being analysed.'[12] One thing that helped to disseminate these techniques to Britain was the growth of the international conference-hosting industry, aided in turn by the jumbo jet. In the 1960s, most of the top London hotels built conference halls to house the American businesses who were increasingly holding their conventions abroad.

But there was still a clash of meetings cultures, a collision between new types of American management science and the more traditional, British approach to committees. As late as 1974, one UK business journalist was complaining about IBM's use of the inhuman verbs 'to task force' and 'to

Any other business?

flip chart'.[13] British meetings were still more likely to have seating protocols which put the most senior people next to the chairman (it almost always was a man) and a certain formalisation of unpunctuality which meant that people arrived at meetings in order of rank, with the chair arriving late and last, an extension of the middle-class custom of appearing slightly late for social gatherings.[14] In the late 1950s, C. Northcote Parkinson called semi-humorously for a 'science of comitology' which would examine the ways in which British meetings and committees developed self-perpetuating conventions whose only purpose was to confer status upon their members. Parkinson devised a quasi-mathematical formula, the 'coefficient of inefficiency', to measure how committees acquired more and more members, all in search of the prestige of membership, until they became wholly ineffective. The first principle of comitology was that 'a committee is organic rather than mechanical in its nature: it is not a structure but a plant. It takes root and grows, it flowers, wilts, and dies, scattering the seed from which other committees will bloom in their turn.'[15]

Parkinson developed this idea while serving in the British army during the war. While a member of various military committees, he noticed that these committees simply generated work for each other, 'reading each other's minutes and criticizing each other's grammar'.[16] He focused on government and company committees, but in popular mythology this kind of unproductive meeting was linked with the labour movement and the trade unions. According to trade unionist Walter Citrine's classic book *The ABC of Chairmanship* (1939), the procedures of meetings were a solemn social contract meant to embody democracy and egalitarianism.[17] As caricatured in figures like the pompous shop steward Fred Kite (Peter Sellers) in *I'm All Right, Jack* (1959), however, these rules came to be associated with a love of procedure for its own sake.

What finally did for this rule-bound meeting was the wholesale Americanisation of British work culture that took place during the Thatcher era. This new work culture had a more informal etiquette: it jettisoned the most visibly hierarchical relationships and rigid rules in favour of more subtle forms of psychological duress. The workers were not being disciplined and regimented as they had been in the bad old days; they were now being 'incentivised' to become the entrepreneurial, creative people they were always meant to be. The ideal place to do the incentivising was the meeting.

By the early 1980s, the American human-relations management that first gave rise to the member-centred meeting had mutated into an even more evangelical new concept: corporate culture. In their book *In Search of Excellence* (1982), Tom Peters and Robert Waterman argued that the best companies had strong cultures, in which all employees felt part of the firm and bought into a common ideal.[18] This book, the first management text to make the *New York Times* bestseller list, appeared at an opportune moment – in the middle of a recession in America, when the Japanese work model of company songs and other rituals of belonging seemed to be the future.[19] Britain was also going through a recession at this time, as well as supposedly suffering from the more chronic 'British disease' of hidebound management and demotivated workers. Fostering a strong corporate culture soon became a ruling motif in British as well as American business life. At the same time, recession-hit firms cut costs by flattening management hierarchies, which required more team meetings to discuss issues once dealt with by middle managers.

This new touchy-feely ethos had its coercive side. A buzz phrase of transatlantic white-collar life in the 1980s and 1990s was 'Total Quality Management'. Companies committed to TQM promised to innovate constantly, work more efficiently and satisfy their customers more completely – and to demonstrate all this to each other and to shareholders. Firms became obsessed with providing documentary evidence of what they did, made easier by the increasing flow of information pouring out of computers. The meeting became the point at which this data was distributed and analysed. Meetings also allowed companies to police their employees' work patterns. One 1980s handbook advised that meetings direct 'scarce management resources to some issues rather than others' and create 'successive deadlines to ensure that managers stay on task'.[20] A meeting generated a cycle of preparation and follow-up ('action points'), so arranging a meeting on a particular topic was a way of making sure employees concentrated their efforts on that topic.

Meetings became confusingly multifunctional. They were about sharing information and fostering a co-operative environment, what Peters called 'social atmospherics'.[21] But they were also about pushing through tough decisions and monitoring workers closely. When working at the 'BritArm' bank in 1994, the ethnographer John Weeks found that the first half-hour of every Wednesday morning was given over to a 'communication meeting', where all employees were meant to disseminate good ideas and compare notes. But Weeks discovered that senior people were so worried about this time being wasted that they sent weekly 'briefing packets' to line managers, sometimes accompanied by videotapes, which the line managers would often simply read out or show without comment.[22] In this weekly meeting, the 'soft' issues about attitude and culture had become mixed up with the 'hard' issues about profit and performance, in a way that was all too apparent to the bank's cynical employees.

By now, meetings were not simply a way of doing business; they were a gigantic, multinational business in themselves. Across America and Europe, the planning and hosting of meetings became a lucrative branch of corporate hospitality. The British descendant of those NTL summer sessions in Bethel, Maine in the 1940s was the departmental 'away day' held in a cheap chain hotel near a motorway intersection, with mints, biscuits, notepads and pens laid on like tea-making facilities in hotel rooms. The business shelves of bookshops were now full of how-to titles like *We Have to Stop Meeting Like This* and *Stop the Meeting, I Want to Get Off*, which promised to relieve the tedium of meetings by creating 'empowered' and 'proactive' participants. The office supplies industry, meanwhile, had been marketing new kinds of member-centred meeting tools like easel pads and flip charts since the 1950s. One of the pioneers of the overhead projector, 3M, realised that 'you can't sell business meeting tools unless you can show the customer why they are needed and how to use them'.[23] So it formed the 3M Meetings Management Team to publish meetings manuals and conduct workshops stressing the importance of visual aids like OHPs and electronic whiteboards. But by the end of the millennium one visual aid began to dwarf all others in popularity: slideware.

Slideware is any sort of computer graphics program used for presentations. One of the earliest models, Presenter, was created by a small software house in 1984. When Microsoft bought it three years later, they rebranded it PowerPoint (the word 'power' presumably denoting thrusting executive energy, as in other 1980s terms such as 'power breakfast' and 'power dressing'). But when its version 1.0 went on sale, the *Guardian*'s computer correspondent, Jack Schofield, was unimpressed. 'How many British businessmen really spend that much time making presentations?' he asked. 'When I worked for a large corporation it was about once every three years.' Schofield predicted that there would be little take-up from businesses that had taken several decades to get the hang of the overhead projector.[24] Of course, Schofield was writing in the pre-laptop and data projector era, when all that slideware could do was generate black-and-white pages to make into transparencies. He also assumed that the market would behave rationally, and only respond to an existing need. But slideware's USP was that it made presentations easier to make, whether they were needed or not. It allowed meetings to be increasingly preceded by presentations, designed to steer proceedings in a particular direction. An LSE study found that, in the period between 1992 and 1997, the time spent making speeches or presentations in British firms increased by 31.9 per cent.[25] Slideware also benefited from the global standardisation of corporate life. Wherever you went in the world, you no longer had to worry if there would be an OHP in the room or if the slide projector would be broken. Slideware was everywhere.

Slideware companies stoked the market by launching more and more features. PowerPoint's 'Auto Content Wizard', introduced in the mid-1990s, offered a series of defaults that chose the style (and in some cases the content) of the presentation for you. There were now ways of gradually building up a slide, in the optimistic hope that this would generate audience interest – like bullet points whizzing across the screen, or 'typewriter text' appearing one letter at a time until the whole text was displayed. Good news could be signalled by the sound of people cheering and a happy tune, bad news by the sound of booing and breaking glass. Edward Tufte, a Yale professor specialising in visual communication and information design, argued that PowerPoint presentations 'too often resemble the school play: very loud, very slow, and very simple'.[26] But slideware was a boon for nervous public speakers because it was much more than a visual 'aid': it virtually substituted itself for the speaker. If all you had to do was start the slide show and read the bullet points out loud, it was almost impossible to dry up.

Slideware's valuing of presentational fluency over intellectual substance encapsulates a more general condition of the modern meeting as a fertile ground for bullshit. For the philosopher Harry Frankfurt, 'bullshit' is language that simply evades conventional categories of truth and falsehood, and is thus much harder to pin down than lying. Bullshit is likely to occur 'whenever a person's obligations or opportunities to speak about some topic are more extensive than his knowledge of the facts that are relevant to that topic'.[27] Modern meetings are precisely these sorts of occasions, requiring you to give a smooth impersonation of someone who knows what they are talking about. They often value unanchored thought, sometimes called 'blue-sky', 'outside-the-box' or 'upside-down' thinking to suggest its lack of boundaries and constraints. During a brainstorm or 'thought shower', the facilitator may remind the group that 'all ideas are good ideas' or invite them to 'run a few ideas up the flagpole and see if they get a salute'. People are actively encouraged to play roles and change their views according to their different areas of responsibility ('with my resources hat on ...'). Fluency, even if it is made up of bullshit, is more valued than awkward silence, even if it inspires thoughtfulness. Bullshit is always more likely to occur when business culture stresses the importance of enthusiasm, passion, creativity, energy, buzz – rather than, say, the ability to ground ideas in knowledge or logical thinking.

If a meeting is full of bullshit, though, why waste time and money having it at all? Why do companies tolerate so many pointless meetings, when they are supposed to be concerned with making profits? In the early 1990s, some American firms started to calculate the cost of meetings by computing people's hourly salaries and the overhead costs of equipment, accommodation and so on. One management consultant invented the Meeting Meter™, a software program that would make these calculations and then start ticking away like a taxi meter, displaying the cost of the meeting as it went along.[28] Others began to undertake 'meeting systems audits', using observations of meetings to determine how effectively they were being run, and to advise firms how to 'out-meet' the competition.[29] After one of these audits, a Minneapolis-based consultancy prescribed 'training for managers in problem-solving, decision-making, conflict resolution, and other meeting management techniques', as well as 'cross-functional meetings' which would 'establish a mechanism for tracking variations in meeting processes and outcomes across the organization'.[30] The cure for sick meetings, in other words, was more meetings.

This touching faith in the power of the meeting to make good its own inadequacies is puzzling. Free-market capitalism's fiercest critics and champions tend to agree on one thing: the market may be ruthless but it is rational, drowning superstition and mysticism in what Marx and Engels called 'the icy water of egotistical calculation'.[31] If this were always true, though, these meetings audits would surely have cut down on the number of worthless meetings by now. The reality is that the market is as susceptible to irrationality as any other form of social organisation. As the anthropologist Helen B. Schwartzman puts it, 'meetings are valuable because they are not what they appear to be'.[32] They seem to be a waste of time because we focus on their content rather than their form. The stated purpose of a meeting – making decisions or exchanging information – is quite different from its actual function.

Anthropologists of tribal societies have suggested that the meeting is an inherently ritualistic occasion. In the 1960s, Maurice Bloch conducted fieldwork among the Merina people of Madagascar, examining the 'prestige auction' of the village council or *fokon'olona*. The time of each council meeting would be set several hours too early. Every elder wanted to arrive at exactly the right time to make it seem as though the meeting was starting because he had arrived – a more intense version of the traditional British association of status with unpunctuality. This entailed much waiting around in nearby houses and sending children on spying missions. Then 'as if by magic the *raiamandreny* [elders] all appear at once at a time little related to the originally appointed hour'. The meeting itself opened with a long series of speeches by the elders, full of general platitudes such as the need for kinsmen to love each other, and after each speech there was a brief period of respectful silence. When junior members finally joined in the discussion, they exchanged mutually contradictory statements rather than arguing directly with each other. Often people went away from the meeting not having a clue what had been decided.[33]

No doubt there are meetings consultants who think that the status-seeking tactics of the Merina elders would all be resolved by a team-building away day, finished off with a game of paintball. If the *fokon'olona* is an extreme example of procrastination, though, anthropologists who have attended meetings and councils have all discovered these resilient rituals.[34] One comparable ritual performed in modern business culture is the Japanese practice of *nemawashi*, which literally means 'tending the roots' and refers to the groundwork – sounding out opinions and negotiating concessions – that is done before the meeting proper begins, like digging round the roots of a tree before transplanting it.[35] Scholars of linguistic politeness have examined similar conflict-avoidance tactics in meetings in western countries. For example, people might preface their comments with qualifiers like 'I'm not sure if this will work, but …' or 'someone's probably thought of this already, but …' One linguist calls these expressions 'butterfinger buts' (children say 'butterfingers' when they pick up a stone in hopscotch, so it doesn't matter if they drop it).[36] Another example is the kind of fudging management speak used in meetings that is a symptom of the more flexible, insecure working practices of the post-Thatcher era. This type of speech avoids questions of ownership or blame for ideas or policies, and searches for consensus, if only rhetorically. So we are urged to be 'on message', 'on the same page', 'aligned', or have 'our ducks in a row'.

The modern meeting remains the most formal occasion in our daily lives. It has introductory rites (apologies for absence, matters arising), a liturgy (agenda items for discussion) and concluding rites (any other business, date of next meeting). Everything is recorded for posterity in the holy book known as 'the minutes', which are typed up, circulated and agreed at the next meeting. The meeting takes place in a designated space (the meeting room), and is presided over by a kind of priest or elder (the chair) who may begin with a recitation (on PowerPoint). The participants break bread together (triangular sandwiches or shortbread biscuits) and dress in ceremonial garb (business suits and ties). Like many rituals, the meeting is rooted in the politics of daily life but aims to transcend the difficult issues of power and status through the use of formality and ceremony.

We are often unaware that the meeting is a ritual because we have become so bored and disenchanted with it. Disenchantment inspires its own clandestine rituals, like 'narcolepsy chicken', the game of brinkmanship in which meeting participants see how close they can come to nodding off without actually doing so; or 'bullshit bingo', in which they print out a mock bingo card containing nefarious examples of management-speak and tick them off until they get a full house. These subversive rituals never fundamentally challenge the nature of the meeting itself, though; they simply give people ways of coping with its tedium. For however much we hate it, the meeting, like all ritual, is repetitive and self-perpetuating. Meetings seem to assume that time is infinite – they generate agenda items for yet more meetings, extending into a never-ending future. Someone will be around to follow up that action point, even if it is not us. But if meetings are immortal, the working day is fortunately not, and sooner or later the cleaners will be here to hoover the carpet. Can we park these issues but leave the motor running? This meeting is adjourned.

10 The ministry of sensible walks

'Hundreds of thousands of salaried employees throng
the streets of Berlin daily, yet their life is more unknown
than that of the primitive tribes at whose habits those
same employees marvel in films'

Siegfried Kracauer[1]

You see it most in the evening rush hour, a strange, improvised street dance you could call 'the pedestrian shuffle'.
Thousands of workers stream out of city offices after work
and, in the hurry to get to the railway station or to the bar,
they weave between the cars on busy roads, using little
head swivels, swerving movements and quickened steps,
often not waiting for traffic lights or using pedestrian
crossings. Crossing the road is a social habit that people
do almost unconsciously. You might hear the occasional
honked horn or see the odd two fingers raised in anger,
but the rival parties generally manage to work things out
amicably enough – a testament to the power of instinctual
actions and non-verbal signals.

Crossing the road is a simple routine, but a rather
important one: after all, getting it wrong can get you
killed. We forget how crucial this routine is because there
are so few legal constraints on pedestrians in Britain. The
Highway Code (which is simply that – a code of good
behaviour – only some of which is backed up by statute law)
contains several pages of instructions on how pedestrians
should behave, but they are mostly unenforceable. You can

jaywalk with impunity – unlike in both North America and much of Western Europe, where there are hefty fines for naughty pedestrians, handed out with varying degrees of alacrity. In the US, the pedestrian is brusquely ordered by the lights simply to 'walk' or 'don't walk', although natives of certain American cities, like New York, are inveterate jaywalkers, a tradition threatened only slightly by Mayor Rudolph Giuliani's zero-tolerance approach at the end of the 1990s. Crossing the road in Germany in defiance of the red standing man is almost as serious an offence as a driver ignoring a red light. In Singapore, the capitalist dictatorship and traffic management capital of the world, it can land you in jail.

These cultural differences are sometimes taken as a sign of the British reliance on good manners rather than rigid rules. But there have been many abortive attempts to police the movements of pedestrians in this country, and their relationship with drivers has often been difficult. Like queuing, crossing the road operates through unspoken rules, and these rules have emerged gradually in response to the sometimes fraught history of the motor car in Britain. One 1937 newspaper leader encapsulated the intractability of this problem with the mock epitaph:

Here lies the body of William Day,
Who was killed disputing a right of way.
He was right, dead right, as he walked along,
But he's just as dead as if he'd been wrong.[2]

Pedestrian crossings were first introduced after the 1934 Road Traffic Act, at a time when the growing number of deaths on the roads was seen as a national scandal. To make the crossings conspicuous, they were marked at kerbside by 'Belisha beacons', named after the minister of transport, Leslie Hore-Belisha. These seven-foot-high striped poles with amber-coloured globes on top were garish additions to the streetscape and produced a great deal of both amused and hostile public interest. The *Spectator* protested that they made London look like it was 'preparing for a fifth-rate carnival'.[3] In the four months after their introduction, 3,000 of the 15,000 beacons installed in London had been destroyed, by people throwing stones or taking pot shots at them with air rifles.[4] Perhaps these guerrilla foot soldiers were protesting at the way in which the crossings conceded the rest of the highway to the motor car. By the end of the 1930s, both local authorities and the government began to restrict pedestrian movement. Miles of pedestrian barriers were erected in London, making it harder not to use the provided crossings.[5] In a pilot project in the capital, policemen stood on the roofs of police cars in busy streets during the rush hour, shouting advice and admonishments at pedestrians through megaphones.[6]

The next major innovation was the zebra crossing, invented in the late 1940s after a series of studies by the Road Research Laboratory on the conspicuousness of different road markings in different conditions like wet roads and night-time.[7] The future prime minister James Callaghan, then a junior at the Ministry of Transport, came up with 'zebra' as a name for the crossing that would be easily remembered, particularly by children. A thousand sets of zebra stripes were painted on roads in preparation for 'pedestrian crossing week', held in April 1949 to test the new zebras and promote the use of crossings generally.[8] There were also painted footprints on the pavement leading up to the zebras, silently urging pedestrians to follow their example.

The Ministry of Transport believed that there were now so many crossings that they were not being observed by either motorists or pedestrians.[9] So the Belisha crossings not converted to zebras were gradually abandoned, reducing the overall number of crossings by about two-thirds. In many towns, parents protested against the removal of crossings, forming human barriers and holding up traffic while their children crossed the road to school.[10] The zebra crossing also failed to get rid of the long-standing confusion over rights of way. The 1954 version of the Highway Code informed pedestrians that they had precedence on the zebra but should 'be sensible; wait for a suitable gap in the traffic so that drivers have time to give way'.[11] It is easy to see how, in heavy traffic, this could lead to a game of chicken.

By the early 1960s it was clear that the zebra could not cope with the growing volume of urban traffic. The post-war office boom had created huge rush-hour congestion in city centres, as more white-collar workers drove to work in cars, many donated by their firms as non-taxable perks. So the government experimented with a 'hybrid' crossing that would stop cars more emphatically but would not disrupt the traffic flow as much as traffic lights. Instead of the zebra's parallel stripes, these new 'panda' crossings had triangular black-and-white shark's teeth, supposedly resembling panda markings. The pedestrian pressed a button at the roadside, which produced a flashing amber light followed by a pulsating red light for drivers, warning and then ordering them to stop, followed by a 'cross' sign for the pedestrian. This was a new concept of road-sharing, which gave pedestrians and cars priority on the same section of road at different times.[12] Panda crossings were introduced in April 1962, when the minister of transport, Ernest Marples, switched on the first one, opposite London's Waterloo station. There is a curious piece of BBC news footage of this event in which, deprived of any ribbon-cutting moment, Marples simply walks over the crossing, holding a toy panda presented to him by the Mayor of Lambeth's wife. Ominously, he has to wave the traffic on again once he has crossed the road.[13]

The panda was a flop. Motorists were baffled by the flashing and pulsating lights and did not realise that, if there was no light at all, it meant 'go ahead'. Many of the new crossings broke down and were covered in sackcloth only hours after being unveiled, which created more confusion about whether a panda whose lights weren't working became a zebra by default. Guildford had all thirteen of its zebras converted to pandas, this stock-broker suburb being selected by the Ministry of Transport as a show town, allegedly because of 'the high standard of intelligence of its inhabitants'. But its local newspaper soon dismissed the experiment as a 'farce'.[14]

London pedestrians had a particular reason to be angry with the pandas: their introduction coincided with the first serious attempt to penalise jaywalking in the capital. In September 1962, the Ministry of Transport proposed an experiment in three metropolitan boroughs (Ealing, Paddington and Tottenham) to make it an offence to cross the road other than at pedestrian crossings. One corre-spondent in *The Times* wondered if 'Mr Marples's next brainwave will be jay-walker wardens on roller skates', and another asserted his 'rights as a freeborn Englishman' to cross the road wherever he liked.[15] While the panda was quickly abandoned, the experiment of punishing badly-behaved pedestrians stuttered on for a few more years. The Metropolitan police tried a new tactic in 1966, painting red lines by the kerb and threatening jaywalkers with £20 fines. 5,000 people received verbal warnings but no one was fined, and the police dropped the scheme three months later, claiming it was 'absolutely unworkable'.[16]

The next pedestrian crossing innovation after the panda, announced in September 1964, was more successful: shielded lights for pedestrians at kerbside showing the silhouetted figures of a red standing man ('wait') and a green walking man ('cross'). The introduction of these matchstick figures followed the 1963 Worboys report, which recommended using symbols rather than letters in traffic signs. The green and red man symbols were inspired by the work of Otto Neurath, a member of the Vienna circle who in the 1930s devised a graphic language known as Isotype (International System of Typographical Picture Education) in the belief that universal visual symbols could transcend cultural and national differences.[17] (In fact, apart from their colour there is nothing universal about the way green and red traffic-light men look – East Germans are very fond of their cute, jauntily-hatted *Ampelmännchen* ('little traffic-light man'), a residue of the old GDR regime, and have fought long campaigns against his replacement by his blander West German cousin. More recently, a little green woman, nicknamed 'Sophie', has appeared at crossings in Germany and Holland.)

Even with little green and red men to guide pedestrians, there was still a lot of confusion about who had right of way, particularly when the various lights were flashing or unlit. Finally, in July 1969, the Ministry of Transport came up with a workable solution: a new crossing called the 'pelican' or 'pelicon', a compression of 'pedestrian light-controlled crossing'. It was clearer for motorists than the earlier green-man crossings because it had a full green signal showing for them all the time, except when someone pressed the button to cross the road. The push-button box also had a plaque explaining to pedestrians how to use the crossing. These instructions are still there today ('Pedestrians: push button and wait for signal opposite'), read by no one except the occasional foreign tourist or bored child.

Unlike the earlier crossing experiments, the pelican received little press attention, perhaps because it was jostling for news space with the moon landings. Television adverts about the pelican focused on the still-ambiguous period when the little green man was flashing. One 1974 TV advertisement used characters from the most popular sitcom of the period, *Dad's Army*, creating the rather incongruous image of the Home Guard marching through a 1970s suburban street. The platoon is crossing on a pelican when the green man starts to flash. As Corporal Jones begins to panic, Sergeant Wilson, the embodiment of patrician calm, says that 'one continues to cross if one's already on the crossing. There's plenty of time.' He then restrains Captain Mainwaring from stepping out, warning him that 'one shouldn't start to cross'. A voiceover instructs the viewer to 'learn your blinking pelican signals'.[18] This film was released five years after pelicans were first introduced, suggesting that the government was still not convinced that pedestrians had got the hang of them. As late as 1976, there was an advert with a 'pelican crossing song' in the style of an American hoedown:

> When the green man's flashing and the amber too
> This is what you've got to do
> Pedestrians, don't start to cross
> Your life's more important than the time that's lost.[19]

The sixties innovation of the push-button crossing – which meant, in a sense, that pedestrians had to ask for permission to cross the road and then wait until permission was granted – was part of a growing attempt to limit their access to busy roads. Around the same time, the new science of traffic engineering, which had first emerged in America in the 1950s, began to have a big influence on British transport policy. Traffic engineering preferred to focus on road design and traffic data rather than more contentious issues like penalising jaywalkers or punishing speeding motorists. It was a car-centred discipline, treating pedestrians largely as impediments to traffic flow. With the rise of this new science, the trend shifted towards changing the street landscape in order to separate pedestrians from drivers.

Colin Buchanan's influential government report and unlikely bestseller, *Traffic in Towns* (1963), epitomised this new approach. In part, this book owed its success to its author's personal charisma and vivid turn of phrase. 'We have taken a bull into the china shop,' Buchanan said, 'and to that old problem there are only two answers – shoot the bull, or more creatively, build a new china shop especially designed for bulls.'[20] Buchanan's report was widely blamed in subsequent years for recommending the complete segregation of pedestrians and traffic.[21] This was unfair. Buchanan simply argued that towns had a finite capacity to absorb cars. He suggested limiting the number of cars going into centres by restricting parking spaces and imposing a congestion tax, long before these ideas achieved political currency. But he also advocated designing 'traffic architecture', which would accommodate cars and pedestrians in multi-tier streets. Pedestrians would walk around on elevated pavements (because humans are easier to raise than vehicles) with most roads at ground level, and some major roads and car parks built underground. In London's Oxford Street, for example – a 'civic disaster' where 'even old ladies have to be spry as matadors to avoid the snapping bonnets of cars'[22] – Buchanan proposed a six-lane freeway, with shops and pedestrians raised above it.

Whether inspired by Buchanan or not, there were some hugely ambitious plans for segregating pedestrians and cars in the 1960s and 1970s, not all of which came to fruition. In London there was a blueprint for a whole network of urban motorways smashing through the Georgian terraces of Islington, Hampstead and Notting Hill, stopped only by the pressure-group power of a growing band of middle-class gentrifiers. In the City of London today you can still see evidence of the aborted 'pedway' system, a network of elevated pavements inspired by New Town planning, which would allow pedestrians to walk for miles without ever descending to street level.[23] But Oxford Street remained (and remains) a traffic-clogged morass for both drivers and pedestrians. What did get built were lots of urban expressways, crossable only via footbridges and subways. Subways were not a post-Buchanan invention, but these dark, urine-stained, graffiti-sprayed tunnels symbolised the failures of urban planning in this era. Aside from their inherent design problems, they tended to be sited on the edges of city centres, underneath ring roads, so they came to be associated with inner-city crime, especially muggings.[24] Margaret Thatcher spoke to her party conference in 1987 about the 'arrogant' post-war planners who had 'cut the heart out of our cities':

> They swept aside the familiar city centres that had grown up over the centuries. They replaced them with a wedge of tower blocks and linking expressways, interspersed with token patches of grass and a few windswept piazzas, where pedestrians fear to tread … they simply set the municipal bulldozer to work. What folly, what incredible folly.[25]

In the 1980s and 1990s, there was a backlash against the subway era as planners and architects began to stress the importance of 'walkability' and 'legible cities'. But the areas earmarked for greater pedestrian-friendliness were generally the central shopping and tourist districts. Pedestrians might be valued as consumers, but they were not allowed to get in the way of traffic flow elsewhere in the city. The pedestrianisation of city-centre areas was another way of segregating walkers from motorists – albeit a free-range solution which gave the former a little more room to roam around.

At the turn of the millennium, the government, and major cities like London, began developing what they called 'walking strategies'. Commissioned by the Central London Partnership to look at the problem of walkability, the Danish architect Jan Gehl concluded that London suffered from 'pedestrian jams', movement that was beyond comfortable walking capacity, a condition that Americans call 'pedlock' (pedestrian gridlock). He recommended removing urban 'obstacle courses' made up of guard railings, staggered pedestrian crossings and pavement clutter such as sign poles and ticket machines.[26] But the possibility of a national strategy for walking was met only with press ridicule. Journalists dismissed 'the ministry of silly walks', and lamented the loss of taxpayers' money spent on promoting 'this miracle method of loco-motion, called putting one foot in front of the other'.[27] Wasn't walking a rather simple, idiot-proof activity? It was certainly none of the business of meddling planners and politicians.

How times have changed. When cars first arrived in the early years of the twentieth century, newspaper journalists were on the side of pedestrians, who made up the majority of their readers. Drivers were seen as over-privileged yobs trying to take over the road at the expense of everyone else. The aristocratic road hog, immortalised as Mr Toad in *The Wind in the Willows* (1908), and, even worse, the nouveau riche businessman who spent his ill-gotten gains on luxury items like cars, were common hate figures.[28] As the car became an increasingly middle-class rather than aristocratic possession throughout the 1920s and 1930s, however, public opinion shifted and the free movement of cars became paramount. Nowadays most journalists are not so much hostile to pedestrians as oblivious to their existence. Walking is statistically almost invisible, particularly since all trips under one mile are discounted by the government's National Travel Survey. But the best estimate is that, in the last quarter of the twentieth century, the amount of walking in Britain declined by about 25 per cent.[29] Given this context, a walking strategy does not seem quite so ludicrous.

From the point of view of public safety, government policy on crossing the road has been a great success story.

In 1927, the earliest year in which statistics are available, 2,774 pedestrians were killed in road accidents. Despite a huge increase in the number of cars and roads since then, the number of deaths in 2004 was 671.[30] But the policy of segregating drivers and pedestrians, building ever more sophisticated crossings and bombarding pedestrians with road safety propaganda has also sidestepped thornier issues about the dominance of the car and the decline of walking in our society.

So what do we have instead of a walking strategy? We have intelligent technology. In the mid-1990s, two new pedestrian crossings were introduced which aimed to take all the remaining hassle out of crossing the road. Carrying on the tradition of lame puns around an avian theme, they were named the puffin ('pedestrian user-friendly intelligent') crossing and the toucan ('two can') crossing, which was basically a puffin that could be used by both pedestrians and cyclists. Both these crossings use infrared sensors to detect pedestrians, ensuring that the traffic is stopped until they have finished crossing, but giving drivers a green light as soon as the crossing is clear – so there is no need for intermediate flashing lights or amber stages, just constant red or green. Compared with their predecessors, these new pedestrian crossings generated little public interest, perhaps because their interactivity makes them so easy to use. But they were specifically designed with the eternal conflict between motorist and pedestrian in mind. The steady red signal meant that pedestrians were not harassed by drivers revving up during the flashing green/ amber period, and drivers were not irritated by having to stop pointlessly at crossings after pedestrians pressed the button and then crossed in a gap in the traffic, or even pressed it just to annoy drivers.

In order to broker this ceasefire between driver and pedestrian, the pedestrian crossing has had to become an incredibly complex and expensive piece of technology.

Government guidelines about its design and installation – on the diameter of lamps, the rate at which lights should flash, the width of zebra stripes, the colour of beacons, the slope of the ramps for wheelchair users, the pitch and tone of the bleep for blind people – now fill entire volumes. This technology works so well that the crossings are, as engineers say, 'black-boxed' – that is, they perform complex functions automatically, with all the workings hidden inside. We do not have to think about how they operate, or about the fierce debates and power struggles that have brought them into being. Nor are pedestrians forced to use them. The only legal requirement imposed on pedestrians is that they must not dawdle on a crossing (although what constitutes dawdling is, of course, not easily defined).

So we are left with this improvised rush-hour ballet, as errant pedestrians take their chances in the busy city traffic. Observational studies of pedestrians have shown that many of them simply disregard the traffic architecture designed to segregate them from cars. They jump over and walk on the outside of guard railings, steer clear of subways and footbridges, ignore the white-painted signs on the road telling them to 'look left' or 'look right', walk across roads just yards away from pedestrian crossings and cross when the little red man is ordering them to wait.[31] Since British traffic law has preferred to appeal to our sense of civic duty rather than the threat of punishment, the only real sanctions against pedestrians are the laws of physics. We cannot rebel too much against the ascendancy of the car, for one very good reason: those several tons of speeding metal racing towards us. We may be in a hurry, but we are also very soft and fleshy. So the pedestrian shuffle is a habit we all have to learn.

11 Not just here for the beer

'Rigid, the skeleton of habit alone upholds the human frame'

Virginia Woolf [1]

Although there is a slight risk of colliding with a car, it is probably worth braving the mean streets to make your way to the pub. A recent study by economists at Stirling University found that workers who drink have higher salaries than their teetotal workmates. Moderate drinkers earn an average of 17 per cent more than abstainers, and even heavy drinkers, consuming more than fifty units a week, earn 5 per cent more. Your earnings start declining only if you drink very large quantities in single sittings; if you 'steadily soak yourself in alcohol' it seems to have the opposite effect. [2] How do we explain this statistical relationship? You could argue that drinkers are just naturally better at their jobs, or at getting on with their colleagues (although I wouldn't advise you to do so in the company of a teetotaller). The most plausible explanation, however, is that the after-work drink is an important if unstated part of work itself. The emphasis on teamwork and networking in modern office jobs tends to blur the boundaries between work and non-work. Even if you are feeling tired and grumpy, it might be politic to pop along for that swift half before you catch the train, just to show your face.

When Mass-Observation conducted research in north-west pubs in the 1930s, it similarly discovered that drinking was not the main motivation for going to the pub. Pub-going was a social habit, a temporary liberation from the 'time-clock factory-whistle dimension of living'.[3] Tribal societies used music, dancing or some other ceremony to achieve this kind of transitional release from work-life rhythms. In Britain, it was the pub, a sort of halfway house between work and home, which served this function for the working-class man. (Women were not usually so welcome in the pub, although they were grudgingly allowed in the more expensive saloon bar.) When the main author of Mass-Observation's *The Pub and the People*, John Sommerfield, returned to Bolton in 1960, he was struck by how little pub culture had changed: 'Go into almost any pub and you would never deduce that this is the era of nuclear fission, computer thinking, sputniks, the cold war and all the rest of it. The winds of change *have hardly ruffled the surface of a single gill of best mild*.'[4] But things *were* changing. Pub-going had been falling steadily since before the First World War in the face of new amusements like cinema, the radio and the football pools, and television seemed to be dealing it a death blow. By 1962, there were 30,000 fewer pubs than in 1939.[5] Many of the surviving pubs were bought up by the big breweries, which wanted to appeal to newer customers like young people, white-collar workers and women. Their strategy was two-fold.

First, they tried to change what people drank. Even in the inter-war period, the pint of mild had acquired an unfashionable image as an old working-class man's drink. After the war, brewers marketed more expensive drinks like bottled beer and bitter. One 1958 newspaper article concluded that 'traditionally bitter is looked on as the bosses' drink. Any man reckons he's as good as his boss. So he chooses bitter.'[6] The most successful new drink was Babycham, a perry served in a special glass, which on its introduction in 1952 did much to turn the pub into a respectable destination for women. But the most significant long-term innovation was lager, which brewers loved because it was easy to keep. After being marketed first at women (Skol's first ad campaign promoted it as 'a blonde for a blonde'), it eventually found its niche among young male office workers, who wanted a less filling drink than bitter after their day's sedentary labours.

By far the most controversial trend was the apparently inexorable rise of keg beer from the mid-1950s onwards. Unlike traditional cask beer, keg is no longer alive and fermenting: it is chilled, pasteurised and pumped with carbon dioxide to make it last longer. It was first drunk in 1936, after the East Sheen Tennis Club complained to Watneys that its beer was not keeping until the weekend, when most of its customers came in. Watneys, then working on a prototype beer called 'Red Barrel' meant for troops in India, swiftly redirected it to the less exotic surroundings of leafy Surrey.[7] Until the 1960s, keg was mostly sold in a few clubs that only opened at weekends. But by the mid-1970s, three-quarters of British pubs offered only keg beer and lager.[8]

Watneys Red Barrel, nicknamed 'Grotneys' by the Campaign for Real Ale (CAMRA), was the most reviled example of keg. Apart from its allegedly awful taste, all evidence of which is now lost to history, many drinkers hated the coercive marketing that accompanied it, from irritating advertising jingles to entire pub refits. In 1971, in a misguided search for radical chic, Watneys urged beer drinkers to 'Join the Red Revolution'. Pubs were painted corporate red, bar staff wore red socks, and posters featured lookalikes of Chairman Mao, Nikita Khrushchev and Fidel Castro supping Watneys.[9] Trying to discover why its keg beer was not selling as well as expected, one brewery conducted what it described as 'the most detailed product research ever undertaken into consumer beer drinking habits'. This research found that its keg beer lacked 'drinkability' (a fundamental failing, one would think).[10] But drinkable or not, keg beer was often the only option for pub-goers in the face of a complex monopoly that made brewers producers, wholesalers and retailers rolled into one.

The brewers' second strategy was to change the ambience of the pub. Of course, when it comes to complaints about the contrived atmosphere of modern pubs, nostalgia is never what it used to be. In *The Road to Wigan Pier* (1937), George Orwell laments the 'dismal sham-Tudor places fitted out by the big brewery companies' in the massive programme of inter-war rebuilding.[11] In a 1946 essay, he rhapsodises about his ideal pub, 'The Moon Under Water'. This pub is 'quiet enough to talk ... the house possesses neither radio nor piano'. The furnishings have 'the solid, comfortable ugliness of the 19th century'. There are 'no glass-topped tables or other modern miseries, and, on the other hand, no sham roof-beams, ingle-nooks or plastic panels masquerading as oak'. Games are only played in the public bar, so 'in the other bars you can walk without constantly ducking to avoid flying darts'.[12] Orwell finally admits what more perceptive readers have already guessed: this perfect pub does not actually exist.

After the war, the modern trends that Orwell hated were consolidated. Brewers refurbished their pubs, targeting younger, richer customers over older regulars. The class and gender divisions between public and saloon bars began to be abolished. 'Special treatment' or 'theme' pubs appeared as early as the late 1940s, although the theme at first was usually 'local pub', with prints, trophies and brasses designed to reflect the surrounding area.[13] The campaign against theme pubs did not begin in earnest until the 1970s, when it became indelibly linked with CAMRA's fight against the 'mass-produced fizzy pap' of keg beer.[14] In 1978, the beer writer and CAMRA campaigner Roger Protz complained:

Not just here for the beer

While the brewers' real estate men go about their business of closure ... trendy young architects are also ruthlessly engaged in the business of 'modernisation'. The regular users of street-corner locals find to their horror that their pub has been re-designed as a large pineapple, a sputnik or a Wild West saloon to attract the gin-and-tonic and lager-and-lime trade. Public bars are ripped out and replaced by lounges with soft lights, soft carpets, wet-look mock leather – and several pennies on the price of a pint.[15]

It was the city-centre 'circuit' pubs (so-called because they were meant to attract a peripatetic crowd who would patronise several of them in an evening) that were refurbished most frequently, and these pubs particularly targeted after-work drinkers during 'happy hours'. The term 'happy hour', originating in the US navy to describe a rest and refreshment period, began to be used in American bars in the 1950s. The concept owed something to the cocktail hour, that staging post between work and home when the man in the grey flannel suit downed a couple of dry martinis before catching the train. The British 'happy hour' – which really took off in the 1980s, as commemorated in a rather preachily disapproving song of that name by the Housemartins – was not quite so urbane. Starting about 5.30, it often lasted several hours, and was a way of plying after-work drinkers with cheap drinks until they were sufficiently relaxed to stay for more expensive drinks, and perhaps less happy hours.

If Orwell hated unruly games like darts, he would surely have loathed the electronic amusements of the theme pub – but they are really only a continuation of longer-term trends. In the 1930s, Mass-Observation noted that most London pubs prohibited any singing or live music, and that radio and slot machines had taken their place.[16] In the late 1940s, the journalist Maurice Gorham complained that the jukebox had already 'closed' several pubs to him, and 'there is another where the monster crouches ready to be called into hideous life; the regulars have the sense to leave it alone, but any day a Frankenstein may walk in.'[17] By 1960, Mass-Observation reported that some London pubs had televisions, although they were rarely switched on.[18] Eventually, the capital's taste for artificial entertainment in its pubs extended to the whole country. Pubs directly managed by brewers, rather than run by landlords, were quicker to introduce such amusements to make money and attract younger customers. 'What can one say of the miscellaneous, extraneous, intercutaneous infestation of the juke boxes, one-armed bandits, pin tables and amusement machines which now buzz, click, bleep, chatter, and caterwaul in almost every bar of the land?' lamented the architectural historian Ben Davis in 1981. 'Like vermin they multiply, and like parasites they threaten the essential bodily functions on which the health of the pub must depend.'[19]

In the 1980s, as pubs faced fiercer competition from other attractions like wine bars and restaurants, they drew in customers with noisier activities like karaoke, quiz nights and televised sport. Pub theming became more organised, with contract furnishing companies springing up with the sole aim of refurbishing pubs in a particular style such as 'Country Cottage' or 'Highlander'. Increased commercial pressures accelerated these changes. Up until the late 1980s, the pub trade was dominated by the tied estates of the big brewers, who owned the pubs and rented them out to landlords. Then, in 1989, after an investigation by the Monopolies and Mergers Commission, the Thatcher government introduced the Beer Orders, which banned any brewer from owning more than 2,000 pubs. In a complicated compromise, aimed at breaking the monopoly while retaining the goodwill of the traditionally Tory-supporting 'beerage', the brewers were allowed

Not just here for the beer

to sell off their pubs while retaining sweetheart supply deals with the new owners.

If the aim was to give more choice to drinkers, it failed. Many pubs got taken over by massive pub companies or 'pubcos', which then simply bought the bestselling drinks from the big brewers. The themed pub turned into the branded pub. The Irish Pub Company was established in 1991, and soon became the largest supplier of Irish pubs in the world. Several British brewers had their own Irish brand, from O'Neill's to Scruffy Murphy's to Finnegan's Wake (and James Joyce would have spluttered into his Guinness at the misplaced apostrophe). The McIrish pub cashed in on the early 1990s thirst for all things Hibernian, from Riverdance to the Irish success in the 1994 World Cup, which no one would have noticed if England hadn't failed to qualify. This pub looked the same wherever it was in the world: lots of timber beams, stone floors and open turf fires, combined with assorted paraphernalia like porcelain Guinness toucans, old street lamps, bags of grain and road signs to Cork.

The confusing thing about the new pub chains and branded bars was that they were selling the idea of 'authenticity' itself. New pub names offered a quirky variant on the English tradition: Rat & Parrot, Tap & Spile, Hedgehog & Hogshead, Newt & Cucumber. Firkin pubs mimicked the spit-and-sawdust decor of 'real ale' boozers, with the added draw of hilarious puns like 'I'm a Firkin Bar Steward' printed on staff T-shirts. J D Wetherspoon, the largest of the chains, specifically targeted customers who did not like theme pubs. Its outlets had no jukeboxes, dartboards or pool tables, and the fruit machines were turned down low. Television was finally introduced in 2005, but only with the sound off. In conscious homage to Orwell, many of Wetherspoon's early pubs were given names like 'Moon Under Water', 'Moon and Sixpence' and 'Man in the Moon'. They particularly tried to appeal to a clientele that the industry had been after for years: women. Large, clear windows, instead of the traditional frosted glass of the pub, allowed women to check out the interior before entering. There were fresh flowers, plants, hanging baskets and clean toilets. Bar stools were banned, so the bar ceased to be a male preserve and the Darwinian struggle to catch the bartender's eye was over. Each bartender had a set of beer pulls and a separate till behind the bar, so none of them ever turned their backs on a customer.[20]

J D Wetherspoon pubs were the close relation of another concept, the 'new bar', which was essentially a corporate reinvention of the earlier wine bar. Before the early 1970s, wine was rarely drunk outside restaurants or a few traditional wine houses. Then new wine bars emerged in the capital, with a more sophisticated ambience and quirky names like 'The Nose' or 'The Cork and Bottle'. During the Thatcher years, wine bars spread across the country. Their stereotypical patron was a flash yuppie stockbroker, conspicuously glugging Bollinger champagne ('Bolly') or Beaujolais Nouveau. But these bars were mainly successful because they appealed to professional women as calm, unthreatening places to meet after work. Opening a wine bar was a common fallback for what Richard Hoggart called 'the redundancy-payment entrepreneurs',[21] the group of people who had been laid off from their city jobs in the periodic recessions of the 1980s and 1990s, and used their pay-offs to start their own businesses. As good wine became more common, though, there was less need for specialist wine bars. Chain-bar concepts emerged, like the 'Pitcher and Piano' and 'All Bar One', which offered other drinks and food as well. The mood to which they aspired was part-Continental and part-American, like the friendly bar in *Cheers* or Central Perk in *Friends*.

The new bar bore the stamp of one of the most influential works of sociology of recent years. In the late 1980s, the American academic Ray Oldenburg wrote a book called

Not just here for the beer

The Great Good Place which suggested that pubs, bars and coffee houses could offer a reassuring 'third place' between home and work. Work offered money and status but was competitive and unfair; home was nurturing but full of the demands and expectations of intimate relationships. The third place was a neutral ground where an 'informal public life' could flourish.[22] Oldenburg's ideas were mainly applied to upmarket chain cafés and bars. They inspired Howard Schultz, the Starbucks CEO, in his vision of the coffee bar as a 'third home away from home, an oasis between home and the workplace where you meet friends'.[23] New bars similarly market themselves as comfortable refuges for middle-class professionals from the strains of modern life. There is a large range of good quality (but pricey) wine, which you can buy in a small or large glass or a bottle. The baristas might mix you a cocktail, but they are more likely to call themselves 'molecular mixologists' than go in for Tom Cruise-style flair bartending. Pine tables and couches are arranged in an artfully casual way, large mirrors create a feeling of space and transparency, and security-conscious women can use the handbag clips under the tables. These bars are found in central, high street sites, so they are a good meeting point for the after-work crowd, perhaps before they decide to go on somewhere else.[24]

The antithesis of the new bar is the city-centre superpub, which is simply about getting people, particularly the young, to drink as much as possible. Young people's favourite drinks are now bottled, premium lagers or RTD (ready-to-drink) spirits such as Bacardi Breezer or Smirnoff Ice. The problem with drinking from a bottle is that it cuts off the drink's aroma, an essential part of the taste (although for certain modern drinks, this may be an advantage). But a bottle is a good way of identifying with a 'cool' brand, is easy to hold in crowded bars, and is a useful theatrical prop, providing ample opportunities for what Mass-Observation called 'swiggling', the kind of affected

were a social phenomenon, group drinking being much quicker than solitary drinking. A group of men all drank roughly the same amount from their glasses at the same time, and emptied them simultaneously, a pattern observed even when blind and sighted men drank together.[29] The main reason for this level drinking was round-standing, an important act of social solidarity and compulsion, similar to gift-giving in tribal societies. In order to avoid the terrible stigma of being accused of not standing his round, the drinker whose turn it was to treat the others set the drinking pace, draining his glass slightly before everyone else so that they did not have to wait for him. Naturally, this high-speed drinking suited the brewers very nicely.[30]

The rule of synchronised drinking seems to be less rigidly followed today. (I am inferring from general observation: I am not quite brave enough to go round pubs with a stopwatch and clipboard, timing people drinking pints – a highly inadvisable activity in some of the pubs I frequent.) The round has lost some of its psychological coercion since people now consume such a wide variety of drinks, so-called 'repertoire drinking'. But pubs have always had other ways of making people drink more quickly. In the 1930s, the techniques were fairly primitive, like offering salty snacks at the bar. Pubs have since become cannier. In the late 1990s there was a big growth in the number of pubs and bars in town centres, and in many towns there were simply not enough drinkers to fill the amount of licensed space. Managers of superpubs tried to draw in customers by selling larger measures, cutting prices and offering special promotions ('women drink for nothing' or 'buy two glasses of wine and get the rest of the bottle free'). 'Speed drinking' bars offered unlimited alcohol for a set entry fee. Pubs also used the techniques of behavioural psychology to speed up drinking. Louder music made people hoarse from shouting and therefore thirsty, or simply made it easier to drink than talk. Removing tables and seating fitted more customers into the pub, and also made them drink standing up. Getting rid of flat ledges meant that drinkers could not even rest their arms by putting their drinks down. Superpubs also sold inexpensive cocktails like the Cheeky Vimto (double port and WKD Blue) or the Slippery Nipple (Baileys and sambuca), often served as 'shooters', designed to be downed like tequilas in a single, theatrical gulp to the cheers of onlookers.

The methods of the superpubs fed into a larger discussion in the British media about 'binge drinking' – afterwork or weekend drinkers going out specifically to get drunk as quickly as possible. In 2003, the prime minister's strategy unit put the blame on 'vertical drinking' dens that tried to cram in as many drinkers as possible; and it praised the more sedentary, Continental style of drinking found in quieter establishments like All Bar One.[31] Fearful of impending regulation, pub chains began to scrap their happy hours, banning many special offers and marketing techniques. At the end of 2005, however, the government finally allowed pubs to apply for 24-hour licences, arguing (more by assertion than from evidence) that the end of closing time would produce more civilised, open-ended drinking. The newspapers predicted bacchanalian street orgies and drunken riots, which generally did not materialise (at least, no more than usual).

These are old anxieties in new bottles. The 1932 report of the Royal Commission on Licensing also attacked unsavoury national customs such as '"perpendicular" drinking', or standing up to drink at bars. It criticised the large numbers of pubs that were 'poor and cramped in structure, gloomy and often insufficiently ventilated', and where 'the predominating, and very often the exclusive, emphasis is on the sale of intoxicants'. It suggested that, while making allowances for our ingrained national customs and weather, the English pub could borrow the best features of the Continental café, such as 'the open and

147

airy surroundings, chairs and tables, and the service of all kinds of refreshments, alcoholic and non-alcoholic'.[32]

The perennial dilemma that the brewers have faced since those years has been whether to cram in customers and ply them with cheap drinks, or foster this more sophisticated, Continental-style ambience and charge them more. In a sense, the dilemma has been solved as the pub-going market has fragmented. Pubs now practise the kind of retail anthropology pioneered by the supermarkets, using the look and feel of particular outlets to cater for carefully differentiated markets, not unlike the supermarket distinction between budget own-brands and gourmet ranges. As with the targeting of particular customers by the supermarkets, pub chains claim that they are simply appealing to different consumer 'tribes', defined solely by their lifestyles and attitudes. But in the chasm between the superpub and the new bar, divisions of age and class seem equally important.

In the understated middle-class ambience of the new bar, you can sit and wonder what all the CAMRA-inspired fuss about the decline of the great British pub is all about. It is not exactly Orwell's paradisiacal vision of 'The Moon Under Water', but it is nice enough. There are whitewashed walls, wooden floors, big squishy sofas and glass tables; the gentle sound of clinking glasses, unraised voices and perhaps a man playing old standards on a Steinway; no vulgar drink promotions and certainly no 'theme', just a soft, subliminal branding which, no doubt with the approval of the prime minister, has turned you into a civilised Continental. 'Drinking in the raw' it isn't. Here you virtuously sip your glass of dry white wine, have intelligent conversation about work and other matters, and gently unwind after the day's labours. Then, before you can line your empty stomach with too much drink, you make your excuses and go home to eat.

12 Your dinner is ready

'Those who forget the pasta are condemned to reheat it'
anon., after George Santayana

For some, it is their occasional standby when they are late home from work. For others, it is their signature dish. Either way, the ready meal is their guilty secret. No one has a good word to say about convenience food any more, apart from the fact that it is convenient. Rubbishing the ready meal is an international ritual. Just read the bleakly comic novels of the French writer Michel Houellebecq, with their recurring figure of the bored, single man who goes home alone to eat gourmet TV dinners (*plats cuisinés*) in front of vapid television shows. Or *Bowling Alone* (2000), in which the American social scientist Robert Putnam uses the decline in meal preparation times, and the rise in solitary dining on TV dinners, as indicators of the loss of 'social capital', the sense of solidarity that binds American society together.[1] America has the biggest market for TV dinners in the world, but Britain is second, and eats more of them than the rest of Europe put together.[2] Our ambivalence about the TV dinner, and its perennial attempts to persuade us that it is anything other than what it is, explain its complex history.

The British anthropologist Mary Douglas's 1972 essay 'Deciphering a meal', outlines the nature of the problem. To save time one evening, Douglas suggested to her family that she make them all a dinner consisting of a thick, nutritious soup and some pudding, only to be met with the complaint that this meal had 'a beginning and an end and no middle'.[3] Instead of telling her family to go and make their own dinner if they weren't happy with hers, Douglas was inspired to write her classic essay, which argued that there were deep-seated ideas in any society about what form a meal should take. A meal had a certain grammar and architecture, a series of elements based on repeated patterns and analogies. A meal's main course, for example, typically had a tripartite structure with a centrepiece (meat or fish) covered with liquid dressing (gravy or similar), a staple (potato, rice or bread) and trimmings (one or two vegetables). The whole meal involved a series of plate and cutlery changes, and savoury/sweet, hot/cold and liquid/ dry contrasts which were 'as formally structured as a Bach cantata'.[4] Even the most convenient of convenience foods has had to gesture towards these deeply ingrained habits of the dinner table.

The oven-ready meal naturally originated in America, the pioneer of both convenience food and commercial television. In 1953 Gerald Thomas, an employee of the Omaha food company Swanson, came up with the TV dinner as a way of using up 270 tons of turkey left over after the Thanksgiving holiday. Thomas was inspired by the heated-up frozen meals on trays, so-called 'Strato-Plates', that he had been served on Pan Am flights. It was the airlines which pioneered methods of successfully reheating pre-cooked food; they discovered, for example, that potatoes reheated better when they were made into croquettes, and that covering a meat entrée with gravy (made with new thickeners that did not curdle) kept it from drying out. Like the airline meal, the Swanson dinner was arranged in a three-compartment metal tray, packaged in a box made to look like the front of a television set. In July 1954, Swanson applied for a US patent for the 'TV Dinner', a frozen turkey meal comprising 'Turkey, Dressing, Giblet Gravy, Sweet

Potatoes, and Green Peas'.[5] (A cynic might have said that this meal had already been invented; it corresponds fairly closely with Mary Douglas's definition of a meal.) By 1955, Swanson was producing 25 million frozen dinners a year.[6] Its well-known advertising slogans – 'Have a Swanson night' and 'Have dinner with the Swansons' – suggested that a TV dinner could be a gourmet occasion. In America they are proud of this frozen-food heritage: when Swanson replaced its aluminium trays with plastic ones suitable for microwave ovens in 1986, Gerald Thomas placed his hand-prints in a block of cement, along with an imprint of the original Swanson tray, on Hollywood's Walk of Fame. The hallowed tray itself was donated to the Smithsonian Institution museum.

When TV arrived in most UK households in the 1950s, eating in front of it soon became commonplace. (Americans and Britons brought the meal to the TV, whereas French people have traditionally done the opposite, bringing the TV to the dining table.[7]) Firms marketed customised plastic trays like the 'Tea-V-Tray' or the 'Armchair tray', which replaced eating on laps with a special tray hooked to the arm of the sofa.[8] But those Britons who did eat in front of the telly were not quite ready for the ready meal. Television viewing was highest among the over-forties, who were more likely to cook from scratch.[9] Cookery books and magazines were full of recipes for 'television entertaining', meals that could be eaten on a tray so as not to miss a show. The first British TV dinner was probably coronation chicken, a dish created in 1953 by the royal florist Constance Spry and the cookery writer Rosemary Hume for Elizabeth II's corona-tion. Many people bought their first television to watch the coronation, and this dish – a pre-prepared snack of cooked, cold chicken in a curried mayonnaise sauce – was easy to combine with television-watching. Designed to appeal to all the new queen's subjects across the Common-wealth, it combined convenience with exoticism in what would become a classic ready-meal combination. But TV cookery programmes at the time were still dominated by elaborate cooks like Fanny and Johnnie Cradock, who always dressed in evening wear and devised recipes to match. Fanny's 'TV-meal menu', for example, consisted of iced tomato juice, a dip'n'dunk platter, stuffed baked snails, chicken liver sauté, raspberry tartlets with orange cream sauce and a Chablis cup. A 1957 Mass-Observation survey found that housewives with TVs spent an average of a half-day a week *more* preparing the dinner.[10]

It did not take long for Swanson imitations to arrive in Britain, such as the 'Birds Eye Roast Beef Dinner for One' with Yorkshire pudding, peas and creamed potatoes. But two things prevented the all-in-one frozen dinner becoming as popular in Britain as in the US. First, in the mid-1950s only 2 or 3 per cent of British homes had a fridge, let alone a freezer.[11] Second, housewives still seemed to want to assemble the meat, fish, vegetable and potatoes for their returning menfolk or children, even if the individual items were all tinned or frozen. A classic example was the phenomenal success of Birds Eye Fish Fingers (the story that they were about to be called 'cod pieces', until someone realised the possible confusion, is probably an urban myth). They arrived in September 1955, a fortnight before the start of ITV, which would advertise this new foodstuff and give people something to watch while they were eating it. By 1962, fish fingers had the honour of becoming the first frozen food to be listed in the Retail Price Index, which uses staple goods to calculate inflation rates. They encouraged children to eat fish and grown-ups to buy fridges. Without the fish finger, frozen convenience food might not have developed in Britain on such a large scale, as it didn't for a long time in the rest of Europe.[12]

Another watershed was crossed in 1961 with the launch of Vesta ready meals, a product of the new art of accelerated freeze-drying. Named after the Roman goddess of the hearth, they were little boxes of dehydrated meat granules, rice and noodles which could be magically rehydrated into exotic curries. ('Expert chefs have done all the hard work for you … All you do is cook it … and take the credit!'[13]) But a Vesta ready meal wasn't very ready. It came with two types of noodle, one lot being placed in boiling water to make soft white noodles, the other in a frier to make crispy noodles. You needed separate pans for the meat granules and the rice, and there were lots of fiddly sachets containing sauce and flavourings. By today's standards, it was hard labour – inconvenience food, even. In fact, it was only in the early 1960s that the phrase 'convenience food' arrived in Britain from the US, in the sense of food that allowed people to save and rearrange their time conveniently. By 1963, *Good Housekeeping* magazine was warmly recommending quick-cook pasta, frozen peas and the ominous-sounding 'pizza in a bag'.[14]

As the 1960s went on, convenience food developed a somewhat plebeian reputation, not simply because it was now cheaper but also because cookery had been reinvented as a middle-class pastime – albeit one which did not involve the elaborate preparation of Cradock-style hostess-trolley cookery. The most influential cookery writer of this era, Elizabeth David, appealed to the now servantless middle classes with the maxim of the French chef Escoffier: 'Faites simple.' David was appalled at a vision of the future she encountered at the 1956 Olympia Food Fair: a frozen TV dinner with everything on a plastic tray, 'so that the awful fag of transferring the frozen chop and two frozen veg from shopping basket to dish is eliminated'.[15] David's meals could often be described in a few lines and prepared in minutes, but they were also supposed to be a labour of love and to use fresh, in-season ingredients. 'The deep freeze appears to have gained over the minds of the English housewife and restaurant keeper a hypnotic power such as never was exercised by the canning factories,' she complains in *Summer Cooking* (1955), in an attack on frozen peas.[16] Those people who bought into the promise of convenience were coming to be seen as indolent and slobbish. By 1972, the critic Barry Norman was referring casually to 'the average pleb, dozing in his carpet slippers in front of his set with his pre-frozen dinner congealing on his lap'.[17]

By the mid-1970s, dedicated freezer centres were arriving on the high street and supermarkets had more freezer space. The most popular frozen foods were still not the all-in-one TV dinners, however, but meat and fish portions, which could be served with another recent innovation, frozen oven chips. 'Ovenability' was the new marketing concept used to promote food that could taste fried simply by heating it up in the oven. The bestselling Birds Eye Crispy Cod Steak, introduced in 1982, was an ovenable piece of fish in batter which did away with 'the fuss, bother and unpleasantness of deep-frying'.[18] It had a memorable advertising campaign featuring the actor Gemma Craven in 1920s flapper gear, feeding her flannelled beau with a fork, and singing, 'Goodbye old frying pan' to the tune of 'Thoroughly Modern Millie', in a knowing reworking of the old Swanson idea of convenience food as posh treat. The other great oven-ready innovation of this era was the frozen pizza, which came from nowhere in the late 1970s to become, in the words of one excited marketing director, 'the beans on toast of the eighties'.[19]

Into this eclectic situation entered our old friend, the re-inventor of the sandwich: Marks & Spencer. When M&S launched its Chicken Kiev in 1976, it single-handedly created the middle-class market for what it called, in a neat piece of ready-meal rebranding, 'recipe dishes'. Ironically, the origins of this bourgeois dish lie behind the Iron Curtain in the form of Chicken à la Kiev, which the food writer Lesley Chamberlain describes as a 'Soviet hotel and restaurant classic' unknown before the Russian Revolution.[20] M&S's ready meals were 'cook-chill', a move away from the American tradition of the frozen dinner. After being cooked in the factory, the meal would be chilled rather than frozen and transported to stores in refrigerated lorries.

Although M&S recipe dishes could be heated up in the oven, what Peter York named 'the Chicken Kiev revolution'[21] relied fundamentally on the microwave. The early 1980s was a boom period for microwaves, with sales rising from 45,000 in 1978 to 900,000 in 1984. According to John Lewis, 1984 was the 'microwave cooker Christmas'; it was 'this year's most fashionable present from husband to wife'.[22] The microwave had arrived in Britain in 1959, but it took much longer to catch on than in America, because of both cost and Cold War suspicion of its nuclear techniques, particularly the fear that it might 'leak' radiation. Many Britons thought that it was dangerous to look through the oven door while it was cooking food, or to open the door in mid-cycle to stir the food[23] – concerns that do not seem to have troubled appliance-loving American consumers. But it is easy to see how those now familiar actions – pulling the ready meal out of its cardboard sleeve, pricking the plastic film with a fork and sticking the tray in the microwave – must have seemed alarmingly space-age when done for the first time. It was only in the late 1980s that this futuristic process began to seem normal and domesticated.

'Ready-made meals, once the tinned provender of elderly widowers and young boozy bachelors, are climbing the social ladder,' reported the *Guardian* in 1987. 'The advent of exotic recipes, low-calorie concoctions, new chilling techniques and the ubiquitous microwave have all helped give market cachet to the instant sachet.'[24] The cookery writer Nigel Slater identified a new generation of 'Thatcher's bachelors', affluent single men who could afford to pay more for convenience with quality.[25] Of course, M&S Chicken Kievs were not solely, or even mainly, eaten by wealthy young city dealers in their trendy, loft-style apartments. But what mattered was the new perception that the ready meal was no longer for sad singletons or lower-class layabouts. Margaret Thatcher gave M&S her well-publicised support, and made its chairman, Marcus Sieff, a life peer in 1980. Later in the decade, she announced that her favourite meal was a frozen lasagne heated up in the microwave.[26]

M&S ruled over the middle-class kitchen in the 1980s in the way that Elizabeth David had in the 1960s, drawing on its established reputation as 'the retailer that would never let you down'. One woman said that if she had an M&S meal and it was not as nice as she had hoped, she thought she must have 'done something wrong in heating it up'.[27] If you had a posh dinner party, you could easily disguise some M&S prepared food as the product of your own labours, or simply confess brazenly, a favourite expression being that you were 'dining with Lord Sieff tonight'.

M&S also cornered the market because, as with its wedge sandwiches, it could offer reassurance to the customer, making its ready meals appear safe and reliable. This issue became particularly sensitive in the late 1980s, when the microbiologist Richard Lacey created a media storm by claiming that the salt levels in ready meals meant that microwaving did not destroy toxic bacteria.[28] Lacey was also a general campaigner against the ready-meal lifestyle:

> What are the two things that Britain spends more on per head of population than any other country? Videos and microwave cookers. That says a lot about what has happened to our society – a culture that is TV-dominated and puts convenience, speed and price above quality, desirability and enjoyment. Eating food has become like going to the lavatory – something private to be got over with as quickly as possible.[29]

Lacey was the slow food movement's John the Baptist, a voice in the wilderness speaking to our nascent anxieties about convenience. In the meantime we had reliable old M&S, who could safely channel the food through the whole 'cool-chain' system of temperature-controlled depots, refrigerated lorries and in-store chill cabinets.[30]

Where M&S led, the supermarkets soon followed, realising the huge mark-ups they could make on own-brand ready meals. Soon they were the supermarkets' prestige item, placed in well-lit refrigerator cabinets near the entrances, next to the fruit and vegetables to give them an aura of freshness and healthiness. The supermarket cook-chill meal also skilfully aligned itself with a particular type of consumer: the young, middle-class professional. This hard-working individual was the target for what the industry calls 'basket trade' – the small, top-up shopping done after work in the new 'metro' or 'local' supermarkets in city centres. The image has become a familiar one: 'Haughty, power-dressed and still running on adrenalin after a 12-hour day in the office, young professionals in modish suits stalk the aisles of late-opening supermarkets looking for comfort food – and usually comfort alcohol as well – with which to settle on the sofa and relax for what little is left of the day.'[31]

The packaging and content of the meals themselves are clearly designed to differentiate them as much as possible from the traditional, primitive rectangular box of the slob's TV dinner. Frozen dinners – which are more likely to be time-honoured Swansonesque affairs with meat, gravy, two veg and sage-and-onion stuffing balls – are now marketed at poorer shoppers, which is one reason why the freezer section of the supermarket is always furthest from the entrance. Ambient ready meals, the canned and freeze-dried products stored at room temperature, are almost as unfashionable. But chilled meals are marketed as premium ranges, with distinctive graphics and telling descriptions

– 'fresh', 'slow-cooked', 'restaurant', 'home-grown' – to appeal to food-conscious professionals. You've had a hard day at the office. What you need is a microwaveable meal in a transparent plastic bowl that doesn't need washing up, a bland salad in a bag, a half-carafe of overpriced wine, and a soggy, single chocolate éclair for pudding. Go on, be good to yourself; you deserve it.

We want food preparation to be quick and easy without losing the associations of mealtime with conviviality and good taste. The majority of chilled meals consist of international recipes such as Italian, Indian and Chinese, for which we have developed a taste through eating out, cookery programmes or books, but are too busy or incompetent to make ourselves. An unintended side-effect of our so-called 'foodie' culture has been to expand the market for the cosmopolitan ready meal – although in more recent years the arrival of the 'gastropub' (now the name of an M&S ready-meal range) has made more traditional British meat recipes trendy again. The ready-meal market is sophisticated and responds quickly to changing tastes. It is certainly a more reliable indicator of our shifting culinary habits than all those unread recipe books, unused new kitchens and unheeded cookery programmes.

This foodie culture assumes that the kitchen is where we unleash our creative, sociable selves. Market analysts are more pessimistic, dividing food consumers into three types. First, there are the 'scratchers', the goody-goodies who always cook from scratch with fresh ingredients. Second, there are the 'helpless avoiders', who cannot or will not cook under any circumstances. Finally, there are the 'help seekers', a growth sector of up to 30 per cent of consumers.[32] Not as energetic or virtuous as the scratchers, they still like to feel they are doing more than simply waiting for the ping of the microwave. They want convenience without its connotations. Sainsbury's first discovered this in 1991, when it ran successful one-minute ads in which celebrities like Selina Scott and Ian McShane rustled up pasta with mozzarella or salmon en papillote from part-prepared ingredients. Help-seekers buy 'meal centres' with 'vegetable accompaniments', giving themselves the arduous task of opening two packets instead of one, and assembling their boeuf bourgignon and creamy mash together on a plate. If they're feeling intrepid, they buy ready-to-cook foods such as stir-fry mixes, cooking sauces or meat that has been deboned, pre-stuffed and marinated; if they want to impress, they buy gourmet meal kits under a celebrity chef's imprimatur, with prepared ingredients and idiot-proof instructions. The trade-off between foodiness and convenience means that we have invented an activity somewhere between microwave instantaneity and cooking from scratch: food assembly. But opinion is divided as to what this actually entails. A survey by the Co-op, for example, discovered that 60 per cent of interviewees thought that chicken nuggets and beans, and pasta in a cook-in sauce, constituted 'home-cooked meals', and that 44 per cent thought the same applied to heating up a frozen pizza.[33]

Today's market analysts might go on about 'flexi-eating' and 'pit-stop dining', but the idea of the meal has survived all this innovation. Mary Douglas's stipulation that a meal requires 'a table, a seating order, restriction on movement and on alternative occupations'[34] now seems outmoded. But her central point that the meal contains a number of contrasting, hierarchically organised elements remains true. Some modern forms of convenience food seem bizarre (*frozen* baked beans on toast? Roast beef and Yorkshire pudding *in a can*?) precisely because they are still attached to this idea of a complete meal. Even if you eat it by yourself with a tray across your knees, dinner is a social event laden with cultural expectations. Your little plastic tray is acknowledging a collective

13 Behind the sofa

> 'The extent to which we take everyday objects for
> granted is the precise extent to which they govern and
> inform our lives'
>
> Margaret Visser[1]

He is a familiar folk devil for our times: an overweight
slob eating a TV dinner with a fork in one hand, remote
control in the other, slouching in semi-darkness on the
sofa. Perhaps he is watching *The Simpsons*, in which the
family arranges itself on the sofa in front of the TV at the
end of the title sequence; or *The Royle Family*, the opening
credits of which show a blank screen coming to life, and
different family members appearing one-by-one on the
living-room couch. Unaware of the irony, this slob slumps
on the sofa, facing his fictional counterparts on their tele-
visual upholstery. But there is a contrasting set of images,
familiar from the glossy inserts for sofa companies that fall
out of the colour supplements, or from the TV commercials
shown at bank holiday periods: female models contort
themselves into various unlikely positions on their sofas,
or couples laugh and joke, holding glasses of wine (or, for
some reason, half-eaten melons) with their bare feet tucked
under their thighs. The last thing these beautiful people
would be seen doing is slobbing out in front of the telly.

Our modern interest in the sofa is somewhat strange.
Historically it was a low-status item, a bastard child in
the history of furniture design. In 1783, William Cowper's

friend Lady Austen tried to alleviate his chronic melancholy by challenging him to write a poem in blank verse about the most mundane thing she could think of: his sofa. The resulting long poem, *The Task* (1785), begins with a mock-Georgic history of this item of furniture before becoming a hymn to the joys of domesticity: 'I sing the Sofa. I who lately sang / Truth, Hope and Charity ... / Now seek repose upon an humbler theme.'[2]

In 1822 the critic Richard Brown declared that, while the design and manufacture of chairs had improved in the hands of more specialised tradesmen, 'sofas are as ridiculous and unmeaning in their forms as ever'.[3] The chair has traditionally been the ultimate expression of the designer's skill and creativity, but the sofa is a shapeless, multifunctional object, an affront to our modern fixation with 'clean lines'. The various efforts to introduce good design to Britain in the twentieth century – such as Scandinavian-influenced 'soft' modernism, Festival of Britain contemporary, or Habitat-inspired minimalism – have either ignored or looked down on the sofa. It has stood for a whole range of undesirable English values, from snobbery to prissiness, epitomised by those possibly mythical people who worry about whether they are sitting on a 'couch' or a 'settee', and keep it forever wrapped in the cellophane in which it was delivered.

The real appeal of the sofa is that it is simultaneously a very commonplace and a rather luxurious item. It still retains associations with bespoke luxury, partly because upholstery has resisted mechanisation longer than many other trades. The sofa is the one piece of furniture that cannot come in flat-pack form, and it sits rather uneasily within our instant-gratification, throwaway consumer economy. Making a sofa remains a labour-intensive and skilled job, despite the introduction in the last century of pneumatic staple guns, foam fillings and ready-made spring units. In 2006, the average spend on a three-seater sofa was £1,118 for a leather one and £900 for a fabric one, making it one of the most expensive items we can buy for the home.[4] But almost every home has a sofa of some description.

In this sense, the sofa mirrors the entire history of seating, a narrative of the democratisation of comfort, as progressively more people have sat down on purpose-built objects rather than simply kneeling or squatting. In eastern and Arabic countries, the *sopha* or *suffah* was a part of the floor raised about two feet, covered with sumptuous cushions, and reserved for the wealthiest, most important people.[5] In Britain, too, the sofa was initially an opulent item, but over the last two centuries it has filtered down the social scale. At the end of the 1950s, Richard Hoggart imagined the ritual of bonfire night in a working-class northern community: 'It is a truly urban fire, with very little wood that has known a tree for the last few years, a fire composed of old mattresses and chairs – replaced now that someone's club turn has come up – or a horsehair sofa displaced by a modern one on hire purchase.'[6] What really transformed the sofa into a classless purchase in the post-war era, as Hoggart's quote suggests, were the invention of the cheap filling of polyurethane foam and the rise of consumer credit. The easing and then abolition of government restrictions on hire-purchase arrangements meant that, by the end of the 1950s, four out of five British families had consumer debts, owing a total of £1,000 million.[7] Hire purchase was used for all large items, from cars to washing machines, but it particularly transformed furniture retailing, which relied on HP for three-quarters of its trade.[8] The set of soft furnishings bought on the 'never-never' was one of the symbols of growing affluence in this period.

The sofa truly arrived as a stand-alone item in the 1970s and 1980s, when it broke free from the increasingly outmoded three-piece suite. A British institution, the three-piece suite had originated as a slimmed-down version of the seven or nine-piece sets in well-to-do homes in the nineteenth century.[9] Symbolically, a matching set meant that you were wealthy enough to buy all your furniture in one go.[10] Betrothed couples saved up for years to begin their married lives with a sofa and two armchairs, and the new members of the middle class who settled in suburban semi-detached houses in the inter-war years were particularly prone to what snobbish design critics called 'suite-itis'. The three-piece suite eventually died for three reasons. First, the arrival of central heating in many homes meant that sofas and armchairs no longer needed to be placed around a fireplace in the conventional three-piece arrangement. Second, the larger number of smaller and single-person households needed fewer items of furniture. Third, the lone sofa – or, more commonly now, an identical pair – managed finally to escape the three piece's associations with lower-middle-class suburban taste, which the success of stores like Habitat and Heal's had rendered so unfashionable.

In part thanks to these stores, the sofa became plainer and simpler in its design. Sofas made for prosperous households before the twentieth century were highly decorative, with rolled arms, spooned backs, curved legs and ornamental carvings. The classic three-piece suite gestured towards the exotic eastern origins of the sofa in its floral chintz covering, velvet trimmings and fringed edges. In the 1960s and 1970s, artificiality was in vogue, with brightly coloured vinyl and PVC sofas, like the 'leather look' endorsed by Beverley in Mike Leigh's play *Abigail's Party* (1977). But such flashiness then became rather passé. Compared to the American Lay-Z-Boy recliner – the chair that, at the push of a button or the pull of a lever, puts you in a horizontal position and has built-in gadgets like refrigerators, remote controls and snack trays – the British sofa of the last quarter-century has been remarkably low-tech. There is an almost universal modern style, with a low back, tall cushions and very little pattern or ornament. Only three things are left to distinguish sofas from each other – colour, fabric and size – and they therefore assume an excessive symbolic importance.

Despite this lack of variety, our interest in the sofa continued to grow with the consumer revolution of the Thatcher years. By then people were spending much more time in their living rooms, not only watching telly but playing with their music systems and computer games, and the sofa was the living room's centrepiece. Sofas were also the perfect product to sell in the retail parks that were springing up on the outskirts of towns – they are so big and tactile that people want to see them properly before buying them, and they need a lot of space to be displayed. The commercial breaks began to fill up with sofa ads, with celebrities like Michael Aspel and Bruce Forsyth walking around furniture warehouses promising us unbeatable bargains and interest-free credit, and reminding us about the sale that was always about to end. Since the life of upholstered furniture is potentially endless, advertising is vital because it has to persuade people with a serviceable sofa that they need to buy another one.

The firm that did most to popularise the modern, no-frills sofa towards the end of the century was IKEA, which, in the words of its founder, Ingvar Kamprad, aspired to 'provide a better everyday life for the many' and bring the benefits of good design to all.[11] IKEA opened its first shop in Britain in Warrington in 1987, and its hold on the UK consumer was complete by the mid-1990s. In 1996 it launched a famous TV advert, with a song on the soundtrack called 'Chuck out your chintz'. In this ad, an enormous, IKEA-blue skip falls down from the sky into a street of stock-brick Victorian terraces in what looks like an up-and-coming area of London's East End. Women emerge from their houses, throwing their flowery furnishings – candlewick bedspreads, frilly lampshades and tasselled sofas – into the skip. At the end they are seen chatting together happily in their stripped-down homes with their new laminate flooring, tasteful prints and plain IKEA sofas. The menfolk are nowhere to be seen and the song lyrics evoke 1970s feminist struggles: 'We're battling hard and we've come a long way, in choices and status, in jobs and in pay.'As a final act of liberation, the song suggests, all women have to do is dispense with their petit-bourgeois taste: 'That sofa's so girly, so silly and twirly.' One director of IKEA's advertising agency, St Luke's, was explicit about the political message, claiming that '"Chuck out your chintz" is the modern equivalent of "burn your bra".'[12]

But the chintzy sofa had been an object of opprobrium long before IKEA put this sentiment to song. In *Barchester Towers* (1857), Anthony Trollope dismissed a new sofa as 'a horrid chintz affair, most unprelatical and almost irre-ligious',[13] and George Eliot wrote in an 1851 letter that 'the effect is chintzy and would be unbecoming',[14] apparently using the word in its modern sense to mean vulgarly suburban. Since its heyday in the nineteenth century, chintz – which is not a pattern, as is commonly believed, but a material, a glazed Indian cotton on which it is easy to print designs – has had various returns to vogue, notably during the 'country house' revival of the 1980s, but it has long been a minority taste. IKEA's stroke of genius was to latch on to a battle that was already won, presenting its own brand of mild minimalism as thrillingly revolutionary.

The following year, IKEA produced another commercial which featured a team of 'researchers' knocking on people's doors to discover the link between furniture choices and personality traits. The ad purported to discover that 'when people had flowery settees, they often had snooty tenden-cies' and that 'people with green sofas were adventurous in bed'. IKEA did not just want us to buy its furniture; it wanted us to buy into an attitude and a lifestyle. The IKEA sofa was disposable furniture for urban nomads and serial monogamists. It was light, unfussy and stylishly impermanent, with none of the baggage of the family heirloom or the bought-for-life wedding present.

But the sofa's egalitarian, informal associations created their own anxieties, particularly if they extended beyond the home into the workplace. When Lord Butler, in his 2004 report into the intelligence used to justify the Iraq War, noted the 'informality and circumscribed character of the Government's procedures',[15] it was widely interpreted as a criticism of Tony Blair's eschewing of boring Cabinet meetings in favour of unofficial chats on the office sofa with his inner circle (although Butler never used the famous term 'sofa-style' to describe Blair's government, and nor would any other mandarin; this was a journalist's invention). But anyone who has attended a meeting conducted on sofas will know that they do not necessarily encourage easiness and informality. Sitting the full complement of people on a supposedly three-person sofa is tricky: the piggy in the middle has no armrest and is in danger of being squashed.

Even in the privacy of our own homes, there is the same, long-standing dilemma: how do you sit on a sofa? In *Can You Forgive Her?* (1865), Trollope describes Lady MacLeod thus: 'She had been educated at a time when easy-chairs were considered vicious, and among people who regarded all easy postures as being so; and she could still boast, at seventy-six, that she never leaned back.'[16] Chairs did not 'give' at all until springs were introduced in the 1820s. In many homes, the closest thing to a sofa was an ottoman – a long, stuffed, backless seat considered too plush for anyone except invalids and the elderly.[17] The Victorians wanted more luxurious seating. The sofa began the movement backwards, displacing the less upholstered 'settee' because the sofa was more suited to reclining.[18]

When springs arrived, seats and backs became deeper and people began to sit back, which meant that crocheted anti-macassars – small lace and cloth circles and squares – had to be placed on the headrests to protect them from the oil on men's hair.[19] But Victorians still firmly discouraged slouching, in keeping with traditional courtly etiquette and their own concern with gentility and self-control.

The historian Kenneth L. Ames argues that the rocking chair, which allowed the sitter to tilt back, was a form of American resistance to the European obsession with an upright posture[20] – a resistance that arguably continues today in the Lay-Z-Boy. Up until at least the Second World War, perfect young ladies were taught at British finishing schools and deportment classes to perch on the ends of sofas rather than lean back, and to cross their legs at the ankles rather than the knees. The 'keep fit' craze of the 1930s added a medical dimension to this traditional injunction to sit up straight. Advising against slouching, the *Daily Mirror*'s posture expert wrote in 1944: 'Muscles and joints get "set" and awkward stiff movements become habitual. Round shoulders and narrow chest are two figure faults which follow on from "sitting in a heap".'[21]

The modern sofa finally grants permission to slouch; indeed, some of the squidgier kinds render it a necessity. While the office chair has been ergonomically refashioned, we are still allowed to ruin our backs in the privacy of our living rooms. What we expect from the modern sofa, apart from good looks, is comfort; but what exactly *is* comfort? Architects and designers have never been able to agree on a definition. Is comfort merely the absence of discomfort, or does it have a quality all of its own? People's opinions about what constitutes a comfy chair vary considerably, and rarely tally with the ergonomically recommended posture.[22] We never simply 'sit' on a sofa; we 'lounge', 'curl up', 'slouch' or 'sprawl'. The words suggest both comfort and laziness, a confusing message in a society which is itself confused about the proper relationship between leisure time and good health. Our uneasiness about the kinds of habits encouraged by the sofa is encapsulated in the phrase 'couch potato', coined in California in the 1970s and used in Britain since the 1980s. In June 2005, representatives from the British Potato Council demonstrated outside the offices of Oxford University Press and in London's Parliament Square, campaigning for the use of the word 'couch slouch' instead of 'couch potato', which they claimed was insulting to potatoes. To no avail: the 'couch potato' or 'sofa spud' lifestyle has become universal shorthand for our supposedly inactive lives, prey to obesity, back problems and mental vegetation.

This is part of a larger anxiety about the sofa's relation to time, and the discomforting evidence it provides that we have spent so much of our lives simply sat down not doing very much. For the lived-in sofa has a memory all of its own. After its occupant gets up, its seat leaves a temporary trace of that person's shape and warmth. As the springs loosen and the foam hardens, it remembers the contours of our backs and the indentations of our bottoms. Eventually these patterns become embedded and the sofa sags irreparably. Sofas also remind us of past times by accumulating the detritus and marginalia of our lives. Pet hairs, dirt and food stains settle on them; and pens, crumbs and remote controls fall underneath them, or down the gap between the cushions and the upholstery. (The financiers Jonathan Wren recently estimated that nearly £1 billion in small change lies forgotten in British homes, much of it presumably down the backs of sofas.[23]) Family homes now tend to have deep plum or chocolate-coloured sofas that cover stains, or leather ones that are wipeable and age well. But even the leather sofa lets itself go eventually, by sagging, fading and cracking in the sunlight.

When confronted with this embarrassing confirmation of physical decline, there is only one thing to do: make a trip to the retail park and buy another sofa. If you want an idea of the high emotion that this can produce, then cast your mind back to that terrifying night in February 2005, when north London erupted into the infamous 'IKEA riots'. For its opening of a new store in Edmonton, IKEA advertised an offer of three-seater sofas, normally priced at £325, for £49. The subsequent rush to reach the store in time for the midnight opening caused traffic chaos on London's North Circular Road. People drove across roundabouts, reversed up the dual carriageway, parked on pavements and, eventually, abandoned their cars on the road itself. When the doors opened, 6,000 people barged their way to Soft Furnishings. Shoppers 'bagsied' sofas by diving on them, only to have others pull them off by their feet. Two people tugged at opposite sides of the same sofa, both shouting, 'It's mine, it's mine'. One woman grabbed a sofa only to be pinned against a wall by a man with a wooden mallet. Another woman waiting at the checkout queue was 'mugged' for her sofa. As security guards fled from the scene in panic, police and paramedics were called, and twenty people were hospitalised with crush injuries.[24]

What on earth is going on, when people are prepared to surrender their dignity and safety to scramble over domestic furniture? A leather sofa, however cheap, is not a De Beers diamond or a truffle from a Tuscan forest. Our attachment to this rather straightforward object – which is, after all, just a wooden frame, a few springs, assorted stuffing, a bit of fabric and some cushions – makes no obvious sense. Anthropologists have used the term 'fetish' to describe objects to which we attach this kind of irrational significance. The word was first used by early Portuguese traders in West Africa to describe the amulets which were thought to have magical properties in tribal societies. In the first volume of *Capital* (1867), Karl Marx drew on this concept to argue that capitalist societies suffer from 'commodity fetishism', the semi-mystical qualities we project on to the products that we buy. The commodity fetish dissociates itself from the mundane labour that goes into producing and purchasing it, and reinvents itself as a desirable object that will bring beauty and meaning to our lives. In nineteenth-century Britain, in particular, Marx identified 'a mania for possessions', a 'fetishism' which 'clung to the products of work once they became wares'.[25] In fact, you did not need to be a revolutionary to notice this Victorian passion for things. An 1854 magazine article noted that 'it is a folly to suppose that when a man amasses a quantity of furniture it belongs to him. On the contrary, it is he who belongs to his furniture.'[26] The modern sofa fulfils a similar role. It is not just something to sit on. It has acquired all the associations of a better life: good taste, easy opulence, social belonging. A heavy burden to bear for a humble item of upholstery.

Unlike the fetishes worshipped in tribal religions, however, the magical, incandescent properties of the commodity fetish do not last. The sofa will survive long after its lifespan as a commodity is over. Even the IKEA-crazy citizens of north London will have to calm down eventually. They will realise that items of furniture have a mundane purpose, and the way that a sofa looks in the showroom is not necessarily how it will sit in the lounge. The sofa adverts may shout at us to buy this thrilling, fashionable item (unbeatable offer! nought per cent APR!), but the alluring lifestyle they promise will soon subside into the comforting boredom or mild disappointment of daily habit. When a sofa arrives in the living room for the first time, it will look like a glamorous intruder, its brand-new smell will linger for a while, and when we first sit down it will seem rather strange and unyielding. After a while, though, we will stop feeling it or even noticing it. It will become like the 'purloined letter' in Edgar Allen Poe's story of the same name: invisible by virtue of being so clearly on display. Whatever those excitable adverts say,

14 Please do not adjust your set

*'The everyday is what we never see for a first time, but
only see again'*

Maurice Blanchot [1]

Of all our daily habits, watching TV is the one we are most
confused about. Since entering mainstream culture in the
1950s, it has been the most popular way of spending our
free time. But synonyms for the television – goggle box,
idiot box, plug-in drug, chewing gum for the eyes – are
rarely flattering. Is watching television a harmless pleasure
or a mindless addiction? The confusion arises from the
dual nature of telly-watching as both a personal choice
and an unthinking habit – something that we have actively
decided to do, but that consists of things we all do and see
over and over again. A night in with the television is taken
up not just with watching programmes but with routine
activities, like flipping through channels or viewing those
repetitive in-between bits – trailers, adverts, announce-
ments, theme tunes and closing credits – that take up more
time in the schedules than we imagine.

Ever since they invented the art of scheduling in the
1950s, broadcasters have exploited the habit-forming
nature of watching television. In these early days, watching
TV was an evening ritual with its own familiar longueurs.
Much time would be spent waiting for the set to warm
up and hum into life, and fiddling with the aerial to get a
good reception, which could be affected by anything from

bad weather to car ignitions. The first onscreen continuity announcers – women in evening gowns, men in dinner jackets – would guide the viewer gently through the night's entertainment. Since programmes often finished early, viewers also had to sit through a stock series of visual fillers, such as a turning windmill, waves crashing on rocks and a clay pot being fashioned on a potter's wheel.[2] Until 1957, there was a 'toddler's truce' between 6 and 7 p.m. to allow parents to put their young children to bed, on the pretence that TV had finished for the night – a collective white lie as zealously maintained as the existence of Santa Claus.[3] Television even told the grown-ups when to go to bed. Programming stopped between 10.30 and 11 p.m. with evening prayers, the National Anthem and the instruction to remember to turn off your set. Perhaps it was the novelty of these new rituals that kept people watching; with only one channel, the range of programmes was rather limited. In the week leading up to the first night of ITV in September 1955, primetime BBC highlights included a programme about the presenter Wilfred Pickles' silver wedding anniversary, the world speedway championships, the searchlight tattoo from Woolwich Stadium, 'Puzzle Corner' and a documentary about Hawick knitwear.[4]

The arrival of commercial television created a new ritual: sitting through the ad breaks. Opponents of the new commercials saw them as a virulent foreign invasion, specifically an American one. The BBC's founding director-general, Lord Reith, compared the arrival into Britain of 'sponsored television' with previous influxes of smallpox and the bubonic plague.[5] The Postmaster General had to reassure the public that Hamlet would not 'interrupt his soliloquy to tell us the brand of toothpaste popular at Elsinore';[6] British television commercials would be 'spot' ads, slotted between the programmes so they could not influence them. The ad breaks could not exceed an average of six minutes an hour over the course of the day, with no more than eight minutes at peak time.[7] When the first commercials were shown on ITV on 22 September 1955, the *News Chronicle* commented that these subdued ads for mundane items like toothpaste, drinking chocolate and margarine were 'muffled, as if making their entrance like well-mannered tradesmen at the side door'.[8]

The 1954 Television Act had ruled that adverts could be inserted not only at the beginning and end of programmes but also in 'natural breaks' in the middle of them. Of course, the ads in the middle of programmes were the hardest to miss and the most coveted by advertisers, but no one could agree what constituted a 'natural' break. The Labour MP Christopher Mayhew thought that adverts were being inserted willy-nilly, and introduced a bill to ban breaks that interrupted programmes. The critic Milton Shulman disagreed, arguing that the normal viewer could only concentrate for about fifteen minutes, after which 'he wants to put the cat out, brew some tea, go to the bathroom – without missing anything.' Shulman pointed out that ending programmes on the hour or half-hour was just as arbitrary: 'Has Mr Mayhew never heard the BBC Brains Trust arbitrarily interrupted in the middle of a fascinating discussion to make way for something like Sooty?'[9] This argument won the day and Mayhew's bill failed.

In fact, there has never been any serious opposition to adverts from viewers. Some find them irritating, others find them entertaining – but a large majority has always considered them a good way of funding programmes. A 1967 survey discovered that more than half of viewers continued to watch during the ad breaks – although, among the 'best educated groups', a small majority did not.[10] Researchers soon found that viewers had outstanding recall of the commercials.[11] This was the age of advertising jingles, those short, simple tunes designed to drill themselves into the collective unconscious like grown-up nursery rhymes.

As one advertising executive said at the time, 'If you've nothing to say, then sing it.'[12] One tune, composed by the classic jingle-writer Howard 'Boogie' Barnes ('Murray mints, Murray mints, too good to hurry mints') became a sort of unofficial national anthem, chanted in school playgrounds and whistled on building sites.

The advent of commercial television produced another habitual accompaniment to watching the box: the channel 'identification'. ITV was organised regionally, and its separate companies had to identify their own 'channel' (a word rarely used in Britain until the mid-1950s, except by engineers in its original sense of a band of frequencies used for a radio or television signal). Almost all of them came up with a musical and visual fanfare similar to those used by Hollywood studios at the start of films, like the seminal one for 20th Century Fox, with searchlights shining on the company logo, set in stone, accompanied by the sound of a crescendo of drums, horns and fortissimo strings. The fanfare for Anglia Television, for example, showed a revolving silver hunting trophy of a knight on horseback (seen by the company chairman in a New Bond Street jewellers shop window the day after Anglia had won the franchise[13]) over a soundtrack of Handel's *Water Music*. Non-Anglia viewers mainly saw the revolving knight before the syndicated quiz show *Sale of the Century*, when the fanfare ended with the anti-climactic declaration, 'And now ... from Norwich.'

These Hollywood-style fanfares were slightly jarring because waiting for a programme to start was now a banal routine, not at all like the light-dimming, audience-hushing start to a film in the cinema. When few people had TV sets, watching them had been a social event. The *Manchester Evening Chronicle* claimed in 1949 that putting an aerial outside your house was a guarantee of a social life. It found one man who had installed eight tip-up seats in his drawing room to create a mini-cinema for his neighbours.[14] Where houses had both a living room and a front 'parlour' reserved for 'best', the TV was often put in the parlour, on the assumption that it would be watched on special occasions.[15] Early press adverts for television sets show families dressed up in their smartest clothes to watch TV, with amazed expressions on their faces.[16] But it did not take long for the television to become just another item of living-room furniture. TV sets were sold in domesticated wooden or Bakelite cabinets, and people put knick-knacks and mementos on top of them. A television set was the most complex piece of technology in people's homes, but it was also one of the easiest to use, and its operation soon became routine.

According to one social historian, television was the 'social solvent' of the 1950s in the way that the war had been in the 1940s. It 'put the nation into a sort of trance, soft and shallow, from which it presently emerged to find itself living its dream'.[17] Television-watching became normal, perhaps rather 'common'. Before about 1950, having a television aerial signalled your social superiority to the rest of the street. But by 1957, the working classes watched telly most of all, 45 per cent of them for an average of four hours every night, compared with an average of 1 hour 41 minutes for the population as a whole.[18] As the TV insinuated itself into people's daily routines, some critics began to evoke a prelapsarian era before its arrival. The novelist Doris Lessing wrote later in her autobiography that 'television had arrived and sat like a toad in the corner of the kitchen. Soon the big kitchen table had been pushed along the wall, chairs were installed in a semi-circle and, on their chair arms, the swivelling supper trays. It was the end of an exuberant verbal culture.'[19] Doctors identified new ailments like 'TV Neck', 'TV Crouch', 'TV Dyspepsia' and 'TV Stutter'. Dentists warned that children could get buck teeth from watching TV lying on the floor with their chins in their hands.[20]

On his return visit to Bolton in 1960 (Mass-Observation's large-scale survey of the town having ended twenty years previously), Tom Harrisson refused to join in the moral panic. He wrote that, for the man who had just returned to Britain from several years in Borneo – which, as a matter of fact, he had – one of the most visible changes was the number of television antennae on roofs, and the growth of shops selling televisions, with signs in the window saying 'Slot TV, 96 hours for 1 shilling' and 'Generous allowance on your old set against advance payments'. But he did not believe that television had destroyed a rich communal life:

> What did people do on a winter's day or a Sunday afternoon of rain before TV – especially if they hadn't much money? The short answer for millions of people then: 'NOTHING MUCH'. They 'messed about' or did odd things (e.g. read pulp mags and Westerns, argued, titivated each other), which can hardly be said to be 'worse' than looking into polypact television.[21]

What the telly-watcher did seem to like was habit and routine. Kenneth Adam, then the BBC's director of television, spoke in 1964 about the most common cause of outrage among viewers: not sex, violence or indeed anything to do with programme content, but late running and rescheduling. Adam claimed that a sizeable minority of TV viewers were 'addicts'. These were the people who wrote 'somewhat illiterately' to complain that TV closed down too early for the night. They made up the several hundred thousand viewers who, during a recent television strike, had turned on to watch the test card.[22]

Test cards were there to test flicker, focus and proportions when there were no programmes – a frequent occurrence, since the government limited the number of hours that channels could broadcast. The number had gone up throughout the 1950s, but even in 1960 it was only sixty hours a week.[23] When colour TV arrived in Britain in 1967, the BBC needed a new test card that would incorporate flesh tones. This was 'Test Card F', the famous image of a BBC technician's daughter, Carol Hersee, playing noughts and crosses on a blackboard easel (so that one of the crosses could mark the centre of the card). Even after the government ended all restrictions on programme hours in 1972, there were still many gaps between the programmes, leaving ample time for Test Card F, accompanied by cheesy lounge music.

The arrival of colour TV also revived two themes associated with television ever since ITV arrived to challenge the BBC's middle-class hegemony: anti-Americanism and class distinction. American television had used colour since 1953, and throughout the 1960s there were long discussions, in Parliament and elsewhere, about whether to use the American NTSC (National Television System Committee) colour system or to wait for more advanced European technology offering subtler tones and a wider range.[24] When the British government eventually adopted the European PAL (Phase Alternating Line) system, there was much patriotic celebration about the quality of the colour on British TV when compared with the primitive hues of American TV, which according to the *Spectator* made 'human complexions look like accidents in the embalmer's workshop'.[25] But in 1969 another critic, George Melly, attacked this 'self-induced hysteria' about colour. He prophesied a 'small resistance movement of middle-class intellectuals, the children of those who in the early fifties wouldn't have the telly at all' who would 'equate black and white with high seriousness'.[26] This guerrilla organisation never quite materialised, but the monochrome set did become something of an unofficial symbol of middle-class asceticism. By 1972, despite the much greater cost of the colour sets and the colour TV licence, there were more of them in working-class households (52 per cent) than in middle-class ones.[27]

As well as the all-colour Test Card F, one of the familiar sights on television in the 1970s, the great era of strikes and shutdowns, was a screen apologising for the interruption in programming. Sometimes this was due to events outside of television's control. In the winter of 1973–4, during the last months of Edward Heath's government, the shortage of power created by the miners' strike and a worldwide oil crisis conspired to end television at 10.30 p.m. every night, one of many events at the time that must have seemed, to the middle-aged and older, like a return to wartime privations. More usually, the loss of television resulted from union strikes over extended programming hours or extra pay for transmitting colour signals. Like the test card, the standard apology caption had a certain hypnotic allure, and was rumoured to get good ratings.[28]

Test cards and apology captions were seen much less in the 1980s. Teletext services began to fill in more of the gaps between the programmes, and there were fewer of these gaps anyway, as daytime TV arrived in 1986 and all-night television a year later. This was the period when academics began to study systematically what people actually did when they watched TV, either by placing cameras on top of televisions or conducting questionnaires and surveys. What they discovered, perhaps because TV-watching had by now become so routine, was that viewers rarely gave the set their undivided attention. While the telly was on (which was most of the time), people also ate dinner, knitted, argued, listened to music, did their homework or hoovered the carpet.[29]

In 1988, the British Film Institute added to this ongoing television research by asking volunteers to help them document 'the impact of television on the life and culture of the nation on a single day: November 1'. The BFI distributed 620,000 free diary leaflets through bookshops, newsagents and supermarkets, with volunteers asked to record what they watched and how they felt about it.[30] Some of the 22,000 diary entries submitted were collected together in a book, *One Day in the Life of Television*. It was clear from the entries that the diarists constantly discriminated between what they saw as high-quality and tacky television, and felt guilty about watching the latter.[31] In a sense, they had internalised the historical anxiety that watching television was a time-wasting activity – a view that has also influenced the unfairly disdainful response to 'media studies', which is supposed to waste academic time investigating it. It was also clear that, although the diarists' attention to television was peripheral and their attitudes ambivalent, they felt that it formed part of the shared history and daily conversation of the nation. As the TV critic Sean Day-Lewis recognised in an elegiac conclusion to the book, the expansion of cheap channels threatened this sense of national community.[32] Thatcherism had always been suspicious of the BBC–ITV duopoly, and especially the BBC's licence-fee monopoly, and the 1990 Broadcasting Act consolidated the arrival of cable and satellite TV by making outside commercial intervention into the industry much easier.

The gadget that cemented these changes was the remote control. Primitive remotes had been around in America since 1950. The first model, the Zenith Corporation's hand-grenade-shaped 'Lazy Bones Station Selector', was a motor-driven tuner attached to the set via a cable. It was envisaged less as a channel-changer than as a device to switch off the set as viewers fell asleep, or to mute the adverts, which the Zenith company president loathed.[33] Later models, marketed like boys' toys as 'Flash-Guns' and 'Space-Commanders', used light beams or ultrasonic waves. But it was not until the introduction of infrared remotes in the mid-1970s that they became more common in the UK. From the late 1980s onwards, the rising number

Please do not adjust your set

of channels helped to universalise the remote: when there were only three or four channels, no one realised they needed a zapper. Meanwhile, academic surveys reinforced the popular folklore that men were remote-control control freaks. Many men used the remote 'obsessively, channel flicking across programmes when their wives were trying to watch something else'.[34] Later studies qualified these early findings, suggesting that men rarely exercised a veto on what to watch. The remote might be the 'symbolic possession of the father', but the power he gained was 'relatively illusory'.[35]

The remote is a semi-invisible technology. It only works in tandem with other appliances like televisions and DVDs, and we don't give it much thought unless we are looking for it down the back of the sofa or moaning about other members of the family hogging it. Although mainly designed for flipping through channels, its most significant effect has been to change the nature of scheduling. In the schedule in today's newspaper, for example, I read that the UKTV History channel is showing seventeen hours of continuous programming featuring the late broadcaster and ex-steeplejack Fred Dibnah, from *Fred Dibnah's World of Steam, Steel and Stone* to *Fred Dibnah's The Building of Britain*. If this conjures up the unlikely image of an army of Fred Dibnah fanatics settling themselves down on the sofa for an all-day viewing marathon, it is indeed unlikely: this channel has simply given up the traditional role of structuring a varied evening's entertainment for the viewer. The schedule is contained not in the TV listings but in the zapper, which allows you to select your evening's entertainment by scrolling down menus. Digital recording devices like Sky Plus allow you to watch programmes when you like, draw up wish lists and even zap through the ads. Viewers live in constant anticipation of some other programme that is better than the one they are watching.

Broadcasters and advertisers, of course, want to stop

you zapping. In a classic diversionary tactic, like distracting a baby with a squeaky toy, the noughties innovation of interactive TV is a way of deterring viewers from flipping channels by keeping them preoccupied with the remote ('press your red button now'). Commercial channels now often leave out the ad break at the end of a programme, carrying you straight into the next one before you can reach for the channel-changer. In order to dissuade you from zapping out of credit sequences, broadcasters employ the 'squeeze and tease', a method pioneered by the American channel NBC, whose audience research found that a quarter of viewers switched channels during the credits. This method squashes the closing credits into part of the frame (which is bad news for the vision mixer, whose name is now too small to read) and uses the rest of it for 'promo-tainment', previewing next week's episode or advertising the accompanying DVD.[36]

As the transitions between programmes have become more important, the notion of the continuity announcer as master of ceremonies has all but disappeared, replaced by a new preoccupation with 'television brand identity'. Announcers play second fiddle to the visual and sound interludes known as 'idents' which fill in the gaps between programmes. The inventor of the modern ident is Martin Lambie-Nairn, whose design company devised the famous 'flying bricks' logo for Channel 4 in 1982. In 1987, despite a spirited 'Save Our Knight' campaign in a Norwich newspaper, Lambie-Nairn replaced the Anglia Knight with a computerised billowing pennant.[37] Then, in 1991, the BBC asked him to help them alter the focus-group view of the typical BBC2 viewer as 'a Volvo-driving schoolteacher with leather patches on the sleeves of his tweed jacket'.[38] Lambie-Nairn's new idents were variations on the number '2': a metallic 2 splashed by paint, a 2 dropping into flour (or some other unspecified white powder) and the outline of a 2 underneath shimmering silk. Eventually, the 2 acquired an animated personality: it became a fluffy, somersaulting toy, a remote-control car, and a plane gliding across a wooden floor. The 2 began to receive fan mail, and focus groups now identified the channel not as snobbishly highbrow but as 'sophisticated, witty and stylish'.[39]

Soon all the channels were using idents, many of them Lambie-Nairn's work. BBC1 had basketball players in wheelchairs, Haka-dancing rugby players and acrobats suspended from ceilings; Channel 4 had hedges, skyscrapers and pylons magically aligning to form the number 4; ITV1 had, for more obscure reasons, people hugging trees, examining their beer bellies in front of mirrors, and falling asleep on trains. Modern idents were like visual poems, accompanied by ambient music and sound effects rather than old-fashioned fanfares. Their Zen-like calm was a creative response to channel multiplication, founded on the hope that people would tire of this dizzying choice and simply stick with one channel, with its familiar ident and the reassuring voice of the announcer saying, 'You're watching BBC1.' Some people complain about how much money they cost, particularly to BBC licence-payers, but idents do their job: like the jingles and fanfares of the 1950s, they have become part of the everyday, repetitive experience of watching telly.

In George Orwell's *1984* (1949), written just as the BBC was resuming its post-war broadcasting, Winston Smith's life is ruled by a two-way television called the telescreen, which both broadcasts programmes and provides a live feed to the authorities. Everyone has to 'live, from habit that became instinct – in the assumption that every sound you made was overheard, and, except in darkness, every movement scrutinised'.[40] In the early days of television, critics attributed this kind of Orwellian influence to the box in the corner. Some people thought that the people on TV could see into their living rooms. One woman wrote to the newsreader Robert Dougall, 'I wonder what you think of me in my cosy chair by the set?' Another wrote to him to ask if she was sitting too near to the television.[41] After a while, people got the hang of the technology, and complaints about TV's pernicious effects began to receive the stock answer: 'If you don't like it, there is always the off switch' – a switch soon joined by buttons to change channels, mute and fast-forward. But Orwell's vision still transfixed us. Viewers watching Channel 4 in the early 2000s would come across a brief, almost subliminal ident (called, appropriately enough, a blink) of a large eye: a silent reminder that the next series of *Big Brother* was imminent. Big Brother is not watching you. You are watching Big Brother, and he is terrified you are going to change channels.

Big Brother could learn a lot from the economist Albert Hirschman's classic book, *Exit, Voice, and Loyalty*, which outlines two contrasting ways of responding to dissatisfaction in companies and organisations. The first, exit, involves a customer switching to another brand or an employee leaving an organisation. This strategy, traditionally favoured by classical economists, is straightforward and impersonal, like the anonymous choices you make in the aisles of a supermarket. But while exit helps individuals in the short term, it may not alter the underlying reasons for their dissatisfaction. The second strategy, voice, allows employees or customers to express their views and try to produce change from within – a messier and sometimes painful process but one that may address these deeper reasons.[42]

In broadcasting, the contrast between exit and voice is stark. BBC Radio 4 listeners, for example, rely on voice. They are loyal whingers: if they do not like an announcer's accent or a new theme tune, they respond with righteous indignation as dedicated listeners to the station, and exercise real influence as a result. The television-watcher,

15 Watching the weather

> 'History appears as the derailment, the disruption of the
> everyday … History changes, the everyday remains'
>
> Karel Kosík [1]

The writer and politician Michael Ignatieff once complained that 'most of us no longer watch television; we graze, zapping back and forth between channels whenever our boredom threshold is triggered … A new culture has taken shape which caters for people with the attention span of a flea.'[2] But there is one programme that seems to have survived and prospered in what Ignatieff called this 'three-minute culture', perhaps because it lasts only about three minutes: the weather forecast. Watching or listening to tomorrow's outlook remains an undying national ritual. There has been a forecast on the BBC almost every day since 26 March 1923. The exception was during the Second World War, when the radio forecast was suspended in case it was helpful to the enemy, although the government partially relented in October 1944, allowing information to be given about the weather the day before yesterday. 'Most people,' the BBC bulletin stated laconically on the day the ban was lifted, 'will have cause to remember it because in most parts of the country it just rained and rained.'[3]

The forecast is now one of the longest-running programmes on British television, and, despite all the competing sources of weather information, it remains popular: 26.3 million people will see at least one BBC weather forecast in any one month.[4] The forecast after the late-evening news is the most popular of all, with hundreds of thousands of people tuning in at the end of the news especially to watch it. 'Popular' is perhaps the wrong word, though, for moaning about the supposed inaccuracy and poor presentation of the forecast is also something of a national pastime. The problem is that viewers have always wanted clarity and predictability in a weather system that is essentially opaque and unpredictable. And how do you represent a dynamic phenomenon like the weather in summary form? Early BBC television forecasts used simple charts and captions, with only a disembodied, Monty-Pythonesque hand coming in from one side to point at the relevant bits. When George Cowling presented the first manned forecast in 1954, he and his colleagues would draw the weather symbols on cardboard charts with felt-tip pens, then he would roll them up and take them by tube train from the London Weather Centre in Kingsway to the BBC's Shepherd's Bush studios. During the bulletin itself, Cowling scribbled over the chart with a charcoal stick to show the weather changing.

The forecasters drew all their own charts until 1967, when they introduced magnetic rubber symbols filled with iron filings, which could be stuck on to steel maps. The symbols themselves were not exactly viewer-friendly, being based on international meteorological iconography such as triangles for showers, round dots for rain and black strips for isobars. In 1975, these symbols were dramatically simplified. Now we had the weather as drawn by a technically proficient six-year-old: fluffy clouds (both white and black, to indicate the chance of rain), pear-like raindrops, white asterisks for snowflakes, and suns with orange circles and lines radiating outwards. But the magnetic symbols were not much better than hand-drawn charts at indicating changing weather. When the forecaster tried to place a black cloud on top of a white one to indicate incoming rain, the magnetic polarity was often reversed and it would fall off.

In 1985, the BBC replaced these symbols with a computer system known as 'colour separation overlay'. In CSO, the forecaster stands in front of a large blue screen, and any area that the camera detects as blue is replaced by a feed from a computerised weather map. Anything non-blue remains the same, so forecasters seem to be standing in front of the map (if they wore blue clothing, they would disappear). At last, television had found a way of integrating a moving weather map with a human narrator. What has really transformed the weather forecast in recent years, however, is not technology but the commercialisation of television and the rise of the personality forecaster. This reflected a classically Thatcherite challenge to traditional professional expertise by market values – but the contest was not quite as straightforward as it first seemed.

The BBC Met Office forecasters were (and remain) career civil servants with corresponding ranks in the RAF, but they also became celebrities by default, simply because they entered people's living rooms for a few minutes every day. Along with the onscreen continuity announcers, the weather forecasters were some of the first TV personalities, and this eventually made it easier to accept newsreaders as personalities as well – a significant cultural shift. Lord Reith had created the traditional news announcer in the 1920s in an attempt to give the corporation a responsible public face and thus shake off government controls. News announcers, he ordered, would be 'shadowy personalities ... aloof and mysterious, who must forgo the desire for notoriety and recognition'.[5] They had to wear evening dress (on the radio), speak in received southern pronunciation and remain strictly anonymous. Reith wanted BBC news to avoid the strident voice and restless search for drama and human interest found in newspapers. A Good

Friday news bulletin in 1930 simply stated, 'There is no news tonight.'[6] Anonymity inspired a presenting style which Collie Knox, *Daily Mail* journalist and fierce BBC critic, described as the 'bored, listless manner of a dying duck'.[7] During the war, news announcers gave their names so that they were less likely to be confused with enemy saboteurs, but on 4 May 1945 the announcer said, 'Here is the news – and this is Stuart Hibberd reading it' for the last time, before returning to obscurity.[8]

Even on television, the BBC did not initially provide pictures for the news. When the first in-vision newsreaders appeared in 1955, they kept their heads down and remained expressionless. According to an audience survey of June 1957, viewers supported the idea of 'dispassionate news reading' but complained that newsreaders often 'sounded uninterested'.[9] Eventually, news producers realised that it was incongruous to strive for complete impersonality when the weather forecasters who followed the news were becoming personalities.[10] Not that they were necessarily captivating performers. 'Weather men on television usually walk on looking like a depression over Iceland,' complained one newspaper columnist in 1968. 'They point at maps and chat about isobars. Even their smiles seem frozen.'[11] In the early years of television news and weather forecasting, viewers were eager to have more of a relationship with these familiar faces. For various reasons the presenters remained standoffish, but it was the forecasters who thawed first.

Bert Foord, who joined the BBC weather team in 1963, was the first forecaster to achieve celebrity status, largely because of his distinctive northern accent and avuncular manner. On one occasion, Foord had to follow a farming programme about lambing techniques. He opened with the line 'From soapflakes to snowflakes', which caused a minor scandal when the easily amused continuity announcer, Valerie Singleton, laughed on air. The children's programme *The Magic Roundabout* often ended with Florence reminding Zebedee and Dougal that Bert Foord was waiting to give the forecast.[12] When Foord left the BBC in 1974, Terry Wogan launched a 'Bring Back Bert Foord' campaign on Radio 2, claiming that the weather itself had got worse since he had stopped forecasting. Tellingly, his professional career had won out over media stardom: Foord had simply given up television after being promoted within the Met Office.[13]

The launch of breakfast television in 1983 was a key moment in the rise of the personality forecaster. The BBC had the Met Office dreamboat and housewives' favourite Francis Wilson. ITV had a member of the old school, a retired naval commander called David Philpott. But it soon shunted him to weekends to make way for Wincey Willis, who would intersperse her weather reports with little anecdotes about her dog or her mother's arthritis. The new breakfast and satellite stations gave disproportionate time to the weather, because it was cheap and could be endlessly repeated for channel-hopping viewers. As the weather took up more airtime, the late 1980s saw a new breed of glamorous 'weathergirls', like TV-am's Ulrika Jonsson and Sky TV's Tania Bryer, who were cruelly nicknamed 'Brolly Dollies' and 'Tracey Sunshines'. Programme makers realised that the novelty weather forecast was a cheap way of drawing viewers into a programme. On the daytime show *This Morning*, the weatherman Fred Talbot did his forecast from a floating map of Britain in Liverpool's Albert Dock. With his weather-themed woolly jumpers and hyperactive manner, Talbot became a cult figure. The most famous part of his forecast, a not particularly death-defying leap over the water to Northern Ireland, was described by one excitable commentator as 'subliminal propaganda for an end to the Union'.[14]

The inspiration for these light-hearted forecasts came from American television, where meteorological expertise had never quite taken hold. In the 1950s, US weather-casters delivered the forecast in verse or with the aid of puppets. One attractive female weathercaster, dressed in a short nightie, tucked herself into bed each night while delivering the late forecast.[15] The American Meteorological Society tried to establish a Seal of Approval programme in 1957 to promote reliability and professionalism among forecasters, but it was largely ignored by ratings-conscious broadcasters. Gimmicky forecasting waned slightly in the 1960s, but American stations still dressed their forecasters in demonstrative costumes – umbrellas and mackintoshes for rain, bathing suits and flip-flops for sun – or sent them outside in gales and blizzards for comic effect.[16] Often a dog or cat would appear as the weathercaster, dressed appro-priately for the weather, with an off-camera announcer providing the voice.[17]

But the arrival in Britain of what Americans call 'weather-tainment' may actually have saved the forecast from obsolescence. In the 1960s, the personalised forecast was an endangered species. There were only three weather bulletins a day on BBC television and there was much managerial pressure to reduce their length to make way for more popular programmes. At one time the length of the main national forecast fell to just thirty seconds. For a week in 1969, the BBC reverted to a weather chart with a voiceover, until viewers responded angrily and the weathermen returned.[18] It was really the putative celebrity of Bert Foord and others that rescued the forecast from being more than just a grudgingly delivered summary.

Under the new commercial pressures of the Thatcher era, many remained worried that public-service items like news and weather would be replaced by cheap fillers and audience-grabbers. In fact, the opposite happened: the 'boring' news and weather forecast were enlisted to fight increasingly fierce ratings battles in the multi-channel environment of cable and satellite TV. ITN, for example, only got round to doing a national forecast in February 1989. They were helped by the Thatcherite liberalisation of programme sponsorship, which allowed the energy company Powergen to affix its logo to the forecast in 1990, promising 'electricity whatever the weather'.

Unlike the more lightweight subscription and breakfast channels, ITN offered a serious competitor to the BBC forecast. Its attitude to the weather was the same as its approach to the news: professional presentation combined with a chatty, human-interest style. For Alex Hill, the Met Office man who made the first ITN forecast, anticyclones were 'highs', precipitation was 'a great, malignant swathe of rain', and frontal systems were 'a baleful banana of cloud'.[19] Around this time, the BBC's producer of weather programmes, John Teather, accepted that forecasters had to make a connection with their audience: 'It's an undefined talent. The term for it in the 1930s was the "It" factor. The presenter is that person who walks into the room and makes everyone's head turn.'[20] It was hard to imagine the older generation of BBC forecasters, with their tweed jackets, kipper ties and seventies haircuts, having the 'It' factor. Rather, it was the ordinariness of the forecasters that made them celebrities – although one of the younger members of the team did become an unlikely youth icon after the 1988 Tribe of Toffs hit, 'John Kettley is a weatherman'.

When George Cowling once let slip in a 1950s forecast that tomorrow would be a good day for drying the washing, he received a reproving phone call from his superior at the Met Office.[21] But in the 1990s, such casual asides became an almost compulsory element of the forecast. The weather was no longer an abstract phenomenon; it had to be related to potential activities like gardening or going to the Test Match. The forecast became distinctly nannyish. We were told to 'go slow on those motorways', 'take care on those icy pavements if you're out and about' and 'put on some layers if you're taking the dog for a walk'. The padded-out forecast also became a source of new, previously unconsidered anxieties about ultraviolet radiation, poor air quality and high pollen counts. But larger anxieties, like climate change, rarely intruded: Britain's weather is actually a poor indicator of global warming because it is so unpredictable.

In fact, the forecast tends to inspire a certain resignation about the weather; certainly, it conveys little sense that our climate could be altered by human intervention. As Mark Twain (or George Axelrod, or numerous other people) is supposed to have said, 'Everyone talks about the weather, but no one does anything about it.' The forecast is similarly fatalistic: coming after the chaotic disruption to diurnal routine represented by the items on the TV news, it calmly restores the timeless rhythms of the everyday. The forecasters are rather apologetic on the weather's behalf ('more rain again, I'm afraid') but quietly insistent about its narrative logic. Tomorrow's weather is an inescapable denouement, described in those strange, unowned verb forms ('rain spreading from the west ... strengthening through the night ... brightening up later ... turning colder'). The news involves us in its problems and dilemmas and invites us to have a position on them; but no one is to blame for the rain. The American author Paul Theroux once noted that the British in particular tend to personify the weather, suggesting that it is either working for or against us, but in a diffident, undramatic way: 'The weather's been letting us down ... It's been trying to rain all day ... The sun's been trying to come out.'[22]

This phlegmatic attitude has traditionally translated into ideas about our national identity. The historian Robert Colls argues that Britain's temperate climate has often been seen as 'the barometer of a true liberal civilization', used to explain our generally placid national character and moderate political system. In 1935, the popular philosopher and broadcaster C. E. M. Joad argued that the 'true spirit of England' could be found in its 'soft, hazy, gentle' climate. In less thoughtful hands than Joad's, this climatological determinism could be used to associate more extreme weather patterns with non-democratic, intolerant political systems. The blazing African sun went logically with slavery and despotism, harsh Russian winters with serfdom and totalitarianism.[23] Even today, the forecast offers a muted form of this national exceptionalism. When we do have extreme weather, it can be blamed on somewhere else, whether it is cold winds from the Arctic or Siberia, rain from the Atlantic or hot winds from the Continent. The language of the British forecast is fuzzily approximate, like those timeless alliterative standbys 'sunny spells' and 'scattered showers'. British weather may be bad but, in contrast to other parts of the world, it is rarely a matter of life and death.

The consoling, cyclical qualities of the weather forecast are not to everyone's taste. In March 2005, BBC2's current affairs flagship, *Newsnight*, decided to introduce a weather forecast at the end of the programme, to the apparent disdain of its presenter, Jeremy Paxman. During one forecast he curtly announced 'a veritable smorgasbord. Sun. Rain. Thunder. Hail. Snow. Cold. Wind. Not worth going to work really.' During another, he raced through a similar list before brusquely concluding, 'It's April, what do you expect?' *Newsnight*'s forecast had replaced the summary of the financial markets, a largely meaningless ritual to everyone but commodity brokers, who presumably have more sophisticated ways of accessing this information. The financial summary is really an upmarket version of the weather forecast: a daily sacrament given at the end of news reports, it sees the fluctuations of the FTSE or the Dow-Jones as an uncontrollable force of nature which only experts can decipher. But *Newsnight* viewers protested on the programme's website about the disappearance of the 'grown-up' market summary and the 'dumbing down' of the programme. In response, *Newsnight* organised an onscreen hustings – with ex-chancellor Norman Lamont speaking up for the markets and ex-forecaster Michael Fish for the weather – followed by a phone-in poll. After a conclusive vote of 68 to 32 per cent, the market report was reinstated and the forecast dropped.

The *Newsnight* controversy was a light shower compared to the storm brewing about the weather forecasts on the rest of the BBC. In May 2005, for the first time in twenty years, the corporation seriously revamped its forecasts, claiming that audience research showed that viewers found the traditional format 'old-fashioned' and 'boring'.[24] It ditched its familiar 2D weather symbols and map for a high-tech, virtual-reality graphics system. Suddenly the forecast was dynamically mobile. Dark shadows moved across the map to represent clouds, shafts of light denoted sunshine, and rain fell down in realistic drops. The graphics system also moved around Britain to give viewers a kind of aerial tour of their own regions. The dull scientific stuff, like those wavy lines representing air pressure, was dumped. Colin Tregear, the BBC Weather Centre's director, explained bullishly, 'It's not a geography lesson, it's a weather forecast.'[25]

The BBC switchboard was deluged with thousands of complaints. Some viewers were getting motion sickness from the fast-moving graphics. The 'fly-through' facility meant that people had to wait too long to see their part of the country. England's green and pleasant land had been turned the colour of a cowpat, a 'sandy' or 'golden' shade having been chosen because it showed up contrasts clearly. Most controversially, the map had a tilt to take account of the curvature of the Earth, which appeared to downsize northern England and Scotland. It had long been a piece of popular folklore that the weather forecast concentrated unduly on the South-East at the expense of the regions, and here at last was hard evidence. The voice of middle

England, the *Daily Mail*, was atypically outraged on behalf of the Celtic fringes. 'Are people in the North,' it wrote, 'going to be offered a reduction in their licence fee?'[26] One Scottish National Party MP tabled a House of Commons motion protesting against the tilt. During a debate in the Lords about the new forecasts, a peer asked, 'Will my noble friend consider looking into the gravely suspicious circumstance that if you pay for it, the weather always seems better on Sky?'[27]

Perhaps conscious of its need to justify the licence fee when its charter was up for renewal, the BBC quickly responded to the furore. In deference to its traditional Reithian mission to educate and inform, it brought back some of the old symbols denoting wind speeds and air pressure; it reduced the speed at which the map zoomed around the country, to appease those with delicate stomachs; and it partially corrected the Earth's tilt, giving the North more prominence. Alex Salmond, the Scottish National Party leader, said proudly, 'The BBC has been undone by the Western Isles whirlwind. It is great to see that Scottish pressure has made the BBC think again.'[28]

Why was everyone so upset about some trivial changes to a programme that lasts only for a few minutes? The controversy is puzzling because, contrary to popular belief, the British are not unusually obsessed with the weather. The American Weather Channel, for example, is regularly in the top-ten cable channels, but when it launched a sister channel in Britain in 1996, viewer indifference closed it down within eighteen months. In a 1992 BBC documentary about the weather, a statistician rang people immediately after they had watched the weather forecast, and discovered that 70 per cent of them could not remember a thing about it.[29] People who actually needed to know the forecast, such as farmers and fishermen, had only marginally better recall. When, in 1976, a similar telephone survey was conducted in Minneapolis and St Paul in America just after the early evening weather forecast, half of viewers 'retained a general notion of what the next day's weather would be'.[30] Perhaps the talking dogs had a mnemonic effect.

Lifestyle changes in recent years have also meant that the weather affects us less and less – at the same time as knowledge of impending weather has become extremely important to the businesses that manage our lifestyles. An interesting example of this disjuncture is the way that producers of forecasts have tried to make the language more precise in recent years, by adopting the American practice of citing probabilities ('an 80 per cent chance of showers'). These percentages are produced by ensemble forecasting, which uses computers to compile different simulations based on minuscule adjustments. The language of probabilities is useful to companies who need figures to enter into software programs that will help them make business decisions. But it is not much help to the rest of us: we just want to know whether to take a brolly. Nowadays, long-term forecasting is the important commodity and is only available to people who are prepared to pay for it. Under the Thatcher government, the Met Office became an executive agency, allowing it to run itself as a business with its own budget. So it was well placed to exploit the emerging business of weather risk management, as our just-in-time economy demanded that products be delivered to their selling points at short notice. The Met Office provides data which tells supermarkets whether to stock up on ice cream, salad and shower gel, or hot-water bottles, women's tights and de-icer. In a sense, these people make it their business to worry about the weather so that the rest of us do not have to, except insofar as it influences our lifestyle choices.

Since we rarely need to know what the weather is going to be like tomorrow, the television forecast is now essentially ritualistic: it follows a familiar format, with the same introductory music, graphics, verbal tics and sign-offs from the forecaster. Linguists call it phatic communication, a more sophisticated version of the pleasantries that people exchange about the weather like 'it's too cold to snow' or 'it's too hot for me', which serve more as conversational fillers than genuine attempts to communicate. Six months after the uproar over the BBC weather map, some confidential new Met Office guidelines for television forecasters were leaked to the press. They advised against overly gloomy descriptions of the weather: 'chilly in areas' should now be characterised as 'warm for most', while 'isolated storms' should become 'hot and sunny for most'. Other terms to be avoided included 'heavy rain' (now to be described as 'rain'), 'occasional showers' ('mainly dry') and 'often cloudy' ('generally clear').[31] An inappropriate spin on bad news, perhaps – but all these guidelines really suggested was replacing one set of vague approximations with another. A statistician recently worked out that, if weather forecasters used the standard, fuzzy phraseology, they could provide an accurate forecast for 41 per cent of the time simply by repeating exactly what they had said the previous day.[32]

Perhaps it is this iterative quality of the weather forecast that explains our emotional attachment to it. Despite the proliferation of TV channels, the BBC still has an important symbolic role as the mediator of national rituals, from special occasions like royal weddings to daily events like weather forecasts. And people do not take kindly to sudden, unrequested changes in their quotidian routines. The persistence of the forecast in all our daily lives invites nostalgic reminiscence. Compared to their predecessors, today's forecasters seem personable but bland, a series of interchangeable Helens and Darrens, of similar ages, mannerisms and haircuts. In time, no doubt, they will become familiar and loved, and we will rail against their successors. But for now this cuts no ice. Where are the

16 At the end of the day

> 'I sometimes think of what future historians will say of
> us. A single sentence will suffice for modern man: he
> fornicated and read the papers'
>
> Albert Camus [1]

In his classic history of manners, *The Civilizing Process*
(1939), Norbert Elias shows how the routine of going to
bed began to be hidden from social life from the Renais-
sance period onwards. The bedroom became an intimate
space, with sleep almost as embarrassing to polite society
as other bodily functions like burping and breaking wind.
The whole-body nightgown came into use in the late
sixteenth century, making it roughly contemporaneous
with innovations like handkerchiefs and the modern
arrangement of table cutlery, which also sought to civilise
our bodily functions. The Victorian period, when ladies
and gentlemen did not go to bed but 'retired', was the high
point of this awkwardness about bedtime habits. [2]

Although things loosened up a little after the First World
War, it was the Second World War that really synchronised
our national bedroom routines and turned them once
more into social habits. The nightly blackout necessitated
the tedious collective ritual of putting up blankets and
brown paper screens to obscure every last bit of window
light. There was no particular reason to stay up late in the
blackout, one MP even suggesting that going to bed early
to save resources was a patriotic duty. [3] With the offshore

commercial stations closed during wartime, BBC radio emerged as the voice of the nation and became the choreographer of bedtime habits, as listeners put themselves to sleep to its background noise. The threat of bombing made sleeping a difficult and sometimes public affair, as families went out each night to their Anderson shelters, public shelters or London Underground platforms. In 1943, Mass-Observation noted that people still slept in Underground stations long after the serious threat of bombing had passed, and commuters were having to pick their way through the 'tube dwellers' on the ground. It concluded that these people stayed there not through fear but out of social habit, and the search for companionship and community.[4]

If you had to go to bed early, or were stuck in a shelter, or could not sleep, one of the few things you could do was read, an activity which grew in popularity in wartime.[5] There was much discussion, both during and after the war, about how to read in bed without getting cold in freezing winter bedrooms. One man patented a device that projected microfilm photographs of a book on to the ceiling, the pages being turned by a camera shutter cable, operated from under the bedclothes, so that you could read while completely tucked in.[6] Other suggestions included choosing a book that was slim enough to hold lightly, and engrossing enough to take your mind off the cold; tucking yourself in with the sheets close to your neck, using your thumb and two fingers to turn the pages; and wearing a ski cap, mittens and a thick cardigan put on the wrong way round and pulled up under the chin.[7]

In the years after the war, the bedroom lagged behind other areas of the house in its embracing of social change. The wartime Utility Furniture Scheme, which ran until 1949, made it against the law to manufacture beds without a government licence. Only priority groups like newly-weds and 'bombees' (those whose houses had been bombed out) could buy the government-sponsored 'utility furniture'. This furniture could not use the design materials pioneered between the wars – aluminium, chrome and plastics – because they were needed for the war effort. For many on the Utility committee, like the designer Gordon Russell, this was an opportunity to educate the public about the beauty of simple, unshowy functionalism. Utility beds were austerely simple items using no nails, no decorative carving or other embellishments, as little wood and other materials as possible, and straight, clean lines. Since utility beds were thin on the ground, however, a side effect of the scheme was to turn the ricketiest old second-hand beds into prized possessions.

Even after these restrictions ended, the bed never became a symbol of the affluent society in the way that the furniture of the kitchen and living room did. In the early 1960s, the president of the National Bedding Federation registered his paternalistic dismay:

> Although we place luxurious sleeping equipment at everybody's disposal, many people are still today sleeping, or trying to sleep, on beds and mattresses in the last stages of senile decay. Why people continue to defy sleep on lumpy, bumpy mattresses is a mystery to me. The same people probably have fine television sets and wonderful refrigerators.[8]

The problem was that the cold British bedroom was unfit for much more than sleeping. In his 1962 history of the bed, *Warm and Snug*, the British historian Lawrence Wright manages to fill more than 350 pages of closely typed text while barely mentioning a rather important secondary function of the bed: sex. Although there is no evidence that Britons have had any less sex than other nationalities, the British bedroom has traditionally been seen as a passionless place where sitcom couples – he in winceyette striped pyjamas, she in a frilly pink nightgown – bicker with each other and imagine hearing strange noises coming from downstairs. 'Continental people have sex life [*sic*],' wrote George Mikes in 1946. 'The English have hot water bottles.'[9] As late as 1963, only 3.5 per cent of British households had central heating, compared to 60 per cent of American homes and 90 per cent of Swedish homes.[10] The delicious habit of warming your feet directly on a hot water bottle was a major cause of chilblains, almost unknown in North America, but still afflicting half the UK population in the 1950s.[11]

One of the key signs of the changing status of the bedroom after the war was the gradual decline of twin beds. Twin beds for married couples had begun to replace double beds in both Britain and the US in the inter-war era and, for a brief period, became more popular after the war, as a symbol of growing affluence. Groucho Marx referred to the warring tribes of 'monobedders' and 'polybedders': the couples who slept in separate, single beds or shared a double.[12] The romantic author Barbara Cartland was a confirmed polybedder:

> I suspect the woman who says that she has chosen twin beds for reasons of decorative effect, sleeping comfort, or hygiene. She is, in fact, excusing the coldness that exists in her marriage ... How much easier is it to make up a row if one is close together in a double bed? ... As the old adage has it, 'No difference is wide, that the sheets will not decide.'[13]

Meanwhile, the Director of the Family Relations Institute argued that twin beds were a conspiracy by furniture manufacturers to make more money, and warned that the movement to twin beds by middle-aged couples was 'often the prelude to a divorce'.[14] The birth-control campaigner and sex expert Marie Stopes was a monobedder, but she also excoriated the twin bed set as 'an invention of the Devil, jealous of married bliss'. For her, the 'truly civilised standard' – an increasingly unrealistic one in cramped post-war houses – was for husband and wife to each have a double-bedded room of their own to 'keep the fresh intensity of their love'.[15]

By the late 1950s the double bed was dominant again and the twin bed in final retreat – and not because of the propagandistic efforts of any of these critics. The double bed came to symbolise the more relaxed, companionate marriage (and other forms of coupling) in this period, consigning the twin bed to a reputation for suburban tweeness which turned out to be terminal. A complicating factor was the scientific evidence now emerging that sleepers changed position twenty to forty-five times a night and needed at least thirty-nine inches of bed-width to do it comfortably[16] – a difficult prospect in a standard double bed. So the double bed also became bigger, expanding to 'king' and 'queen' sizes.[17] The old, four-foot-wide 'three-quarter' bed, nicknamed the 'landlady's double' because it could cram two people into a space fit only for one, became extinct. The polybedders had won, by a length. For no doubt unrelated reasons, the divorce rate carried on rising.

Another activity ripe for change was bedmaking. This ritual involved layering the different elements in strict order – an under-blanket round the mattress, then an under-sheet, a top sheet, pillows, blankets, counterpane, and an eiderdown in winter – distributing them evenly without any rucks, and tucking them into mitred folds at the end of the bed, or 'hospital corners'. In cold British bedrooms, a properly made bed certainly had its comforts. Robert Louis Stevenson eulogised about 'the pleasant land of counterpane' and Rupert Brooke about 'the cool kindliness of sheets, that soon / Smooth away trouble; and the rough male kiss / Of blankets'.[18] But bedmaking was a potential tyranny for the housewife, the unshakeable order of the different layers a way of valuing hierarchy and order in themselves. In the 1960s, as many press articles and consumer surveys began to measure how hard the housewife actually worked, traditional bedmaking was beginning to seem like a chore too many.[19]

If you had to pick one significant date in the history of British bedmaking, it would be 11 May 1964, when Terence Conran opened the first Habitat store in South Kensington. Habitat soon became the most fashionable London shop of the 1960s, spreading to the provinces in the 1970s. The expansion of universities, and generally rising affluence, created a new generation of middle-class baby-boomers who were setting up home earlier. This vanguard of bedsitters and flatsharers did not have time for hospital corners. Conran recognised that this new middle class wanted elegant but low-maintenance housewares: cutlery that did not need endless polishing; tables that looked good without tablecloths; earthenware dishes that went straight from the oven to the dinner table; and beds that could be easily made. Habitat's bestselling item throughout the 1960s was the duvet, which had been used in Alpine and Scandinavian bedrooms for centuries and which the British were now encountering on foreign holidays. Some Habitat shoppers were so fascinated by the duvets that they climbed into the display beds in the stores to see what they felt like.[20] Conran later said it was the best product he ever sold because it was 'symbolic of social change'.[21]

According to one advert, making the bed with a duvet only took eighteen seconds: 'Eight to smooth out the bed, six to plump up the pillows, and four more to s-w-i-s-h over your Slumberdown.'[22] In a photo from a Habitat catalogue of the time, a man is arranging the duvet in the background while a woman is looking straight at the camera, doing her nails at a dressing table.[23] The duvet, this image suggested, was encouraging men to make the bed at last. Perhaps, but one suspects it was still women who had to put the quilt back into the washed duvet cover once a week, a delicate manoeuvre which was a bit like trying to stuff a giant marshmallow into a small envelope. Another new boon for bedmakers was the no-iron, nylon fitted sheet. 'These are the sheets a few years ago only millionaires and film stars could enjoy,' went an advert for Brentford's ('the king of nylon sheets') in 1966. 'So, if they are good enough for them, they are good enough for us all!'[24]

When adverts for duvets promised an 'uninhibited' lifestyle, they meant more than simply that they were light, comfy and convenient. Duvets were the 'luxurious Swedish sleeping sensation'[25] at a time when Scandinavia was synonymous with a liberated sex life. A 1970 advert for Slumberdown duvets showed a pretty blonde woman in bed, the duvet covering her naked front. 'Sleep Swedish – and be free of that blankety-blank bedmaking,' it said. 'The Scandinavian way of sleeping is free, uninhibited.'[26] 'The English have been doing it all wrong for years,' went another advert. 'It's the bedclothes they use. They're so restricting, they're more of a hindrance than a help.' The duvet 'will do wonders for your nightlife – and our reputation. Rule Britannia.'[27] All this nudging and winking went nicely with Habitat's image as unstuffy and anti-suburban. Habitat opened in France in 1973, with a special promotion on duvets ('*vingt secondes pour faire un lit!*') and Conran later claimed, with enviable chutzpah, that this 'undoubtedly changed the sex life of Europe'.[28] Duvets entered the British mainstream in the early 1970s, when they no longer needed to be known as 'continental quilts' to hint at their exotic origins. They soon lost their sexy connotations, but once people had been weaned off blankets they never wanted to return to them.

The central heating boom of the 1960s – by the end of that decade, a quarter of British homes had it installed[29] – should also have encouraged bedroom design to become more playful. There was indeed a brief fashion for novelty, such as PVC water beds with ripple-control and mirrored headboards; Murphy beds that descended from holes in the wall; and 'sleeping centres' with gadgets like undulating massagers, inbuilt alarms, fridges, hi-fis, electric razors and remote controls for curtains and lights. On the whole, though, outside of swanky bachelor pads and James Bond movies the bedroom was never a place of technological invention. Instead it became part of what Nicholas Tomalin, in a prophetic article in *Town* magazine in 1963, identified as a new middle-class aesthetic of 'conspicuous thrift', which was supposedly a reaction against chintzy bourgeois taste. But as Tomalin recognised, the thrifters were also 'distinguishing themselves, distastefully, from the real proletariat', which in an age of consumer affluence now 'guiltlessly enjoys the excesses of conspicuous waste'.[30]

Stripped pine, pioneered by Habitat in the 1960s, was the classic example of this middle-class preference for understatement. In the nineteenth and early twentieth centuries, it was the preserve of poor families who could not afford to paint or stain their furniture. But with the working classes now buying furniture made of modern fabrics and plastics on hire purchase, stripped pine was in no danger of being seen as vulgarly proletarian. The prime site for this manufactured nostalgia, the new bourgeois-bohemian fondness for retro styles, was the bedroom. Here the middle classes adopted a comfortable version of the below-stairs life of the servants they might have employed in a previous era: Victorian maids' cast-iron beds, simple pine bedsteads, bare floorboards, sanded-down old dressers. This was the mass-market, middle-class version of Gordon Russell's Utility aesthetic, which had been born out of wartime privations. It combined the pleasures of mass consumption with older ideals of homeliness, naturalness and simplicity.

In 1955, the *Daily Mirror* had noted that in London only one bedstead was sold for every seven divans, while in the Midlands and North they still clung to the 'traditional' bedstead.[31] But this trend soon reversed and more people began to buy bedsteads than divans, a movement which is only now showing signs of levelling out. 'A bed like grandmama's. Suddenly it's news. They've taken the aspidistra-antimacassar gloom out of Victoriana and turned what is left into the brightest trend in bedroom décor for years,' claimed the *Mirror* in 1959. 'Brass bedsteads are back.'[32] Influenced by eastern traditions and the hippy movement, there was a fashion in the 1960s and 1970s for sleeping on lower, even sparser beds without footboards or headboards, or simply a mattress on the floor. In the 1980s and 1990s, this minimalist tradition continued in the fibre-filled Japanese futon and the unadorned IKEA bed on which, if you believed the adverts, one out of every ten European babies was conceived.

But the bedroom could not entirely escape the acquisitive culture of consumerism. It also became more of a social space, meant not just for sleeping but for relaxation and entertainment. As more people bought multiple TV sets, they usually put the spare ones in their bedrooms. A 1983 survey found that at least a quarter of all households watched television in bed. (In the days when most TVs did not have remote controls, it was the man's job to get up and change channels or switch off – for which he was rewarded with control of the remote when it eventually came.[33]) Bedrooms acquired exercise bikes (used and unused), telephones, bookcases, desks and computers. This newly social dimension of the bedroom created a market for 'relax-at-home' loungewear like kimonos and dressing gowns, which could be worn for longer and in front of more people. It was a reversion to the historical pattern in place before the eighteenth century, when bedrooms were semi-public spaces, which the poor used as multi-occupancy rooms and the rich as reception areas.[34] The bedroom now brought together two countervailing trends: the search for simplicity and the desire for modern comforts. No wonder that one of the new obsessions of makeover programmes and furniture stores was storage and hanging space, to hide all the stuff we had absent-mindedly acquired and to turn the bedroom into a retreat once again.

The bedroom was partly changing because our attitude to sleep was changing. In his 1905 essay *The Protestant Ethic and the Spirit of Capitalism*, Max Weber noted that it had long been common in protestant, capitalist Europe to view sleeping too much as an immoral waste of one's time on God's earth: 'The span of human life is infinitely short and precious to make sure of one's own election. Loss of time through sociability, idle talk, luxury, even more sleep than is necessary for health, six to at most eight hours, is worthy of absolute moral condemnation.'[35] In some ways, the longer-hours culture of the last few decades has institutionalised this idea of sleep as non-productive time. One of this culture's architects, Margaret Thatcher, let it be known that she slept for only four hours a night, in a manner that suggested that going to bed at a normal hour was the unnecessary indulgence of shiftless layabouts.

In a book published in 1987, the American sociologist Murray Melbin claimed that night was 'the last frontier'. Since the birth of gas lighting, he argued, night-time had been colonised in the same way that white Americans had gradually settled the western frontier, and in both cases it had been accompanied by a relaxation of social codes and hierarchies. The first people to lay claim to night-time were misfits and criminals, just like the hunters and outlaws of the wild west. Then, as in the west, came the entrepreneurs, who invented shift work so that the expensive machinery in their factories could be used at night. Finally there came a whole 'afterhours community' of pleasure seekers. Busy roads and flight paths made night-time noisier, and people kept themselves awake with alcohol, nicotine and caffeine. Once shops and broadcasters adopted a 24-hour schedule, Melbin argued, the distinction between night and day would disappear.[36]

But if sleep is a waste of time in this 24/7 culture, it is still rather difficult to avoid. If we are rich enough, many of the most tedious routines of daily life, like cooking, childcare or housework, can be farmed out to minions or purchased in more convenient forms. But sleeping, the most time-consuming routine of all, cannot be outsourced in this way – at least, not yet. Some experts predict that Modafinil and other 'clock-shifting' compounds, used to treat disorders like narcolepsy, will soon become lifestyle drugs that will pharmacologically eliminate the need for sleep. They will not simply knock us out like sleeping pills, but change our 'sleep architecture' so that we enter deep sleep quicker. Two hours' sleep will feel like eight, freeing up more time to check our emails or book cheap flights on the internet. Bedtime will be cancelled. For now, though, most of us seem reluctant to do our civic duty and become 24-hour workers and consumers. Quite unreasonably, we insist on going to bed at a reasonable time every night. The normal time for retiring – between 11 p.m. and midnight, with men going slightly later than women – has remained remarkably consistent since the war.

In fact, one consequence of the so-called '24-hour society' has been a growing interest in sleep. Ever since the scientific study of sleep began with the discovery of REM (rapid eye movement) sleep in the 1950s, our increasing knowledge has produced accompanying anxieties. The specialist language for talking about sleep – some of which has now filtered into general use – borrows the vocabulary of a time-, money- and health-conscious culture. When we do not sleep we are said to be suffering from 'sleep-debt', which we will need to make up by depositing more sleep in our 'account'. Western society itself is 'sleep-sick', suffering from chronic sleep deficiency. To cure our sleep-sickness, we need to practise 'sleep hygiene', which means keeping the bedroom dark with light-proof curtains, cool and free from TVs and other electrical equipment. In a neat mirroring of the Thatcherite work ethic, we are urged to be more 'sleep efficient'. This means maximising the usefulness of our time in bed, making sure we drift into deeper REM sleep more quickly and do not keep waking ourselves up by snagging our clothes or rolling around on bumpy mattresses.

Insomnia has also been pathologised. Science has finally confirmed what most of us suspected, that the time-honoured tricks for falling asleep, such as imagining ourselves building brick walls or counting sheep, are worse than useless, because they do not use up enough brain capacity. Getting people to sleep has become an industry, particularly in the case of over-the-counter remedies like herbal pills, aromatherapies and dilator strips designed to keep our nasal passages open. Insomnia is one of the most common complaints in doctors' surgeries. It is often viewed as a particularly contemporary condition, a product of life-styles that are supposedly more stressful and hectic than they have ever been. But there is actually little agreement among sleep experts about whether we are sleeping less than we used to, and even whether this is a problem. The western tradition of getting seven or eight hours' contin-uous sleep is, after all, a recent development, a product of the arrival of sophisticated forms of artificial lighting in the eighteenth century which encouraged people to stay up late into the evening.[37]

Whether our anxieties about sleep are justified or not, manufacturers and advertisers have cottoned on to them. The bedroom has become a glorious escape from the stresses of the day, a promise of 'sweet and restful slumber' and 'night after night of bedtime bliss'. We can buy different types of bedside light to cast a soft, restful glow on the bed, creating the right mood for sleep. We can ditch our sweaty polyester duvets and nylon fitted sheets, and luxuriate in duck feather or goosedown pillows and duvets, and brushed Egyptian cotton sheets with a lavish 'thread count', which enclose us in their loving folds and creases. We can buy mattresses with individually pocketed springs and delicately responsive fillings which accommodate the uniqueness of our body shapes and our favourite sleeping positions. We can even buy mattresses divided into two halves of contrasting firmness for couples, or ones that adapt to the changing seasons – summer silk on one side, winter cashmere on the other. Falling asleep, and inducing the right kind of sleep, has become a market-driven lifestyle choice.

Right up until the moment we drift off each night, in other words, we are creatures of collective habit. This natural phenomenon of the single day, which we fill up with our quotidian routines, marks out our limits as social animals. If we are lucky, this day will be separated from the next one by a good few hours of lost consciousness – and here, since we are all narcissists in our dreams, the study of our shared daily life has to end. So now I'm just going to creep out, close the door quietly, and leave you to it.

Afterword: Habits of the heart

'What speaks to us, seemingly, is always the big event,
the untoward, the extra-ordinary: the front-page splash,
the banner headlines ... The daily papers talk of every-
thing except the daily ... We sleep through our lives in a
dreamless sleep'

Georges Perec[1]

'You will never look at ordinary things in the same way
again,' promised Charles Warrell to his young redskins.[2]
Warrell was the former headteacher who founded the I-
Spy book series for children in 1948, becoming the first and
most famous 'Big Chief'. During its heyday in the 1950s
and 1960s, the I-Spy club had half a million members.
But it was still going strong when I joined up, for a brief
but intense period, in the late 1970s. All the I-Spy books
had a list of potential sightings on a particular theme,
with points awarded for each spot. They were often
about very everyday things – *I-Spy on the Pavement*, for
example, being entirely devoted to street furniture like
coalhole covers, road signs and traffic lights. The points
you scored depended on how rare a sight was: five points
for a standard red telephone kiosk, say, fifteen for an old-
fashioned police box and thirty for something really rare
like a thatched bus shelter.

After accumulating the requisite number of points,
you got a parent to sign a disappointingly hedge-betting
endorsement ('I certify that I have examined the records in

this book, and as far as I can judge, the entries are genuine') and sent the book in the post to Big Chief I-Spy at the Wigwam-by-the-Green, which turned out, rather incongruously, to be just off London's Edgware Road. By the time I sent off my books, Big Chief was no longer Charles Warrell but a man with the slightly more indigenous-sounding name of Robin Tucek – although I imagine it was one of his braves who handled the paperwork, and who sent me, by return of post, an I-Spy badge. We members of the I-Spy tribe could also read a weekly column in the *Daily Mail* which ended with the coded catchphrase ODHU/NTINGGO (good hunting). As Julian Barnes, another former redskin, writes, 'This sort of enforced looking is … comparatively rare in our lives: on the whole, we seek out the things we are already interested in. Our habits of inspection and our view of the world are reconfirmed each time we concentrate our vision or avert our eye.'[3]

I think it was the I-Spy books that first inspired my interest in the strange invisibility of the quotidian, that unobserved area of our lives which is suddenly rendered exotic when we pay it the compliment of prolonged attention. But when we grow up, we are supposed to put away such childish things, and focus on more significant matters. In fact, we tend to infantilise those (usually male) unfortunates who retain such obscure interests into adulthood as 'geeks', 'anoraks' and 'trainspotters'. In any English thesaurus, the word 'everyday' is found alongside some rather unappealing terms: dull, workaday, common, monotonous, mundane, humdrum, run-of-the-mill. Then there are all those cult books about boring postcards, roundabouts, tea and biscuits, men and their sheds: the British in particular seem to find it hard to look at the everyday without dousing it liberally with irony and bathos (a trap into which I am sure I have also fallen).

Those who lived through the historical crises of the 1930s and 1940s might well have seen this sense of the banality of daily life as a hard-won luxury. During this period, simply getting through the day could be a matter of great discomfort and anxiety. In wartime, daily life was inescapably political. The government bombarded people with propaganda to show them how their everyday routines could be significant and meaningful, whether it was by donating saucepans to build spitfires, making and mending their own clothes or using only four inches of bathwater. But once post-war reconstruction began and shortages of basic necessities like food, housing and fuel became less acute, our social habits also became less troublesome and less visible. A new culture of consumption and affluence promised to relieve the drudgery of mundane life, tapping into the desires – for energy, abundance, stylishness, glamour – that this life did not fulfil. One symptom of this change was the way in which new forms of research into everyday life displaced the kind of domestic anthropology that Mass-Observation had practised. The growth industry of market research studied consumer lifestyle choices rather than our less conscious daily habits. Mass-Observation itself became Mass Observation UK Ltd, a more conventional market research company doing consumer surveys on products like toothpaste, fizzy drinks and washing powder. Like other similar companies, it focused on individual buying habits rather than 'anthropology at home'.

This emphasis on personal preference and self-image in our daily lives would seem very strange even to our immediate ancestors. The concept of lifestyle depends on the principle of individual choice: if you don't like your life, you can purchase a lifestyle. Private pleasures, from new kitchens to garden makeovers, can compensate for public tedium, from bus queues to boring meetings. But what I have tried to show in this book is that we can never be the sole, sovereign authors of our daily lives in this way. We cannot simply buy ourselves out of our involvement in each other's lives by upgrading to a better car or a nicer holiday. Quotidian life, that overlooked area of existence made up of our collective daily habits, always gets in the way. And we might as well start noticing it, because it is the life we have in common, and how we will fill most of the rest of our days.

We need the everyday, the familiar and the predictable: diary full, deadlines to meet, emails to answer, in-tray ticking over, cigarettes to smoke, telly to watch, sofa to slump on. Depressives often find that absorption in accustomed routines helps them to ward off melancholia. Habits allow us to take certain things for granted, put our brains on automatic pilot and get on with our lives. 'Continuity is no accident,' as the sociologist A. H. Halsey writes. 'Social customs, like personal habit, economize human effort. They store knowledge, pre-arrange decisions, save us the trouble of weighing every choice afresh.'[4] But our social habits can also be a hindrance to new ways of thinking and acting – because they are so bound up with collective attitudes and feelings that we simply accept unthinkingly. Our daily habits are, in the words of the nineteenth-century thinker Alexis de Tocqueville, 'habits of the heart'[5] – and when you have learned something off by heart, it is difficult to adapt to a new routine.

Our social habits are so often ignored and taken for granted that they only become truly visible when they are suddenly absent or changing. While I was in the middle of writing this book, two news stories illustrated this very well. In December 2005, London's Routemaster buses – the famous ones with the lopsided fronts and the open back platforms – finally went out of service after operating for nearly half a century. 'The Routemaster bus is being run off London's streets by political correctness,' lamented one of countless valedictory newspaper articles, in a reference to the poor disabled access that was one of the reasons for decommissioning it.[6] Websites like savetheroutemaster.com campaigned for the bus to be retained. The right-wing think-tank Policy Exchange produced a research paper in favour of keeping the bus or producing a 'child of Routemaster'.[7] There was even a well-timed book about 'the bus we loved' which celebrated its 'implacable, if polite, majesty' and condemned the new bendy buses for having 'all the aesthetics of the inside of a Hoover attachment'.[8]

Just as buses bunch up on a busy route, a very similar news story came along only a few weeks later. BBC Radio 4 announced that it was getting rid of its 'UK theme', a five-minute medley of traditional folk tunes which had begun the day's programming at 5.30 a.m. every day since 1973. Everyone seemed to want the UK theme to survive, even if they were always fast asleep when it was being broadcast. Eighteen thousand people signed an online petition against its removal, three MPs tabled motions about it in Parliament, the tune reached number twenty-nine in the UK singles chart and the chancellor, Gordon Brown, told the *Daily Mail* that it was 'one of the symbols of Britishness and a celebration of British culture'.[9]

Whatever the respective merits of the Routemaster and the Radio 4 UK theme, the acreage of newsprint expended on these phenomena was an interesting social phenomenon in itself. The disproportionate attention they received could be ascribed to the particular interests of metropolitan-based, early-rising journalists. But both stories also had a pleasingly melancholic finality – a familiar part of many people's daily routine was about to end for ever with the last bus arriving at the depot, or the last play of the tune before the change of schedule. This is how daily life appears to us – in isolated, fragmentary images and moments, before disappearing again into the endless progression of days. As days come and go, our social habits tend to seem as eternal and inevitable as the sun rising and setting – but as I have tried to show in this book, this is partly a consequence of our neglect of the familiar. We might nostalgically lament the passing of the Routemaster and the Radio 4 UK theme, but perhaps we should also remember to celebrate the end of freezing cold bedrooms, airless railway carriages, endless queuing and nothing to watch on telly but the test card. Daily life is changing all the time for better and worse – and much of it is as tedious, debilitating and unfair as it ever was. But if you can see that it is part of an ever-changing historical process, at least you know that a dull routine need not be a life sentence.

It is only when we start to notice our daily lives a little more that we realise they take place in historical time, not in an eternal present of endlessly recycled routines. One of my favourite true stories is about the East German man who borrowed three books from the American Memorial Library in West Berlin in August 1961, and failed to return them on time. He did have a cast-iron excuse for this very unGermanic dereliction of civic duty: a few days after he had checked the books out, the Berlin wall went up and blocked his route to the library. But the man kept hold of the books, hoping he would be able to return them one day. And so he did, in pristine condition, on 10 November 1989, the day after the wall came down.[10] It is a story that encapsulates the capacity of everyday routines to survive the most dramatic interruptions, the loyalty of people to communal rules – and the way that habits collide unpredictably with history and politics.

But the history of taking back our library books remains an oddly neglected area of study. What Tom Harrisson and Charles Madge argued in 1937 is still true. 'How little we know of our next door neighbour and his habits; how little we know of ourselves,' they wrote. 'Of conditions of life and thought in another class or district our ignorance is complete. The anthropology of ourselves is still only a dream.'[11] Fortunately, it is an anthropology that everyone

Notes

Introduction: The infra-ordinary

1. Raoul Vaneigem, *The Revolution of Everyday Life*, trans. Donald Nicholson-Smith (London: Rebel Press/Left Bank Books, [1967] 1994), p. 21.
2. Humphrey Jennings and Charles Madge (eds), *May the Twelfth: Mass-Observation Day Surveys 1937* (London: Faber and Faber, [1937] 1987), pp. 360–97.
3. Tom Harrisson, Humphrey Jennings and Charles Madge, 'Anthropology at home', *New Statesman and Nation*, 30 January 1937, p. 155.
4. Tom Harrisson, *Britain Revisited* (London: Victor Gollancz, 1961), p. 25; Tom Harrisson, *World Within: A Borneo Story* (London: Cresset, 1959), p. 158.
5. Charles Madge and Tom Harrisson, *Mass-Observation* (London: Frederick Muller, 1937), p. 29.
6. Walter Hood, 'Outing with a girl stranger, 19 April 1938', in Angus Calder and Dorothy Sheridan (eds), *Speak for Yourself: A Mass-Observation Anthology 1937–49* (London: Jonathan Cape, 1984), pp. 39–42.
7. Charles Madge and Tom Harrisson (eds), *First Year's Work 1937–38 by Mass-Observation* (London: Lindsay Drummond, 1938), p. 87.
8. Angus Calder, 'Introduction', in Tom Harrisson and Charles Madge, *Britain by Mass-Observation* (London: Cresset, [1939] 1986), p. vii.

9. Cassandra, 'What were you doing at 8.57 last night?', *Daily Mirror*, 25 June 1937.
10. Georges Perec, *Species of Spaces and Other Pieces*, ed. and trans. John Sturrock (London: Penguin, 1999), p. 210.
11. Siegfried Kracauer, 'Boredom', in *The Mass Ornament: Weimar Essays*, ed. and trans. Thomas Y. Levin (Cambridge, MA: Harvard University Press, 1995), pp. 331–2.
12. Lytton Strachey, *Eminent Victorians* (Harmondsworth: Penguin, [1918] 1986), p. 9.
13. Richard Steele, 'The hours of London', *Spectator*, 11 August 1712, reprinted in Rick Allen (ed.), *The Moving Pageant: A Literary Sourcebook on London Street-life, 1700–1914* (London: Routledge, 1998), pp. 42, 44.
14. Charles Dickens, 'The Streets – Morning' and 'The Streets – Night', in *Sketches by Boz* (London: J. M. Dent, [1836] 1968), pp. 42–46, 47–51.

1. Bacon and eggs to go

1. Perec, *Species of Spaces*, pp. 50, 210.
2. Arnold Palmer, *Movable Feasts: A Reconnaissance of the Origins and Consequences of Fluctuations in Meal-Times with Special Attention to the Introduction of Luncheon and Afternoon Tea* (Oxford: Oxford University Press, [1952] 1984), p. 74.
3. J. C. Drummond and Anne Wilbraham, *The Englishman's Food: A History of Five Centuries of English Diet* (London: Pimlico, [1939] 1991), p. 335.
4. A. P. Herbert, 'Bacon and Eggs', in *A Book of Ballads: Being the Collected Light Verse* (London: Ernest Benn, 1931), pp. 31–2.
5. 'Cooked breakfast', *The Times*, 14 August 1961.
6. Adverts in *The Times*, 17 October 1939 and 6 February 1940.

7. Mass-Observation, *Meet Yourself on Sunday* (London: Naldrett Press, 1949), p. 11.

8. David Pocock, 'Introduction', in Palmer, *Movable Feasts*, pp. xx–xxi.

9. Ron Noon, 'Goodbye, Mr Cube', *History Today*, October 2001, pp. 40–1.

10. Pocock, 'Introduction', in Palmer, *Movable Feasts*, p. xxi.

11. Edmund Leach, *A Runaway World? The Reith Lectures 1967* (London: BBC, 1968), p. 42; Edmund Leach, 'The cereal-packet norm', *Guardian*, 29 January 1968.

12. Ellen Lupton, *Mechanical Brides: Women and Machines from Home to Office* (Princeton, NJ: Princeton Architectural Press, 1993), pp. 5–6; advert in the *Daily Mirror* for Morphy-Richards toasters, 17 September 1964.

13. 'As others see us', *The Times*, 24 July 1961.

14. Paul Fussell, *Wartime: Understanding and Behavior in the Second World War* (New York: Oxford University Press, 1989), p. 47.

15. Miriam Akhtar and Steve Humphries, *The Fifties and Sixties: A Lifestyle Revolution* (London: Boxtree, 2001), p. 107.

16. Derek Cooper, *The Bad Food Guide* (London: Routledge and Kegan Paul, 1968), p. 182.

17. Elizabeth David, *English Bread and Yeast Cookery* (London: Allen Lane, 1977), pp. 35, 542.

18. *Delia's How to Cook*, BBC2, 20 October 1998.

19. Nigel Slater, 'Use your loaf', *Observer*, 13 March 1994.

20. Reyner Banham, 'Household godjets', in Paul Barker (ed.), *Arts in Society: A New Society Collection* (London: Fontana, 1977), p. 165.

21. Sigmund Freud, 'Civilization and its discontents', in *Civilization, Society and Religion*, trans. James Strachey (Harmondsworth: Penguin, 1991), p. 280.

22. Kellogg's Company of Great Britain, *Breakfast and the Changing British Lifestyle* (London: Kellogg's, 1977), no page numbers.

23. *Hansard (Commons), Fifth Series, Volume 852, 5–16 March 1973* (London: HMSO, 1973), p. 578.

24. 'Save your great British brekker!', *Daily Mirror*, 18 November 1974.

25. Pocock, 'Introduction', in Palmer, *Movable Feasts*, pp. xix–xx.

26. Christina Hardyment, *Slice of Life: The British Way of Eating Since 1945* (London: BBC Books, 1995), p. 201.

27. 'Cereal manufacturers may soon be facing a problem', *SuperMarketing*, 29 May 1987, p. 10.

28. Philippa Drewer (ed.), *Breakfast Cereals: Market Report 2004* (London: Key Note, 2004), p. 20.

29. Kellogg's Nutri-Grain packaging, 1997.

30. Andrew Gumbel, 'All set for the feeding frenzy', *Independent*, 3 February 1999.

31. Julian Barnes, *Flaubert's Parrot* (London: Jonathan Cape, 1984), p. 101.

2. Standing room only

1. Virginia Woolf, *Jacob's Room* (London: Grafton, [1922] 1976), p. 79.

2. Simon Garfield, *Our Hidden Lives: The Everyday Diaries of a Forgotten Britain 1945–1948* (London: Ebury, 2004), p. 96.

3. William Hazlitt, *Table Talk: Essays on Men and Manners* (London: J. M. Dent, [1822] 1959), p. 75.

4. *The Railway Traveller's Handy Book of Hints, Suggestions and Advice: Before the Journey, On the Journey and After the Journey*, ed. Jack Simmons (Bath: Adams and Dart, [1862] 1971), p. 62.

5. *The Railway Traveller's Handy Book*, p. 65.

6. 'Overcrowding in motor-omnibuses', *The Times*, 24 March 1906.

7. 'More comfort on the underground', *The Times*, 12 August 1924.

8. Geoffrey Kichenside, *150 Years of Railway Carriages: Railway History in Pictures* (Newton Abbot: David and Charles, 1981), p. 5.

9. Tom Harrisson, 'Demob diary', *New Statesman and Nation*, 28 September 1946, p. 221, quoted in Nick Hubble, *Mass-Observation and Everyday Life: Culture, History, Theory* (Basingstoke: Palgrave, 2006), p. 9; and Judith M. Heimann, *The Most Offending Soul Alive: Tom Harrisson and his Remarkable Life* (Honolulu: University of Hawaii Press, 1998), p. 241.

10. W. H. Auden, 'September 1, 1939', in *Selected Poems*, ed. Edward Mendelson (London: Faber and Faber, 1979), p. 88.

11. Jack Simmons and Gordon Biddle (eds.), *Oxford Companion to British Railway History: From 1603 to the 1990s* (Oxford: Oxford University Press, 1997), p. 96.

12. 'Champion commuter', *The Times*, 23 February 1963.

13. 'Constant seasons', *The Times*, 8 March 1956.

14. Fred Miller Robinson, *The Man in the Bowler Hat: His History and Iconography* (Chapel Hill, NC: University of North Carolina Press, 1993), pp. 166, 168.

15. Andrew Murray, *Off the Rails: The Crisis on Britain's Railways* (London: Verso, 2001), p. 9; Margaret Thatcher, speech representing 1989 Better Environment Awards for Industry, 16 March 1990, in Christopher Collins (ed.), *Margaret Thatcher: Complete Public Statements on CD-ROM* (Oxford: Oxford University Press, 1999).

16. See Christian Wolmar, *On the Wrong Line: How Ideology and Incompetence Wrecked Britain's Railways* (London: Aurum, 2005), p. 44.

17. See Wolmar, *On the Wrong Line*, p. 44.

18. Robert Wright, 'Ideas above their station', *Financial Times*, 22 October 2005; Jack Simmons, *The Victorian Railway* (London: Thames and Hudson, 1991), p. 362.
19. House of Commons Transport Committee, *Overcrowding on Public Transport* (London: Stationery Office, 2003), pp. 4–10, 23.
20. James Tozer, 'Overcrowded trains? OK, we'll rip out half the seats', *Daily Mail*, 2 August 2002.
21. Ben Webster, 'Q. How do you get more passengers on your train? A. Take out the seats', *The Times*, 2 October 2006.
22. Erving Goffman, *Behavior in Public Places: Notes on the Social Organization of Gatherings* (New York: Free Press, 1963), p. 83.
23. Erving Goffman, *Relations in Public: Microstudies of the Public Order* (London: Allen Lane, 1971), p. 125.
24. E. J. Poole-Connor, 'Points from letters', *The Times*, 7 August 1937.
25. 'Disturbance at a station', *The Times*, 19 August 1935.
26. G. I. Rees-Jones, 'Chivalry rewarded', *The Times*, 16 August 1961.
27. Richard Branson, *Losing My Virginity: The Autobiography* (London: Virgin, 1998), p. 358.

3. A lifetime behind a desk

1. Primo Levi, *The Wrench*, trans. William Weaver (London: Abacus, 1988), p. 80.
2. *Business Etiquette Handbook* (West Nyack: Parker Publishing Co., 1965), quoted in Max Nathan with Judith Doyle, *The State of the Office: The Politics and Geography of Working Space* (London: The Work Foundation, 2002), p. 24.
3. Adrian Forty, *Objects of Desire: Design and Society since 1750* (London: Thames and Hudson, 1986), p. 148.
4. Eric Larrabee, 'The cult of work: what is happening to the office?', *Industrial Design*, 1 (April 1954), p. 21.

5. Forty, *Objects of Desire*, pp. 140, 143, 147.

6. Forty, *Objects of Desire*, p. 153.

7. John R. Berry, *Herman Miller: Classic Furniture and System Designs for the Working Environment* (London: Thames and Hudson, 2004), p. 194.

8. Robert Propst, *The Office – A Facility Based on Change* (Elmhurst, IL: Business Press, 1968), pp. 21–25.

9. Philip J. Stone and Robert Luchetti, 'Your office is where you are', *Harvard Business Review*, 63: 2 (March–April 1985), p. 103.

10. Stone and Luchetti, 'Your office is where you are', p. 102.

11. Berry, *Herman Miller*, p. 125.

12. Newspaper clipping exhibited at the 'Office Politics: Women in the Workplace 1860–2004' exhibition held at the Women's Library, London Metropolitan University, 12 February–1 May 2004.

13. 'Why girls prefer "modesty boards …"', *Daily Mirror*, 12 August 1965.

14. J. Manser, 'New thinking in office furniture', *Design*, 236 (1968), p. 16.

15. Joy Hendry, *Wrapping Culture: Politeness, Presentation and Power in Japan and Other Societies* (Oxford: Clarendon Press, 1993), p. 124.

16. Diana Rowntree, 'Desk and chair: basic tools of urban life', *Design*, 105 (1957), p. 17.

17. Berry, *Herman Miller*, p. 130.

18. Berry, *Herman Miller*, p. 133.

19. Berry, *Herman Miller*, p. 203.

20. Tom Newton Dunn, 'MoD wastes millions on posh chairs', *Sun*, 12 July 2004.

21. Darrin Zeer, *Office Feng Shui* (San Francisco: Chronicle Books, 2004), p. 17.

22. See the 'Office Doctors' website at http://www.officedoctors.co.uk (accessed on 3 July 2006).

23. Meredith M. Wells, 'Office clutter or meaningful personal displays: the role of office personalization in employee and organizational well-being', *Journal of Environmental Psychology*, 20:3 (September 2000), p. 246.

24. Samuel D. Gosling, Sei Jin Ko, Thomas Mannarelli and Margaret E. Morris, 'A room with a cue: personality judgments based on offices and bedrooms', *Journal of Personality and Social Psychology*, 82:3 (2002), pp. 379–98. See also Jennifer Drapkin, 'Betrayed by your desk', *Psychology Today*, July/August 2005, pp. 34–5.

25. See Abigail J. Sellen and Richard H. R. Harper, *The Myth of the Paperless Office* (Cambridge, MA: MIT Press, 2002); Malcolm Gladwell, 'The social life of paper', *New Yorker*, 25 March 2002, pp. 92–6; and Eric Abrahamson and David H. Freedman, *A Perfect Mess: The Hidden Benefits of Disorder* (Boston: Little, Brown, 2007).

26. Nathan, *The State of the Office*, p. 22.

27. Stone and Luchetti, 'Your office is where you are', pp. 103, 111.

28. Berry, *Herman Miller*, p. 209.

29. Sana Siwolop, 'Stepping out from its cubicle', *New York Times*, 15 February 1998.

30. Description of Herman Miller furniture at http://www.hmeurope.com (accessed on 4 September 2006).

31. Francis Duffy, *The New Office* (London: Conran Octopus, 1997), pp. 8–10.

32. Nathan, *The State of the Office*, p. 6.

33. John Heskett, *Toothpicks and Logos: Design in Everyday Life* (Oxford: Oxford University Press, 2002), pp. 112–14.

34. Nathan, *The State of the Office*, pp. 24, 28.

35. Nathan, *The State of the Office*, p. 19.

4. The word from the water cooler

1. Jonathan Gathorne-Hardy, *The Office* (London: Hodder and Stoughton, 1970), p. 7.

2. Sinclair Lewis, *The Job* (London: Jonathan Cape, [1917] 1929), p. 229.

3. Entry in the *Oxford English Dictionary*.

4. Mass-Observation, *War Factory* (London: Cresset, [1943] 1987), pp. 30–31.

5. Paul Vaughan, *Exciting Times in the Accounts Department* (London: Sinclair-Stevenson, 1995), p. 12.

6. 'Are vending machines the answer to tea strikes?', *The Times*, 26 September 1962.

7. Anthony M. Perry, 'Vending machines: a special report', *The Times*, 12 February 1968.

8. 'Row brews up over the civil servants' robot cuppa', *Daily Mirror*, 2 June 1969; 'Queue here for a ghost cuppa', *Daily Mirror*, 10 March 1978.

9. Robert Propst speaking in 1998, quoted in John R. Berry, *Herman Miller: Classic Furniture and System Designs for the Working Environment* (London: Thames and Hudson, 2004), p. 125.

10. Jacqueline Simpson and Steve Roud, *A Dictionary of English Folklore* (Oxford: Oxford University Press, 2000), p. 277. See also Michael J. Preston, 'Xerox-lore', *Keystone Folklore Quarterly*, 19 (1974), pp. 11–26.

11. Cahal Milmo, 'After 50 years, KitKat takes a break from the slogan that made its name', *Independent*, 3 August 2004.

12. 'Our favourite ways to waste some time', *Personnel Today*, 25 July 2000, quoted in Judith Doyle, *New Community or New Slavery? The Emotional Division of Labour* (London: The Industrial Society, 2000), p. 8.

13. Robin Dunbar, *Grooming, Gossip and the Evolution of Language* (London: Faber and Faber, 1996), p. 123.

14. John R. Weeks, *Unpopular Culture: The Ritual of Complaint in a British Bank* (Chicago: University of Chicago Press, 2003), p. 3.

15. Weeks, *Unpopular Culture*, pp. 67–73.

16. Weeks, *Unpopular Culture*, p. 10.

17. Dunbar, *Grooming, Gossip and the Evolution of Language*, pp. 204, 207.

18. Richard Sennett, *The Corrosion of Character* (New York: Norton, 1998), pp. 15–31; Ray Pahl, *On Friendship* (Cambridge: Polity, 2000), p. 169.

19. Francis Duffy, *The New Office* (London: Conran Octopus, 1997), p. 61.

20. Michael Moynagh and Richard Worsley, *Tomorrow's Workplace: Fulfilment or Stress?* (Kings Lynn: The Tomorrow Project, 2001), pp. 27–8.

21. Francis Green, David Ashton, Brendan Burchell, Bryn Davies and Alan Felstead, 'Are British workers getting more skilled?', in A. B. Atkinson and John Hills (eds), *Exclusion, Employment and Opportunity* (London: London School of Economics, 1998), pp. 117–18.

22. Barrie Clement, 'Cappuccino crisis almost sent London down tube', *Independent*, 3 December 1996.

23. D. J. Taylor, 'Why everything still stops for tea', *Independent*, 21 August 2001.

24. See Malcolm Gladwell, 'Java man', *New Yorker*, 30 July 2001, p. 78.

25. UCL Space Syntax, 'Work environments' (2001), at http://www.spacesyntax.com, quoted in Max Nathan with Judith Doyle, *The State of the Office: The Politics and Geography of Working Space* (London: The Work Foundation, 2002), p. 9.

26. Nathan, *The State of the Office*, p. 25; see also Philip J. Stone and Robert Luchetti, 'Your office is where you are', *Harvard Business Review*, 63:2 (March–April 1985), p. 108; and Thomas J. Allen, *Managing*

the Flow of Technology: Technology Transfer and the
Dissemination of Technological Information Within the
R&D Organization (Cambridge, MA: MIT Press, 1977),
pp. 238–9.

5. Cashier number *one*, please

1. Siegfried Kracauer, *The Salaried Masses: Duty and Distraction in Weimar Germany*, trans. Quintin Hoare (London: Verso, 1998), p. 62.
2. Thomas Carlyle, *The French Revolution: A History in Three Parts, Volume 1* (London: Methuen, [1837] 1902), p. 307.
3. George Orwell, 'The English people', in Sonia Orwell and Ian Angus (eds), *The Collected Essays, Journalism and Letters of George Orwell, Volume 3: As I Please 1943–1945* (Harmondsworth: Penguin, 1970), p. 16.
4. George Mikes, *How to be an Alien: A Handbook for Beginners and More Advanced Pupils* (Harmondsworth: Penguin, [1946] 1966), p. 48.
5. Ernest Barker, 'An attempt at perspective', in Barker (ed.), *The Character of England* (Oxford: Clarendon Press, 1947), p. 562.
6. Barker, 'An attempt at perspective', p. 562.
7. Ina Zweiniger-Bargielowska, *Austerity in Britain: Rationing, Controls, and Consumption 1939–1955* (Oxford: Oxford University Press, 2000), p. 118.
8. Quoted in James Hinton, 'Militant housewives: the British Housewives' League and the Attlee government', *History Workshop Journal*, 38 (Autumn 1994), p. 129.
9. Gareth Shaw, Louise Curth and Andrew Alexander, 'Selling self-service and the supermarket: the Americanisation of food retailing in Britain, 1945–60', *Business History*, 46:4 (October 2004), p. 572.

10. Louise Curth, Gareth Shaw and Andrew Alexander, 'Streamlining shopping', *History Today* (November 2002), p. 35.

11. '70 new self-service shops a month', *The Times*, 9 March 1959.

12. 'Waits at supermarkets', *The Times*, 27 May 1964.

13. Correlli Barnett, *The Lost Victory: British Dreams, British Realities, 1945–1950* (London: Macmillan, 1995), p. 174.

14. David Butler and Dennis Kavanagh, *The British General Election of 1979* (Basingstoke: Macmillan, 1980), p. 140.

15. '"Epoch-making" poster was clever fake', BBC News Online, 16 March 2001, http://news.bbc.co.uk (accessed on 4 May 2005).

16. George Orwell, 'The lion and the unicorn: socialism and the English genius', in Sonia Orwell and Ian Angus (eds), *The Collected Essays, Journalism and Letters of George Orwell, Volume 2: My Country Right or Left 1940–1943* (Harmondsworth: Penguin, 1970), pp. 75–6.

17. 'Keeping people in line', *Director* (May 1996), p. 18.

18. Barry Schwartz, *Queuing and Waiting: Studies in the Social Organization of Access and Delay* (Chicago: University of Chicago Press, 1975), p. 99.

19. Mintel, *Customer Care in Retailing – UK* (London: Mintel, 2001).

20. Michael Portillo, 'The Conservative agenda' (speech to North-East Fife Conservative Association in Freuchie, 22 April 1994), in George Gardiner (ed.), *Clear Blue Water: A Compendium of Speeches and Interviews given by the Rt Hon Michael Portillo MP* (London: Conservative Way Forward, 1994), p. 38.

21. Shyama Perera, 'Queuing', in *British Greats* (London: Cassell, 2000), p. 186.

22. Professor Cary Cooper, quoted in Jo Revill, 'Queue the Irritation', *Observer*, 26 October 2003; see also David Stewart-David, *The Stressful Queue* (Newcastle: Newcastle Business School, 2003).

6. Dining al desko

1. Michel de Certeau, *The Practice of Everyday Life*, trans. Steven Rendall (Berkeley, CA: University of California Press, 1984), p. 108.
2. 'Graphic of the week: food for thought', *Guardian*, 28 January 2006.
3. Arnold Palmer, *Movable Feasts: A Reconnaissance of the Origins and Consequences of Fluctuations in Meal-Times with Special Attention to the Introduction of Luncheon and Afternoon Tea* (Oxford: Oxford University Press, [1952] 1984), pp. 150–1.
4. Harry Hopkins, *The New Look: A Social History of the Forties and Fifties in Britain* (London: Secker and Warburg, 1963), p. 153.
5. Advert in *The Times*, 22 November 1962.
6. Steve Humphries and John Taylor, *The Making of Modern London, 1945–1985* (London: Sidgwick and Jackson, 1986), p. 71.
7. Robert Bell, 'Luncheon vouchers', *The Times*, 15 August 1960.
8. Cited in Connie Robertson (ed.), *Wordsworth Dictionary of Quotations* (Ware: Wordsworth, 1998), p. 251.
9. H. D. Renner, *The Origin of Food Habits* (London: Faber and Faber, 1944), pp. 223–4.
10. Reader's Digest, *Yesterday's Britain: The Illustrated Story of How We Lived, Worked and Played* (London: Reader's Digest Association, 1998), p. 252.
11. Quoted in Godfrey Smith, 'It's not high noon for lunch', *Sunday Times Magazine*, 17 July 2005.

12. Michael Bracewell, *Perfect Tense* (London: Jonathan Cape, 2001), pp. 125, 127.
13. Paul Nathanson, 'Small business: butties come by runner', *Financial Times*, 1 March 1985.
14. Richard Boston, *Beer and Skittles* (London: Collins, 1976), p. 144.
15. Ralph T. King Jr, 'Sub standard: these sandwich makers aren't seen as heroes', *Wall Street Journal*, 14 May 1997.
16. Judi Bevan, *The Rise and Fall of Marks & Spencer* (London: Profile, 2001), p. 118.
17. Hopkins, *The New Look*, p. 314.
18. Bevan, *The Rise and Fall of Marks & Spencer*, pp. 119–20.
19. Janette Marshall, 'A day in the life of a sandwich in a million', *Independent*, 8 June 1991.
20. Mandy Rowbotham, 'And so to bread – eating in or taking out, the sandwich is big business', *Guardian*, 14 July 1990.
21. Keith Waterhouse, *The Theory and Practice of Lunch* (London: Michael Joseph, 1986), pp. 99, 4.
22. Mintel, *Sandwiches – UK – October 2005* (London: Mintel, 2005).
23. YouGov poll, March 2005, available at http://www.benjys-sandwiches.com (accessed on 3 March 2006).
24. Tony May, 'Using a down-market carat to beat recession', *Guardian*, 23 April 1991.
25. Dominic Fifield, 'Who ate all the prawns?', *Guardian*, 10 November 2000.
26. Barry Schwartz, *The Paradox of Choice: Why More is Less* (New York: Harper Perennial, 2005), pp. 77–9, 225–6.
27. Marshall, 'A day in the life of a sandwich in a million'.

7. The dread of the inbox

1. Quoted in Ben Highmore, 'Questioning Everyday Life', in Highmore (ed.), *The Everyday Life Reader* (London: Routledge, 2002), p. 21.

2. *The eHealth Traffic Accountant* (New York: Concord Business Service Management, 2005), p. 8.

3. Daniel Pool, *What Jane Austen Ate and Charles Dickens Knew: Fascinating Facts of Daily Life in the Nineteenth Century* (London: Robinson, 1998), pp. 129–130.

4. Frank Kermode and Anita Kermode, 'Introduction', in Frank Kermode and Anita Kermode (eds), *The Oxford Book of Letters* (Oxford: Oxford University Press, 1995), p. xx.

5. Victorian, 'Your obedient servant', *The Times*, 9 January 1930.

6. Another Victorian, 'After compliments', *The Times*, 16 January 1930.

7. Neil A. Parker, 'Faithfully whose?', *The Times*, 19 December 1968.

8. Alan S. C. Ross, 'U and non-U: an essay in sociological linguistics', in Nancy Mitford (ed.), *Noblesse Oblige* (London: Hamish Hamilton, 1956), p. 18.

9. Nancy Mitford, 'The English Aristocracy', in Mitford (ed.), *Noblesse Oblige*, p. 43.

10. J. P. W. Mallalieu, 'Forms of address', *The Times*, 24 August 1962.

11. Chris Partridge, 'Electronic mail delivers late', *The Times*, 23 April 1991.

12. S. G. Price, *Introducing the Electronic Office* (Manchester: National Computing Centre, 1979), p. 45.

13. Ken Young, 'Passing on the message faster', *The Times*, 24 October 1988.

14. 'Electronic mail can send character based messages', *Guardian*, 14 March 1988.

15. Katie Hafner and Matthew Lyon, *Where Wizards Stay Up Late: The Origins of the Internet* (New York: Simon and Schuster, 1996), p. 188.

16. 'The usage of electronic mail is rapidly increasing', *Economist*, 8 March 1987, p. 75.

17. 'Electronic mail can send character based messages'.

18. Simeon J. Yates, 'Computer-mediated communication: the future of the letter?', in David Barton and Nigel Hall (eds), *Letter Writing as a Social Practice* (Amsterdam: John Benjamins, 2000), p. 243.

19. Guy Kawasaki, *The Guy Kawasaki Computer Curmudgeon* (Carmel, IN: Hayden Books, 1992), cited in David Angell and Brett Heslop, *Elements of E-mail Style: Communicate Effectively via Electronic Mail* (Reading, MA: Addison Wesley, 1992), p. 3.

20. David A. Owens, Margaret A. Neale and Robert I. Sutton, 'Technologies of status management: status dynamics in e-mail communications', in M. A. Neale, E. A. Mannix and T. L. Griffith (eds), *Research on Groups and Teams, Volume 3: Technology* (Greenwich, CT: JAI Press, 2000), pp. 205–30. See also Bruce Headlam, 'How to e-mail like a CEO', *New York Times*, 8 April 2001.

21. David Crystal, *Language and the Internet* (Cambridge: Cambridge University Press, 2001), pp. 122–4.

22. Mitford, 'The English Aristocracy', p. 42.

23. Ann Barr and Peter York, *The Official Sloane Ranger Handbook: The First Guide to What Really Matters in Life* (London: Ebury, 1982), pp. 54–5.

24. See John Morgan, *Debrett's New Guide to Etiquette and Modern Manners* (London: Headline, 1996), pp. 175–6.

25. David Hewson, 'Why e-mail is now the new first-class post', *Sunday Times*, 30 March 2003.

26. Richard Tyrell, 'The internet is not all listed buildings', *The Times*, 2 March 1999.

27. Barry Collins, 'E-mail trouble', *Sunday Times*, 18 February 2001.

28. Joel Best, *Damned Lies and Statistics: Untangling Numbers from the Media, Politicians, and Activists* (Berkeley, CA: University of California Press, 2001), p. 13.

29. Nic Paton, 'The solution to inbox overload', *Daily Telegraph*, 5 September 2002.

30. Max Nathan with Judith Doyle, *The State of the Office: The Politics and Geography of Working Space* (London: The Work Foundation, 2002), p. 25.

31. 'E-mails prove unfit', *Sunday Express*, 16 October 2005; see also 'Physical perks', *The Times*, 31 October 2005.

32. Paton, 'The solution to inbox overload'.

33. 'Computer horizons: at home with the cabinet secrets', *The Times*, 14 January 1986.

34. Abigail J. Sellen and Richard H. R. Harper, *The Myth of the Paperless Office* (Cambridge, MA: MIT Press, 2002), pp. 13–14.

35. C. Northcote Parkinson, *Parkinson's Law: Or, the Pursuit of Progress* (Harmondsworth: Penguin, [1957] 1986), p. 14.

36. Kermode and Kermode, 'Introduction', p. xxiii.

37. Tom Phillips, *The Postcard Century: 2000 Cards and Their Messages* (London: Thames and Hudson, 2000).

8. Puffing al fresco

1. Mignon McLaughlin, *The Second Neurotic's Notebook* (Indianapolis: Bobbs-Merrill, 1966).

2. 'Smoke abatement', *The Times*, 21 January 1952.

3. Matthew Hilton, *Smoking in British Popular Culture, 1800–2000: Perfect Pleasures* (Manchester: Manchester University Press, 2000), p. 52.

4. Jack Simmons and Gordon Biddle (eds), *Oxford Companion to British Railway History: From 1603 to the*

1990s (Oxford: Oxford University Press, 1997), pp. 454–5.

5. Hilton, *Smoking in British Popular Culture*, p. 28.

6. Virginia Berridge, 'Passive smoking and its pre-history in Britain', *Social Science and Medicine*, 49:9 (November 1999), p. 1,185. See also Hilton, *Smoking in British Popular Culture*, p. 76.

7. 'Smokers, non-smokers and the rest', *The Times*, 1 November 1938.

8. Charles Madge and Tom Harrisson (eds), *First Year's Work 1937–38 by Mass-Observation* (London: Lindsay Drummond, 1938), pp. 12–14.

9. Hilton, *Smoking in British Popular Culture*, p. 124.

10. Harry Hopkins, *The New Look: A Social History of the Forties and Fifties in Britain* (London: Secker and Warburg, 1963), p. 42.

11. Edward Lyttleton, 'Non-smoking carriages', *The Times*, 24 March 1941.

12. Simmons and Biddle, *Oxford Companion to British Railway History*, p. 455.

13. 'Most young men "prefer the sack to a haircut"', *Daily Mirror*, 28 April 1969.

14. Sean Gabb, *Smoking and its Enemies: A Short History of 500 Years of the Use and Prohibition of Tobacco* (London: Forest, 1990), p. 2.

15. Jill Sherman, 'Passive smoking "can be an industrial accident"', *The Times*, 30 August 1990.

16. Francis Elliott and Abigail Townsend, 'Reid in secret talks on smoking ban', *Independent on Sunday*, 11 July 2004.

17. 'New York's defiant band of nicotine addicts', *Financial Times*, 9 April 1988.

18. Peter H. King, 'What have we been smoking?', *Los Angeles Times*, 23 October 1994.

19. Naush Boghossian, 'Anti-smoking area extended', *Los Angeles Daily News*, 3 January 2004.

20. Rachelle Thackray, 'No smoke without gossip', *Independent*, 10 June 1998.

21. Alison Maitland, 'When workers have to take to the streets', *Financial Times*, 7 July 1998.

22. *Smoke-free Premises and Vehicles: Consultation on Proposed Regulations* (London: Department of Health, 2006), p. 29; Philip Webster, 'Move to ban smoking from office doorways', *The Times*, 21 June 2006.

23. Advertisement for smoking shelter at http://www.nobutts.co.uk (accessed on 3 December 2005).

24. Madge and Harrisson, *First Year's Work*, p. 22.

25. Tom Harrisson, *Britain Revisited* (London: Victor Gollancz, 1961), pp. 196–7.

26. Mass-Observation report on 'Man and his cigarette' (1949), quoted in Hilton, *Smoking in British Popular Culture*, p. 125.

27. Harrisson, *Britain Revisited*, p. 199.

28. Richard Klein, *Cigarettes are Sublime* (London: Picador, 1995), p. 26.

29. Klein, *Cigarettes are Sublime*, p. 31.

30. Klein, *Cigarettes are Sublime*, p. 105.

31. Quoted in Hilton, *Smoking in British Popular Culture*, p. 129.

9. Any other business?

1. Marcel Proust, *Remembrance of Things Past, Volume Three: The Captive*, trans. C. K. Scott Moncrieff, Terence Kilmartin and Andreas Mayor (London: Chatto and Windus, [1927] 1981), p. 37.

2. William H. Whyte, *The Organization Man* (London: Jonathan Cape, 1957), p. 55.

3. Bertram W. Strauss and Frances Strauss, *New Ways to Better Meetings* (London: Tavistock, 1966), pp. vii, 3.

4. Strauss and Strauss, *New Ways to Better Meetings*, pp. 75, 8, 10–14.

5. B. Y. Augur, *How to Run Better Business Meetings: A Businessman's Guide to Meetings that Get Things Done* (St Paul, MN: Business Services Press, 1966), p. 7.

6. Whyte, *The Organization Man*, p. 47.

7. Whyte, *The Organization Man*, p. 55.

8. William H. Whyte, 'Group think', *Fortune* (March 1952), pp. 114–17, 145–6.

9. Strauss and Strauss, *New Ways to Better Meetings*, p. 51.

10. Strauss and Strauss, *New Ways to Better Meetings*, p. 59.

11. Alex F. Osborn, *Applied Imagination: Principles and Procedures of Creative Problem-Solving*, 3rd edn (New York: Charles Scribners, 1963), pp. 151–96.

12. '"Brainstorming" as a fount of business ideas', *The Times*, 10 March 1959.

13. Kenneth Owen, 'IBM: a way of life with its own culture', *The Times*, 11 November 1974.

14. John Mole, *Mind Your Manners: Culture Clash in the European Single Market* (London: The Industrial Society, 1990), p. 101.

15. C. Northcote Parkinson, *Parkinson's Law: Or, the Pursuit of Progress* (Harmondsworth: Penguin, [1957] 1986), p. 40.

16. John Algeo (ed.), *Fifty Years Among the New Words: A Dictionary of Neologisms* (Cambridge: Cambridge University Press, 1991), p. 169.

17. Walter Citrine, *The ABC of Chairmanship: All About Meetings and Conferences* (London: Co-operative Printing Society Ltd, [1939] 1948).

18. Thomas J. Peters and Robert H. Waterman, Jr, *In Search of Excellence: Lessons from America's Best-Run Companies* (New York: Harper and Row 1982), p. 77.

19. John R. Weeks, *Unpopular Culture: The Ritual of Complaint in a British Bank* (Chicago: University of Chicago Press, 2003), p. 3.

20. Lynn Oppenheim, *Making Meetings Matter: A Report to the 3M Corporation* (Philadelphia, PA: Wharton Center for Applied Research, 1987), p. 2.

21. The 3M Meeting Management Team with Jeannine Drew, *Mastering Meetings: Discovering the Hidden Potential of Effective Business Meetings* (New York: McGraw-Hill, 1994), p. 171.

22. Weeks, *Unpopular Culture*, pp. 14–15.

23. The 3M Meeting Management Team, *How to Run Better Business Meetings: A Reference Guide for Managers* (New York: McGraw-Hill, 1987), p. vii.

24. Jack Schofield, 'The graphic new business', *Guardian*, 25 August 1988.

25. Francis Green, David Ashton, Brendan Burchell, Bryn Davies and Alan Felstead, 'Are British workers getting more skilled?', in A. B. Atkinson and John Hills (eds), *Exclusion, Employment and Opportunity* (London: London School of Economics, 1998), p. 118.

26. Edward Tufte, *The Cognitive Style of PowerPoint* (Cheshire, CT: Graphics Press, 2003), p. 24.

27. Harry G. Frankfurt, 'On bullshit', in *The Importance of What We Care About: Philosophical Essays* (Cambridge: Cambridge University Press, 1988), pp. 132–3.

28. 3M, *Mastering Meetings*, p. 14.

29. 3M, *Mastering Meetings*, pp. 195, 6.

30. 3M, *Mastering Meetings*, p. 198.

31. Karl Marx and Friedrich Engels, *The Communist Manifesto*, in *Marx and Engels: Selected Works* (London: Lawrence and Wishart, 1968), p. 38.

32. Helen B. Schwartzman, *The Meeting: Gatherings in Organizations and Communities* (New York: Plenum Press, 1989), pp. 44, 4, 42.

33. Maurice Bloch, 'Decision-making in councils among the Merina of Madagascar', in Audrey Richards and Adam Kuper (eds), *Councils in Action* (Cambridge: Cambridge University Press, 1971), pp. 47–51.

34. Schwartzman, *The Meeting*, pp. 13–45.

35. Joy Hendry, *Wrapping Culture: Politeness, Presentation and Power in Japan and Other Societies* (Oxford: Clarendon Press, 1993), p. 144; Deborah Tannen, *Talking from 9 to 5: How Women's and Men's Conversational Styles Affect Who Gets Heard, Who Gets Credit, and What Gets Done at Work* (London: Virago, 1995), p. 305.

36. Charlotte Baker, quoted in Tannen, *Talking from 9 to 5*, p. 279.

10. The ministry of sensible walks

1. Siegfried Kracauer, *The Salaried Masses: Duty and Distraction in Weimar Germany*, trans. Quintin Hoare (London: Verso, 1998), p. 29.

2. 'Pedestrian rights', *The Times*, 20 July 1937.

3. Peter Thorold, *The Motoring Age: The Automobile and Britain 1896–1939* (London: Profile, 2003), p. 206.

4. 'Worst week on record for road deaths', *Daily Telegraph*, 4 January 1935.

5. 'A mile of pedestrian barriers', *The Times*, 28 May 1936.

6. 'How not to cross the road', *The Times*, 9 October 1936.

7. George Charlesworth, *A History of the Transport and Road Research Laboratory 1933–1983* (Aldershot: Avebury, 1987), pp. 104–6.

8. Charlesworth, *A History of the Transport and Road Research Laboratory*, p. 108.

9. 'Contribution to brief for debate on private member's motion: pedestrian crossings', January 1964, National Archives, MT 112/167.

10. 'News in brief', *The Times*, 3 November 1951.

11. Ministry of Transport, *The Highway Code*, 4th edn (London: HMSO, 1954), p. 5.

12. Department of the Environment, *Pedestrian Safety* (London: HMSO, 1973), p. 21.

13. Footage on the BBC 'On this day' website at http://news.bbc.co.uk/onthisday (accessed on 5 July 2006).

14. 'Does a faulty panda become a zebra?', *The Times*, 18 May 1962.

15. Letters in *The Times*, 10 September 1962.

16. Martin Wainwright, 'Zebras get the hump', *Guardian*, 19 August 1986.

17. See Otto Neurath, *International Picture Language* (London: Kegan Paul, 1936); and Nancy Cartwright, Jordi Cat, Lola Fleck and Thomas E. Uebel, *Otto Neurath: Philosophy between Science and Politics* (Cambridge: Cambridge University Press, 1996), p. 85.

18. *Pelican Crossing – Pedestrians – Cast of 'Dad's Army'* (Central Office of Information, 1974).

19. *Pelican Crossing Song – Paul Greenwood* (Central Office of Information, 1976).

20. Colin Buchanan, speech on 'Building and planning in the motor age' at the RIBA conference in Coventry, 11 July 1962, quoted in 'Britain needs the "Traffic Architect"', *The Times*, 12 July 1962.

21. Ministry of Transport, *Traffic in Towns: A Study of the Long-Term Problems of Traffic in Urban Areas* (London: HMSO, 1963).

22. Buchanan quoted in 'Shoppers repudiate Buchanan theory', *The Times*, 21 September 1966.

23. Bob Stanley, 'Taking a walk in the clouds', *The Times*, 24 August 2004; see also David Heathcote, *Barbican: Penthouse Over the City* (London: Wiley-Academy, 2004), p. 71.

24. Robert Davis, *Death on the Streets: Cars and the Mythology of Road Safety* (Hawes: Leading Edge, 1993), p. 200.

25. Quoted in Nick Tiratsoo, 'The reconstruction of blitzed British cities, 1945–55: myths and reality', *Contemporary British History*, 14:1 (Spring 2000), pp. 36–7.

26. Gehl Architects, *Towards a Fine City for People: Public Spaces and Public Life – London, June 2004* (London: Central London Partnership, 2004), pp. 32–5.

27. Paul Eastam, 'The ministry of silly walks?', *Daily Mail*, 4 September 1999; Boris Johnson, 'Face it: it's all your own fat fault', *Daily Telegraph*, 27 May 2004.

28. Sean O'Connell, *The Car in British Society: Class, Gender and Motoring 1896–1939* (Manchester: Manchester University Press, 1998), pp. 119–20.

29. Jake Desyllas, 'The cost of bad street design', in Commission for Architecture and the Built Environment, *The Cost of Bad Design* (London: CABE, 2006), pp. 40–41.

30. Office for National Statistics, *Social Trends no. 36* (Basingstoke: Palgrave Macmillan, 2006), p. 186.

31. Desyllas, 'The cost of bad street design', pp. 35–6; see also Gehl Architects, *Towards a Fine City for People*, pp. 42–3.

11. Not just here for the beer

1. Virginia Woolf, *Mrs Dalloway* (London: Penguin, [1925] 1996), p. 55.

2. 'If you want to get ahead', *Credit Management*, October 2003, p. 12. See also Edward Stringham and Bethany L. Peters, 'No booze? You may lose: why drinkers earn more money than non-drinkers', *Journal of Labor Research*, 27:3 (Summer 2006), pp. 411–21, for a US study with similar findings.

3. Mass-Observation, *The Pub and the People: A Worktown Study* (London: Cresset, [1943] 1987), p. 252.

4. Tom Harrisson, *Britain Revisited* (London: Victor Gollancz, 1961), p. 194 (italics in the original).

5. Anthony Sampson, *Anatomy of Britain* (London: Hodder and Stoughton, 1962), p. 576.
6. 'Pleasing all palates', *The Times*, 29 April 1958.
7. Roger Protz, *Pulling a Fast One: What Your Brewers Have Done to Your Beer* (London: Pluto Press, 1978), p. 50.
8. Protz, *Pulling a Fast One*, p. 51.
9. Pete Brown, *Man Walks into a Pub: A Sociable History of Beer* (London: Macmillan, 2003), p. 285; Martyn Cornell, *Beer: The Story of the Pint: The History of Britain's Most Popular Drink* (London: Headline, 2003), p. 219.
10. J.Y., 'Marketing approach to keg puts cart before horse', *The Times*, 26 April 1971.
11. George Orwell, *The Road to Wigan Pier* (Harmondsworth: Penguin, [1937] 1989), p. 66.
12. George Orwell, 'The Moon Under Water', in Sonia Orwell and Ian Angus (eds), *The Collected Essays, Journalism and Letters of George Orwell, Volume 3: As I Please 1943–1945* (Harmondsworth: Penguin, 1970), p. 63.
13. Brown, *Man Walks into a Pub*, p. 335.
14. Protz, *Pulling a Fast One*, p. 12.
15. Protz, *Pulling a Fast One*, p. 14.
16. Mass-Observation, *The Pub and the People*, p. 218.
17. Maurice Gorham, *Back to the Local* (London: Percival Marshall, 1949), p. 85.
18. Harrisson, *Britain Revisited*, p. 183.
19. Ben Davis, *The Traditional English Pub: A Way of Drinking* (London: Architectural Press, 1981), p. 62.
20. Peter Martin, 'Eat, drink and be merry', *Observer*, 25 May 1997.
21. Richard Hoggart, *Townscape with Figures: Farnham, Portrait of an English Town* (London: Chatto and Windus, 1994), p. 49.

22. Ray Oldenburg, *The Great Good Place: Cafés, Coffee Shops, Community Centers, Beauty Parlors, General Stores, Bars, Hangouts and How They Get You Through the Day* (New York: Paragon House, 1989), p. xi.

23. Christian Mikunda, *Brand Lands, Hot Spots and Cool Spaces: Welcome to the Third Place and the Total Marketing Experience* (London: Kogan Page, 2004), p. 5. See also Markman Ellis, *The Coffee House: A Cultural History* (London: Weidenfeld and Nicolson, 2004), p. 256.

24. Peter Millar, 'Where women may safely graze and swallow', *Financial Times*, 7 August 1999. See also Brown, *Man Walks into a Pub*, pp. 350–51.

25. Mass-Observation, *The Pub and the People*, p. 185. See also Brown, *Man Walks into a Pub*, pp. 306, 308, 326 for the use of bottles.

26. Matthew Engel, 'The lonely death of the British ale', *Guardian*, 29 June 1999.

27. Harrisson, *Britain Revisited*, p. 174.

28. Mass-Observation, *The Pub and the People*, pp. 304–6.

29. Mass-Observation, *The Pub and the People*, pp. 169–70.

30. Mass-Observation, *The Pub and the People*, pp. 176–80.

31. Marie Woolf, 'No 10 unit blames vertical drinking', *Independent*, 8 September 2003.

32. *Royal Commission on Licensing (England and Wales) 1929–31* (London: HMSO, 1932), pp. 45–8.

12. Your dinner is ready

1. Robert D. Putnam, *Bowling Alone: The Collapse and Revival of American Community* (New York: Simon and Schuster, 2000), pp. 100–101.

2. Joanna Blythman, *Bad Food Britain: How a Nation Ruined Its Appetite* (London: Fourth Estate, 2006), p. xv.

3. Mary Douglas, 'Deciphering a meal', in *Implicit Meanings: Essays in Anthropology* (London: Routledge and Kegan Paul, 1975), p. 250.

4. Mary Douglas and Michael Nicod, 'Taking the biscuit: the structure of British meals', *New Society*, 19 December 1974, p. 744.

5. Official Gazette, US Patent Office, 27 July 1954, quoted in the *Oxford English Dictionary* entry for 'TV dinner'.

6. Virginia Barnstorff, 'Swanson', in Janice Jorgensen (ed.), *Encyclopedia of Brands, Volume 1: Consumable Products* (Detroit: St James Press, 1994), p. 572.

7. Harvey Levenstein, *Paradox of Plenty: A Social History of Eating in Modern America* (New York: Oxford University Press, 1993), p. 289.

8. Miriam Akhtar and Steve Humphries, *The Fifties and Sixties: A Lifestyle Revolution* (London: Boxtree, 2001), p. 104.

9. Christina Hardyment, *Slice of Life: The British Way of Eating Since 1945* (London: BBC Books, 1995), p. 52.

10. Akhtar and Humphries, *The Fifties and Sixties*, p. 104.

11. Torin Douglas, 'Fingers point to frozen assets', *The Times*, 2 September 1985.

12. Douglas, 'Fingers point to frozen assets'.

13. Kathy Myers, *Understains: The Sense and Seduction of Advertising* (London: Comedia, 1986), p. 45.

14. Nick Clarke, *The Shadow of a Nation: How Celebrity Destroyed Britain* (London: Phoenix, 2004), p. 167.

15. Quoted in Artemis Cooper, *Writing at the Kitchen Table: The Authorized Biography of Elizabeth David* (London: Penguin, 2000), p. 192.

16. Elizabeth David, *Summer Cooking* (Harmondsworth: Penguin, [1955] 1965), p. 8.

17. Barry Norman, 'Norman Swallow of the BBC', *The Times*, 5 February 1972.

18. Torin Douglas, 'Taking a bird's eye view of marketing success with frozen foods', *The Times*, 12 April 1983.

19. Derek Harris, 'Pizza, English-style, lifts frozen foods', *The Times*, 17 January 1983.

20. Quoted in Alan Davidson, *The Penguin Companion to Food* (London: Penguin, 2002), p. 200.

21. Peter York and Charles Jennings, *Peter York's Eighties* (London: BBC Books, 1995), p. 65.

22. Derek Harris, 'Christmas boom for microwave cookers', *The Times*, 20 December 1984.

23. Ann Kent, 'Can common sense rule the microwave?', *The Times*, 15 November 1990.

24. James Erlichman, 'Instant cachet from the sachet', *Guardian*, 26 September 1987.

25. Hardyment, *Slice of Life*, p. 190.

26. David Nicholson-Lord, 'Kinnock confuses the kids', *The Times*, 22 June 1988.

27. Judi Bevan, *The Rise and Fall of Marks & Spencer* (London: Profile, 2001), p. 138.

28. See Richard W. Lacey, *Hard to Swallow: A Brief History of Food* (Cambridge: Cambridge University Press, 1994), p. 120.

29. Joanna Blythman, 'Mad, bad and dangerous to swallow', *Independent*, 23 March 1991.

30. Jancis Robinson, 'The cool-chain-single-source-M&S-recipe-dish test', *The Times*, 6 October 1985.

31. Angela Lambert, 'Are you lonesome tonight?', *Independent*, 19 October 1995.

32. Datamonitor, *Mealtime Behaviours and Occasions 2004: A Complete Review of Eating Habits and Needs* (London: Datamonitor, 2004), p. 36.

33. Jim Ainsworth, 'We'll eat again', *Observer*, 31 October 1999.

34. Douglas, 'Deciphering a meal', p. 255.

13. Behind the sofa

1. Margaret Visser, *Much Depends on Dinner: The Extraordinary History and Mythology, Allure and Obsessions, Perils and Taboos, of an Ordinary Meal* (New York: Grove Press, 1986), p. 11.

2. William Cowper, *The Task and Selected Other Poems*, ed. James Sandbrook (London: Longman, 1994), pp. 57–8.

3. John Gloag, *The Englishman's Chair: The Origins, Design, and Social History of Seat Furniture in England* (London: Allen and Unwin, 1964), p. 179.

4. Lucy Siegle, 'Urban sprawl', *Observer*, 12 March 2006.

5. *Oxford English Dictionary* entry for 'sofa'.

6. Richard Hoggart, *The Uses of Literacy* (Harmondsworth: Penguin, 1958), p. 68.

7. Juliet Gardiner, *From the Bomb to the Beatles: The Changing Face of Post-War Britain* (London: Collins and Brown, 1999), p. 92.

8. 'Credits for everyman', *The Times*, 23 September 1954.

9. Joanna Banham (ed.), *Encyclopedia of Interior Design, Volume 2* (London: Fitzroy Dearborn, 1997), p. 1,287.

10. Kenneth L. Ames, *Death in the Dining Room and Other Tales of Victorian Culture* (Philadelphia: Temple University Press, 1992), p. 191.

11. Rod Gerber, *Training for a Smart Workforce* (London: Routledge, 2000), p. 61.

12. Max Nathan, 'You burnt your bra, now it's time to chuck out the chintz', *Observer*, 22 September 1996.

13. Anthony Trollope, *Barchester Towers* (Oxford: Oxford University Press, [1857] 1980), p. 34.

14. Quoted in the *Oxford English Dictionary* entry for 'chintz'.

15. *Review of Intelligence on Weapons of Mass Destruction: Report of a Committee of Privy Counsellors* (London: Stationery Office, 2004), p. 162.

16. Anthony Trollope, *Can You Forgive Her?* (London: Oxford University Press, [1865] 1972), pp. 13–14.

17. Daniel Pool, *What Jane Austen Ate and Charles Dickens Knew: Fascinating Facts of Daily Life in the Nineteenth Century* (London: Robinson, 1998), p. 177.

18. Banham (ed.), *Encyclopedia of Interior Design*, p. 1,194.

19. Pool, *What Jane Austen Ate*, p. 177.

20. Ames, *Death in the Dining Room*, pp. 216–31.

21. 'Don't neglect your body', *Daily Mirror*, 27 April 1944.

22. Galen Cranz, *The Chair: Rethinking Culture, Body, and Design* (New York: Norton, 1998), p. 112.

23. 'Hopes of more rate cuts recede', *Independent on Sunday*, 21 August 2005.

24. See Laura Smith, 'Ikea blamed for pandemonium as 6000 turn up for bargains', *Guardian*, 11 February 2005; and Craig Brown, 'My kingdom for a sofa', *Daily Telegraph*, 12 February 2005.

25. Asa Briggs, *Victorian Things* (London: Penguin, 1990), p. 15.

26. Briggs, *Victorian Things*, p. 15.

14. Please do not adjust your set

1. Maurice Blanchot, 'Everyday speech', *Yale French Studies*, 73 (1987), p. 14.

2. Peter Lewis, *The Fifties: Portrait of an Age* (London: Heinemann, 1978), p. 208.

3. Reader's Digest, *Yesterday's Britain: The Illustrated Story of How We Lived, Worked and Played* (London: Reader's Digest Association, 1998), p. 212.

4. Television schedules in *The Times*, 15–22 September 1955.

5. Tony Currie, *A Concise History of British Television 1930–2000* (Tiverton: Kelly Publications, 2000), p. 36.

6. Reader's Digest, *Yesterday's Britain*, p. 213.

7. 'Advertising quota on television cut', *The Times*, 17 May 1960.

8. Asa Briggs, *The History of Broadcasting in the United Kingdom, Volume IV: Sound and Vision 1945–1955* (Oxford: Oxford University Press, 1995), p. 912.

9. Milton Shulman, 'Television breaks', *The Times*, 3 March 1959.

10. 'Attitudes to advertising revealed', *The Times*, 13 June 1967.

11. Peter Black, *The Mirror in the Corner: People's Television* (London: Hutchinson, 1972), p. 170.

12. Alexander Garrett, 'Midlife crisis for the TV ad', *Observer*, 17 September 1995.

13. Martin Lambie-Nairn, *Brand Identity for Television: With Knobs On* (London: Phaidon, 1997), p. 93.

14. Briggs, *The History of Broadcasting in the United Kingdom, Volume IV*, p. 223.

15. Tim O'Sullivan, 'Television memories and cultures of viewing, 1950–65', in John Corner (ed.), *Popular Television in Britain: Studies in Cultural History* (London: BFI, 1991), p. 167.

16. Peter Conrad, *Television: The Medium and its Manners* (London: Routledge and Kegan Paul, 1982), p. 18.

17. Harry Hopkins, *The New Look: A Social History of the Forties and Fifties in Britain* (London: Secker and Warburg, 1963), p. 420.

18. Hopkins, *The New Look*, pp. 403–4; O'Sullivan, 'Television memories and cultures of viewing', p. 168.

19. Doris Lessing, *Walking in the Shade: Volume Two of My Autobiography, 1949–1962* (London: HarperCollins, 1997), p. 16, quoted in Dominic Sandbrook, *Never Had It So Good: A History of Britain from Suez to the Beatles* (London: Little, Brown, 2005), p. 367.

20. Hopkins, *The New Look*, p. 403.

21. Tom Harrisson, *Britain Revisited* (London: Victor Gollancz, 1961), pp. 204–5, 207–8.

22. 'Close view of the average viewer', *The Times*, 3 September 1964.

23. Asa Briggs, *The History of Broadcasting in the United Kingdom, Volume V: Competition 1955–1974* (Oxford: Oxford University Press, 1995), p. 158.

24. Sean Day-Lewis, *TV Heaven: A Review of British Television from the 1930s to the 1990s* (London: Channel 4 Television, 1992), p. 22.

25. Patrick Skene Catling in the *Spectator*, 13 February 1971, quoted in Briggs, *History of Broadcasting, Volume V*, p. 848.

26. 'The colour fanfarade', *Observer*, 16 November 1969, quoted in Briggs, *History of Broadcasting, Volume V*, p. 863.

27. Briggs, *History of Broadcasting, Volume V*, p. 848.

28. Currie, *A Concise History of British Television*, pp. 70–6.

29. Jane Root, *Open the Box* (London: Comedia, 1986), p. 26.

30. '*Broadcast* reviews the various aspects of the BFI's One Day in the Life of Television experiment', *Broadcast*, 25 November 1988, p. 21.

31. Sean Day-Lewis, *One Day in the Life of Television* (London: Grafton/BFI, 1989), p. xiv.

32. Day-Lewis, *One Day in the Life of Television*, pp. 394–7.

33. See Mike Michael, *Reconnecting Culture, Technology and Nature: From Society to Heterogeneity* (London: Routledge, 2000), p. 101; James Gleick, *Faster: The Acceleration of Just About Everything* (London: Little, Brown, 1999), p. 182.

34. David Morley, *Television, Audiences and Cultural Studies* (London: Routledge, 1992), p. 147.

35. Morley, *Television, Audiences and Cultural Studies*, p. 147; David Gauntlett and Annette Hill, *TV Living: Television, Culture and Everyday Life* (London: Routledge, 1999), p. 241.

36. Gleick, *Faster*, p. 184.

37. Lambie-Nairn, *Brand Identity for Television*, p. 97.

38. Stephen Armstrong, 'Your number's up', *Sunday Times*, 11 November 2001.

39. Lambie-Nairn, *Brand Identity for Television*, pp. 122, 129.

40. George Orwell, *1984* (Harmondsworth: Penguin, [1949] 1989), p. 5.

41. 'Obituary: Robert Dougall', *The Times*, 20 December 1999.

42. Albert O. Hirschman, *Exit, Voice, and Loyalty: Responses to Decline in Firms, Organizations and States* (Cambridge, MA: Harvard University Press, 1970), pp. 4–16.

15. Watching the weather

1. Karel Kosík, *Dialectics of the Concrete: A Study on Problems of Man and World*, trans. Karel Kovana with James Schmidt (Dordrecht: D. Reidel, 1976), p. 44.

2. *Three-Minute Culture*, BBC2, 15 January 1989.

3. Asa Briggs, *The History of Broadcasting in the United Kingdom, Volume III: The War of Words* (Oxford: Oxford University Press, 1995), p. 700.

4. Owen Gibson, 'Weather alert: hi-tech front moves in on the BBC', *Guardian*, 14 May 2005.

5. Sarah Stoddart, 'Accent on the voice', *The Times*, 2 November 1972.

6. Ross McKibbin, *Classes and Cultures: England, 1918–1951* (Oxford: Oxford University Press, 1998), p. 461.

7. McKibbin, *Classes and Cultures*, p. 460.

8. Harry Hopkins, *The New Look: A Social History of the Forties and Fifties in Britain* (London: Secker and Warburg, 1963), p. 15.

9. Asa Briggs, *The History of Broadcasting in the United Kingdom, Volume V: Competition 1955–1974* (Oxford: Oxford University Press, 1995), p. 71.

10. Asa Briggs, *The History of Broadcasting in the United Kingdom, Volume IV: Sound and Vision 1945–1955* (Oxford: Oxford University Press, 1995), p. 544.

11. Mary Malone, 'The weather's always sunny in East Anglia', *Daily Mirror*, 9 March 1968.

12. Bert Foord, 'BBC television weather forecasts, 1963–74', *Weather*, 49:11 (November 1994), pp. 390–2.

13. Jack Scott, 'Reminiscences of the history of national television weather forecasts, 1969–88', *Weather*, 49:12 (December 1994), p. 422.

14. Ben Thompson, 'Long runners no. 22: *This Morning*', *Independent on Sunday*, 13 March 1994.

15. Robert Henson, *Television Weathercasting: A History* (Jefferson, NC: McFarland & Company, 1990), p. 8.

16. Mark S. Monmonier, *Air Apparent: How Meteorologists Learned to Map, Predict, and Dramatize Weather* (Chicago: University of Chicago Press, 1999), pp. 179–80.

17. Henson, *Television Weathercasting*, p. 37.

18. Foord, 'BBC television weather forecasts', p. 392.

19. Matthew Engel, 'Barnstorming ITN blows in with the weather show', *Guardian*, 14 February 1989.

20. Julia Llewellyn Smith, 'Weather girls under a cloud', *The Times*, 17 December 1993.

21. 'Our hearts are in our charts', *Daily Mail*, 12 January 1994.

22. Paul Theroux, *The Kingdom by the Sea* (Harmondsworth: Penguin, 1984), p. 20.

23. Robert Colls, *Identity of England* (Oxford: Oxford University Press, 2002), pp. 208–9.

24. Gibson, 'Weather alert'.

25. Adam Sherwin, 'New front opens for tomorrow's forecast', *The Times*, 14 May 2005.

26. Matt Born, 'Outlook, nauseous', *Daily Mail*, 18 May 2005.

27. *Hansard (Lords)*, 24 May 2005, columns 351–2.

28. Adam Sherwin, 'Scotland gets its day in the sun as BBC straightens weather map', *The Times*, 28 May 2005.

29. *High Pressure Heroes*, 9 May 1992, BBC2.

30. David Hyatt, Kathy Riley and Noel Sederstrom, 'Recall of television weather reports', *Journalism Quarterly*, 55:2 (1978), p. 310.

31. Nicole Martin, 'Met Office tells forecasters to give clouds a silver lining', *Daily Telegraph*, 5 October 2005; Adam Sherwin, 'Outlook is suddenly brighter', *The Times*, 5 October 2005.

32. Ivor Williams, 'Viewpoint: what is a weather forecast?', *Weather*, 59:1 (January 2004), p. 21.

16. At the end of the day

1. Albert Camus, *The Fall*, trans. Justin O'Brien (Harmondsworth: Penguin, [1956] 1963), p. 7.

2. Norbert Elias, *The Civilizing Process, Volume 1: The History of Manners*, trans. Edmund Jephcott (Oxford: Basil Blackwell, [1939] 1978), pp. 163–5.

3. 'The extra half hour', *The Times*, 16 December 1943.

4. Mass-Observation, 'The Tube Dwellers' (1943), in Angus Calder and Dorothy Sheridan (eds), *Speak for Yourself: A Mass-Observation Anthology 1937–49* (London: Jonathan Cape, 1964), pp. 101–7.

5. Tom Harrisson and Charles Madge (eds), *War Begins at Home by Mass-Observation* (London: Chatto and Windus, 1940), p. 194.

6. 'The bedroom ceiling', *The Times*, 18 December 1944.

7. Michael Connolly, 'Reading in bed', *The Times*, 2 January 1962; P. Gardner-Smith, 'Reading in bed', *The Times*, 3 January 1962; Basil Ward, 'Reading in bed', *The Times*, 4 January 1962.

8. Lawrence Wright, *Warm and Snug: The History of the Bed* (London: Routledge and Kegan Paul, 1962), p. 337.

9. George Mikes, *How to be an Alien: A Handbook for Beginners and More Advanced Pupils* (Harmondsworth: Penguin, [1946] 1966), p. 29.

10. Denzil Batchelor, 'In the age of the specialist, a new concept', *The Times*, 14 May 1963.

11. 'Clothes or chilblains', *The Times*, 3 December 1956.

12. Wright, *Warm and Snug*, p. 199.

13. Barbara Cartland, *Marriage for Moderns* (London: Herbert Jenkins, 1955), pp. 107–8.

14. Wright, *Warm and Snug*, p. 335.

15. Marie Carmichael Stopes, *Sleep* (London: Chatto and Windus, 1956), p. 38.

16. 'Cold feet in the back that chill romances', *Daily Mirror*, 12 January 1950.

17. Tony Miles, 'The bed', *Daily Mirror*, 11 October 1955; Eileen Harris, *Going to Bed: The Arts and Living* (London: HMSO, 1981), p. 62.

18. Robert Louis Stevenson, 'The land of counterpane', in *A Child's Garden of Verses* (London: David Campbell, [1885] 1992), p. 38; Rupert Brooke, 'The great lover', in *The Complete Poems of Rupert Brooke* (London: Sidgwick and Jackson, 1936), p. 133.

19. 'The 70-hour-a-week wives', *Daily Mirror*, 19 September 1966; see also Dominic Sandbrook, *White Heat: A History of Britain in the Swinging Sixties* (London: Little, Brown, 2006), p. 653.

20. Philip Howard, 'The shop that changed our lives and turned us on', *The Times*, 10 May 2004.

21. Terence Conran, *Q and A: A Sort of Autobiography* (London: HarperCollins, 2001), p. 75.

22. Slumberdown advert in *The Times*, 17 September 1970.

23. Conran, *Q and A*, p. 78.

24. Advert in the *Daily Mirror*, 1 January 1966.

25. 'British duvets better than continental quilts', *The Times*, 24 January 1973.

26. Slumberdown advert in *The Times*, 17 September 1970.

27. Slumberdown advert in the *Daily Mirror*, 14 August 1971.

28. Conran, *Q and A*, p. 75.

29. Patricia Tisdall, 'How the average family spends its income', *The Times*, 14 November 1970.

30. Nicholas Tomalin, 'Conspicuous thrift', in *Nicholas Tomalin Reporting* (London: André Deutsch, 1975), p. 53.

31. Miles, 'The bed'.

32. 'Background to our dreams', *Daily Mirror*, 4 August 1959.

33. 'Television invades the bedroom', *The Times*, 15 June 1983.

34. Akiko Busch, *Geography of Home: Writings on Where We Live* (New York: Princeton Architectural Press, 1999), p. 117.

35. Max Weber, *The Protestant Ethic and the Spirit of Capitalism*, trans. Talcott Parsons (London: Allen and Unwin, [1930] 1970), pp. 157–8.

36. Murray Melbin, *Night as Frontier: Colonizing the World After Dark* (New York: The Free Press, 1987), pp. 14, 40.

37. A. Roger Ekirch, *At Day's Close: A History of Nighttime* (London: Weidenfeld and Nicolson, 2005), p. 324.

Afterword: Habits of the heart

1. Georges Perec, *Species of Spaces and Other Pieces*, ed. and trans. John Sturrock (London: Penguin, 1999), pp. 209–10.

2. Francis Hertzberg, 'I-Spy with a winning eye', *Guardian*, 1 December 1995.

3. Julian Barnes, *Letters from London: 1990–1995* (London: Picador, 1995), p. ix.

4. A. H. Halsey, *Change in British Society* (Oxford: Oxford University Press, 1995), p. 8.

5. Alexis de Tocqueville, *Democracy in America*, trans. George Lawrence (London: Fontana, [1840] 1994), p. 287.

6. Dean Godson, 'I want to hop on a red bus again', *The Times*, 21 July 2005.

7. Dean Godson (ed.), *Replacing the Routemaster: How to Undo Ken Livingstone's Destruction of London's Best Ever Bus* (London: Policy Exchange, 2005).

8. Travis Elborough, *The Bus We Loved: London's Love Affair with the Routemaster* (London: Granta, 2005), pp. xii, 171–2.

9. Benedict Brogan and Matt Born, 'Brown calls the tune', *Daily Mail*, 26 January 2006.

10. Peter Schneider, *Extreme Mittellage: Eine Reise Durch das Deutsche Nationalgefühl* (Reinbek bei Hamburg: Rowohlt, 1990), p. 127.

11. Charles Madge and Tom Harrisson, *Mass-Observation* (London: Frederick Muller, 1937), p. 10.

Index